This Is Your Life

The Story of Television's Famous Big Red Book

Motorcycle world champion Barry Sheene was watching himself in a race on film when Eamonn burst through the screen.

This Is Your Life

The Story of Television's Famous Big Red Book

ROY BOTTOMLEY

Foreword by Michael Aspel, OBE

THAMES METHUEN

Title page: Jazz singer George Melly plays out his Life
in his own inimitable style.

First published in Great Britain 1993
by Methuen London
an imprint of Reed Consumer Books Ltd
Michelin House, 81 Fulham Road, London SW3 6RB
and Auckland, Melbourne, Singapore and Toronto
in association with Thames Television International Ltd
Broom Road, Teddington Lock, Teddington, Middlesex TW11 9NT

A CIP catalogue record for this book
is available from the British Library
ISBN 0 413 67200 X

Printed in Great Britain
by BPCC Hazells Ltd, Aylesbury, Bucks

To the stars in *my* life:

wife Patti, daughter Sally,
sons Steve and Tom, and 'Ivy-Love' (Nan)

Acknowledgements

I would like to thank all Lifers (teams past and present); Stan Allen who took so many of these photographs, Thames Television for permission to reproduce them and Gilly Hartley at the Production Design Company for her help in tracking them down; Michael Aspel for his generous Foreword; all Life's subjects and those who made our surprises possible; Ralph Edwards who started it all; Life's loyal family of viewers for switching on every Wednesday and never ceasing to surprise us by the numbers of millions; and last, but by no means least, the memory of Eamonn Andrews.

Contents

Foreword by Michael Aspel, OBE   9

1   Life Behind the Scenes   11
2   Birth of Life   28
3   New Lease of Life   43
4   Life and Legends   52
5   Variety: The Spice of Life   68
6   Life's Heroes and Heroines   84
7   Hollywood Life   96
8   Life in Coronation Street   110
9   It's a Musical Life   121
10   This Sporting Life   131
11   Life upon the Wicked Stage   150
12   Life and Politics   165
13   Life in Broadcasting   175
14   Life's Best-Sellers   187
15   Living Life Dangerously   195
16   It's a Funny Old Life   203
17   Life's a Party   212

Appendix: an A–Z of Life Subjects
    Featured by Thames Television   215
Index   222

Foreword

When I was a National Serviceman it was explained to me that saluting an officer meant that we were acknowledging the pips on the shoulder rather than the man himself. I think the same applies to *This Is Your Life*'s Big Red Book. The theatre audiences that erupt as they see the star being crept up on from behind are reacting to that familiar ledger with its gold lettering; the man carrying it could be wearing a barrel for all they care.

Having said that, I must admit that I was one of those who believed, when Eamonn Andrews died, that the programme would die with him. After so many years the two, it seemed, were inseparable, and anyone else uttering that famous phrase would sound a very pale imitation. I knew how much Eamonn loved the show. I had helped him more than once to spring the surprise, and had seen the glee that seized him, the joyful anticipation of the subject's reaction. Indeed, the morning that Eamonn died, there was a letter on my hall table waiting to be posted to him – my response to his letter thanking me for being part of a recent Life.

I was flattered and slightly alarmed to be asked to take Eamonn's place. I had followed in his footsteps before with other, lesser programmes, but this took some thinking about. I was persuaded, and so began some of the happiest days, so far, of my professional life.

The team I inherited were an awesomely skilled bunch, working in that fast, confident way that only years of experience, and success, can bring. They were remarkably welcoming and patient as they showed me the ropes. One of the first things I learned was that the person whose tribute we were preparing was always referred to as the subject, never the victim.

There are people who see *This Is Your Life* as an embarrassing intrusion, and there are people who regard it as the ultimate accolade. Nigel Mansell has said that the three things he wanted most were the World Championship, the OBE and the Big Red Book. He got all three, and I was there to see the strong man with a tear in his eye.

I now know how Eamonn felt all those years: the nervous tension, the exhilaration of a successful 'hit', the satisfaction of the moment when, after weeks of planning, all the strands have been drawn together, the story has been told, and everyone goes home happy. I've also learned the mixed pleasures of impersonating Sooty, a British

Rail ticket-collector and a Chinese magician – just a few of the disguises that the devilish production team have dreamed up for me.

I have now come to love the show and the team who work on it, but my devotion was tested, to say the least, when producer Malcolm Morris informed me that we were going to record a programme on Nobby Stiles, of Manchester United and England fame, on the same day as the Rugby Union World Cup Final, England v. Australia, for which I had tickets. I gave Malcolm one of my hard looks and shook my head emphatically. As a result, at the very moment that England kicked off at Twickenham, I stepped on to the pitch at Old Trafford where a pre-match assembly of veterans was gathered, and said, with a brave smile, 'Nobby Stiles, this is your life.' My last defiant words to Malcolm had been 'If he says no, I'm going to kick him all round the park.' But Nobby said yes, and we made a fine show. (England, without my support, lost the Final.) That, as they say, is . . . Life.

When Michael Aspel had tickets for the Rugby Union World Cup Final, the author had an idea which changed the Life's fixture list. It was the twenty-fifth anniversary of England winning the 1966 World Cup. So Michael's venue was Old Trafford, not Twickenham. And the book was for one of those World Cup heroes, Nobby Stiles – seen here disguising the fact that he had his front teeth in – watched by another former Life subject, Manchester United and England's Bobby Charlton.

No one is better qualified to write the history of *This Is Your Life* than Roy Bottomley. He has written almost every word of each series throughout the years, without losing an ounce of his enthusiasm. He has ransacked the archives and his own phenomenal memory to bring you a vivid account of the creation of one of broadcasting's institutions. Let's hope we all continue to enjoy it for the rest of our natural.

Michael Aspel

Chapter One
Life Behind the Scenes

How is someone chosen to be the guest of honour on *This Is Your Life*? And what goes on between then and the moment Michael Aspel surprises that person with the Big Red Book and the four most famous words on British television?

The answers to those questions, and many more, are behind the closed doors of Room 226 at Teddington Studios, riverside headquarters of Thames TV. All the secrets of *This Is Your Life* are here, in this green-carpeted, open-plan office. This is the programme's nerve centre, though it is no place for the nervous; too many things can go wrong between a name being chosen and that person walking on to the familiar set to the signature tune of 'Gala Performance' (specially arranged for the Life by Carl Davis) and thunderous applause.

Two particular examples of what can go wrong are never far from the Life team's memories – soccer star Danny Blanchflower taking one look at the book and doing a runner, and Richard Gordon, author of the 'Doctor' books, blurting out, 'Oh balls!' live in front of millions of viewers. He fled the studio, but was persuaded to return and the programme was transmitted the following week.

And no one in Room 226 answers the telephone with the words 'This Is Your Life office'. Comedy actor Ronnie Barker had become suspicious about his wife taking mysterious telephone calls. When he came across a piece of paper with a telephone number and the name Brian written on it, he decided to ring the number. '*This Is Your Life* office,' answered the researcher, and the show was lost. Now the standard reply is simply: 'Can I help you?'

Happier memories for the Life's researchers are stuck to walls, desks, noticeboards and typewriters. These are replicas of the gilt-on-red-leather names that are revealed on the front of the Big Red Book. There they are, all part and parcel of Life's story: Earl Mountbatten of Burma, Omar Sharif, Joan Collins, Falklands hero Simon Weston, the Bee Gees, Phil Collins, Barbara Cartland and many more.

Also on the office walls are photographs recalling the team's visits to make programmes in Hollywood and New York, and postcards from the globetrotting researchers from all over the world.

Stuck to the inside of the office door is a note from award-winning actor Robert Lindsay: 'Dear All, thank you for a most thrilling night. I hope to pay you all back in some way, as horrible as I can think of.

Love, Bob.' And with that note came a bottle of champagne for every member of the team.

Eamonn stops the show to surprise Evita herself, Elaine Paige.

When you open that office door this is what you see: a large square table around which the team gathers for production meetings and script conferences with Michael Aspel, much enlivened by his natural charm and wit (often mildly risqué and all the funnier for it).

My little office is in the corner of the big room. Here I compose the contents of Michael's Big Red Book on my ancient portable typewriter. This happens, of course, after the researchers have delivered several tons of paperwork with the background to our subjects, likely contributors and surprises. My first task is to sift through all available material, including any books on or by the subject. Then I draw up what in my view is the best possible running order. In television terms it is often best not to tell a story in strict chronological order, and for *This Is Your Life* I like to sprinkle the surprises over our twenty-five minutes and five seconds of running time.

That is in my capacity as scriptwriter. I am also programme consultant, and as such am one of the triumvirate – the others being producer Malcolm Morris and associate producer John Graham – which largely decides the names that will appear on the Big Red Book. This involves suggesting likely candidates and keeping a close eye on early research, looking out for any likely pitfalls or blind alleys we might find ourselves going down if we're not wary.

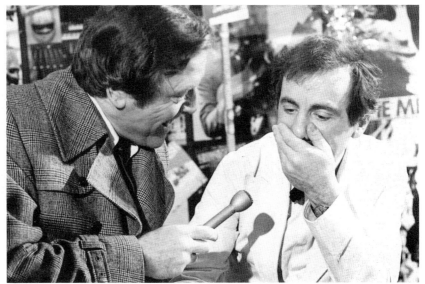

Manuel from *Fawlty Towers*,
Andrew Sachs, stops himself from
putting his foot in it.

In the main office, nearest to the big table, is the desk of programme
co-ordinator Mandy Lee. Her demanding job is to make sure everybody
appearing on the programme reaches the studio and gets back home
again. Often there are scores of people on one programme. And some
of the most moving reunions have involved travel from remote corners
of the world. Little wonder Mandy sometimes looks as though she has
a telephone sprouting from each ear.

Passing her desk, a snatch of one of her urgent telephone calls might
be: 'So she's no longer in Cambodia? She's now where? Moscow. And
she hasn't got a visa. . . .' A roll of Mandy's eyes.

Looking down the length of the office from Mandy's desk, you see
a centre aisle flanked by the desks of the five researchers. Rarely are
all of them in the office at the same time. From Manchester to Miami,
Newcastle to New York, they are on the trail of the programme's
surprises: those offstage voices which will bring a whoop of recognition
from the guest of honour, or an expression of frustrated concentration
as the memory seeks to put a face to the voice.

At the occupied desks, researchers are never off the phone, making
calls or fielding them. The fax machine has steam coming from it.

Fragments of telephone conversations you might overhear as you
walk past the desks:

'We could get a film crew to the President no matter where
he's going to be. . . .'

At another phone: 'Not seen each other for forty years?' A pause.
The researcher listens. 'Until last week. . . .' Elation deflates.

Barbara Windsor, on stage at the Theatre Royal, Windsor, looks as though she quite liked Michael's surprise . . .

To the left: 'Mr O'Toole will join us live? Wonderful.' A thumbs-up signal.

To the right: 'Ideally we would like permission to have the princess in shot. . . .'

Film researcher Sue Tiplady's is the last of the researchers' desks. It is her job to locate and get clearance for use of all those fascinating film inserts you see on *This Is Your Life*, from Hollywood spectaculars to long-lost home movies. Included in her many film-world contacts are amateur movie buffs and collectors, some with priceless footage.

To Sue's right sits the production secretary, Avril Norton. One of her jobs is to make sure every one of the viewers' letters (and there are dozens a day) is attended to. Some propose people the viewer believes might be worthy of a Life tribute; others may request either a repeat of last week's programme, or a cassette, because they were out and missed it. . . .

One of the more bizarre letters came from a man seen in drag on one of our film inserts. He thought a fee of £100 might cover his embarrassment.

We are almost at the end of the lengthy office. The last desk is that of associate producer John Graham. Though only in his late thirties, John is a Life veteran. Himself a former researcher, he knows at first hand every problem that can get in the way of delivering a successful programme. He and Michael Aspel go back a long way. When Michael was a Capital Radio DJ in the mid-1970s, John was the traffic reporter.

One of John's most important roles is to fix the location of the 'pick-up' – Life-speak for the big moment of surprise which has millions switching on at the start of every programme. Then, having copper-bottomed the location, he must make sure there are no security leaks. If the subject of a programme gets the slightest hint of our plans, the whole thing is called off. We 'lost' Derek Nimmo when someone pushed an anonymous note under his theatre dressing-room door – and we haven't caught him since, though you never know. . . . Bernard Braden's six-year-old grandson, leaving after Sunday lunch, blurted out, 'See you on Wednesday at *This Is Your Life*, grandad.' We waited more than a decade before we tried again – this time successfully.

In the early days of *This Is Your Life* we did many more 'live' transmissions than we do now. In his days as a sports commentator, Eamonn Andrews had done a lot of live television and he remained very keen on it. If we were surprising our guest in a television studio, we could even do a 'live' pick-up and go straight into the programme; more often we would film the pick-up and do the rest of the show live.

Nowadays, the programmes are mostly pre-recorded, so if anything goes disastrously wrong millions of viewers are not faced with blank

. . . and so, too, did Juliet Mills, on stage at the Richmond Theatre.

television screens. We are always working on six shows at once, so if need be we can make a last-minute substitution. But there is no second crack at the pick-up – the subjects' reactions that are seen on TV are always completely genuine. And we do try to make the shows as 'live' as possible: we run them to the exact length if we possibly can, to preserve the spontaneity and to cut out expensive time in the editing suite. And we keep the delay between the pick-up and the actual show to a minimum, so that while Michael is announcing the first surprise the adrenaline is still pumping for the subject – and for the Life team.

Behind John Graham's desk is a partition through which is the office of producer Malcolm Morris, a man with more than thirty years' television experience, as producer, director and one-time Controller of Programmes at Tyne Tees Television. Despite his stress-filled role, never have I seen him throw a tantrum. He gets his way with quiet determination and a sense of humour bordering on the style of Woody Allen.

This is the inner sanctum in which decisions are made affecting the lives of hundreds of people.

The first item to catch your eye is the famous wartime poster, pinned to the wall, reminding us that 'Careless Talk Costs Lives'. Seated behind two gossiping ladies on a bus are Hitler and Goering. The slogan continues: 'You never know *who's* listening.'

It's an appropriate reminder to us all. Most of the Life team have been asked, perfectly innocently, in the local, down at the shops, even in the studio canteen: 'Who is it this week?' As one of the prerequisites for working on the programme is a cheerful, co-operative and friendly personality, we always resist the temptation to say, 'That's a stupid question.' Instead, we grit our teeth and smile: 'Watch and find out.'

Who 'it' – the subject, that is – may be for the next few weeks, even months, is on a huge, squared-off blackboard behind the producer's desk. But it would take the genius of a codebreaker from the days of 'Careless Talk Costs Lives' to decipher the names we hope to see transferred to the Big Red Book.

So security conscious are we that every potential *This Is Your Life* subject is given a codename. And that is how they will be known to everyone connected with the programme until the final credits roll over those irresistible pictures of family and friends gathering round the subject at the close. Only then do they discover that they have been known by codename for the past weeks, months and, in some cases, years. The first thing most of them want to know at the party afterwards is 'What did you call me?'

Nothing uncomplimentary, we hope. What we aim for is a total lack of logic in the codename – to make it as unguessable as possible.

Try these: 'Queen' and 'Detective'.

'Queen' was Esther Rantzen (her initials are ER). 'Detective' was Michael Aspel himself. How did the Life tongue-in-cheek geniuses work that one out? Michael was hosting *Give Us A Clue* at the time.

But how does a potential subject reach the stage of being given a codename in the first place?

Malcolm Morris, John Graham and I get together towards the end of June/beginning of July. The production team members are still away. The majority being freelance, they will have been picking up other work if they can find it, or need it. Some will not have been able to shake off the travel bug – even at their own expense.

Over lunch at a local wine bar, Malcolm, John and I plot how the team will spend their autumn and winter, what the Life assignments will be. We have a minimum of twenty-six shows to put together, and we start recording in September. As well as picking our subjects, we have to decide where we'll shoot – we have a Granada studio booked, so we need at least four subjects we can catch in and around Manchester. And we'll be going back to LA, and possibly to Australia, so we need several stars in each of those places.

What are we looking for? Well, *This Is Your Life* is the biggest and best surprise party ever devised, so it could be useful if the potential subject had something to celebrate – a moment of triumph among his or her peers. Personally, I love newly crowned world champions, at anything.

But someone out there might be a totally unsung world champion – simply and selflessly giving the best of themselves in the interests of others less fortunate.

Seeking the right 'mix' of subjects for the twenty-six-week season is the head-banging part of the job. We must try to please all of the people all of the time.

'Why don't you do more stars?' ask some letters. 'Why don't you do more real people who help others?' plead others. Some demand more sports people, others more from theatre and the arts.

In the weeks leading up to this meeting, possible subjects in a wide variety of categories will have been going through our minds; now, Malcolm, Johnny and I talk through our ideas and make a shortlist.

This is all very well, but it cannot, at this juncture, take into account the availability of a certain subject on a certain date, nor the availability of all those people whose contributions could make or break a Life story.

Nor do we shy away from the possibility of certain subjects telling Michael where to go and what to do with his Big Red Book.

So, at our pre-season meetings, optimism is the watchword. Without it, Life would be dead.

Having agreed our mix of programmes for the first five of the series, we write codenames in the allocated squares on the blackboard. The next twenty-one will be added as soon as possible. At this stage it is known as the 'Dream Board' – because actually achieving these recordings on the hoped-for dates is still far removed from reality.

Reality re-enters Room 226 in the middle of July, with the arrival back of the research team, plus the programme's director Brian Klein (a former Life researcher) and his PA Irene Clark, still bubbling with enthusiasm after years on the Life.

Professional collectors of other people's anecdotes for use on the programme, the team go on for some time swapping what-happened-to-you-you'll-never-guess stories of their own. Then it's down to business.

Each researcher is assigned a potential subject to look into. Each will provide, within a few days, a feasibility report, known to all as a 'feeza'. These early reports are not merely potted biographies; they will include points against as well as for going further on a given subject. They will also give a possible 'spotlist' of people likely to appear on the programme.

Occasionally, the 'feeza' will sound early warning bells against going with a Life. There may just be too many skeletons in the cupboard. But this is rare. After all, we are not an investigative programme. The Life is a party. If we can avoid it, there will be no unwelcome guests.

While the 'feezas' are being prepared for the new season, Michael Aspel is taking a well-earned break, not only from the Life but from his live chat show. His keen interest and contribution come at a later date, when we know where we are at and with whom.

The researchers talk through their 'feezas' and everything is looking possible, including a Life on the rock band Status Quo, celebrating their twenty-five years in the business with a tour called 'Rock 'Til You Drop'. Unfortunately, after several weeks, we will have to drop *them*. Various key people turn out to be unavailable and we agree with the band's management that the show will be scrapped. Perhaps we can resume negotiations at a later date.

What happens next is this. Someone very close to our potential subject is contacted by telephone. This could be wife, husband, parent, brother, sister, business partner, closest friend, manager or agent. The conversation usually begins like this: 'Good morning. My name is . . . and I work on the *This Is Your Life* programme. I would ask you, please, to treat this call in the strictest confidence. . . .'

Things can go wrong even at this early stage. We once planned a Life on gravel-voiced American actress Elaine Stritch who, at the time, was living at the Savoy. A researcher telephoned her suite. When a deep American voice boomed out the number of the suite the researcher thought it was Elaine's husband.

'Good morning. We're thinking of doing a *This Is Your Life* on your wife, what do you think?'

Came the reply: 'Great idea, baby, but this *is* Elaine Stritch. . . .'

No such bad luck this particular morning as our researchers make their first approach calls.

One of our most experienced researchers, Sue Green, has produced a 'feeza' on heart-throb actor Nigel Havers, who charmed millions as *The Charmer*. Her first call is to Nigel's wife, Polly, a former model. They arrange to meet for a strictly confidential lunch. Sue is on delicate territory because Nigel's divorce from his first wife hit the headlines.

During lunch, Polly advises Sue to contact Nigel's agent and production company business partner, Michael Whitehall. They have an exciting new project in the pipeline called *Good Guys*, co-starring Keith Barron, with a host of big name guest stars.

Nigel's parents, too, must be contacted before they leave for a holiday in the South of France. Lord Havers was a former Attorney-General, and very much in the public eye. Again a delicate situation. He may not wish for the kind of TV exposure *This Is Your Life* gives.

Sue Green is greatly relieved when Lady Havers turns out to be cheerfully co-operative. Sue told me, 'When Lady Havers said, "Sue, just call me Carol," I knew we were going to be all right. She is such a sweet lady.'

Sue is well into the research when she takes a call from the South of France. Lord and Lady Havers are having second thoughts. Sue arrives at a compromise. Director Brian Klein will make sure the cameras do not linger on them, nor do they have to speak, so minimising any attention they will receive. Sue puts down the phone and stares into space. 'Phew' is all she can manage.

The next stage is the researchers starting to type up their findings, from newspaper cuttings, books, interviews with relatives and friends. Who haven't our subjects seen for a long time, but would genuinely love to see again? Answers can range from school teachers who first inspired them to old pals from the Services. Two teacher brothers at his prep school first fired Nigel Havers's acting ambitions.

Michael Whitehall can get Nigel to a preview of the first episode of *Good Guys* at nearby Twickenham Studios. Keith Barron will be there, and so will Martin Jarvis, Angela Thorne, Hilary Gish and former EastEnders star Leslie Grantham. An unexpected guest will be Michael Aspel.

We are now up and running. Changing my 'programme consultant' hat for my 'writer' hat, I am bombarded with research on half a dozen programmes.

Other researchers have followed the same pattern as Sue Green. They, too, have been seeking the vital piece of information which will give us the best impact start to the programmes. The pick-up is all-important to the Life.

First information on broadcasting chef Keith Floyd is not what we wanted on our menu. It seems he will not be at his Devon pub where we hoped to surprise him with Michael Aspel popping in for a pint. Instead, Keith will be in Dublin. The wheels are set in motion for the pick-up team, with Michael, to be in Dublin on the same day, surprise Keith and fly him back to our studios here at Teddington. His codename is 'Soup', but it looked for a while as though we could be in it. We finally track him down in Dublin – to a pub, and Michael pops in for a pint.

Pam Ferris (codename 'Wheel'), Ma Larkin in television's hit of the season *The Darling Buds of May*, will be filming a new series for Yorkshire Television in Leeds. They are happy to go along with our plan to have Pa Larkin, David Jason, announce an unexpected visitor to the farmhouse, and for Michael to walk into the kitchen where Ma is chatting to her screen daughter, the stunning Catherine Zeta Jones. I have no shortage of male helpers when I brief Catherine on her script at our hideaway hotel.

Next, we have the go-ahead for a spectacular pick-up for Paul Nicholas (codename 'Saint') at the curtain-call at the Bristol Hippodrome, where he is starring in the musical *Barnum*. John Graham gets on to the studios of HTV in Bristol so we can take Paul straight there.

We will be recording a whole batch of programmes out of Granada's Manchester studios, including *Coronation Street*'s own Thelma Barlow ('Till'). We will be taking special care of the Big Red Book this time.

When we went to the Street to surprise its longest-serving star Bill Roache, who plays Ken Barlow, the book went walkabout. We had Eamonn Andrews dressed as an Arab (Bill is a former Captain in the Royal Welsh Fusiliers and served with the Bedouins) complete with camel. Had the camel eaten the book?

It was nowhere to be found. Malcolm Morris grabbed a red plastic folder and shoved it into Eamonn's hands just as Bill came round the corner. He didn't notice the difference, and nor did fifteen million viewers. Oh, and the camel wasn't guilty. Someone had picked up the book out of curiosity and left it behind the bar of the Rover's Return. It was returned to us in the nick of time for the actual show.

We also get the go-ahead to pick up dangerman comedian Bernard Manning in full flight at his own nightclub. Fingers on the 'bleep' machine for that one.

Award-winning television writer Alan Bleasdale (*GBH, Boys from the Black Stuff*) we aim to surprise in his native Liverpool, then we are off to Dundee, to the vast Caird Hall, to tell the story of that wisp of a world champion, 10,000 metres winner in Tokyo and winner of the New York Marathon, Liz McColgan ('Live').

Then it's back to London and the pop scene to surprise Gary Glitter ('Sparkle') at his Wembley concert. What a night that will turn out to be.

A sell-out crowd of twelve thousand chanted 'Leader! Leader!' as Gary's concert came to a climax, and a wall of sound met Michael as he walked on stage with the book. 'I've never heard anything like it in my life,' Michael told me later.

That was after a reluctant Gary had said, 'I don't want to do this, Michael. I'm sorry, but you can all **** off.'

Michael has always said he will never try to persuade a subject to do the show if it is clearly against their wishes, and he was as good as his word. It was Gary's manager and our producer Malcolm Morris who told him his family had all co-operated, and he agreed to go ahead.

As it turned out it was a great night, and Gary himself finished the show with his original Glitter Band.

In stark contrast, researcher Sarah Cockcroft is working on one of Life's unsung heroes – Oxfam's globetrotting troubleshooter Jim Howard, who has saved millions of lives in third-world countries and in the aftermath of the 'Killing Fields' of Cambodia.

A bit of light relief comes from Sue Green, who has been talking to actress Jenny Seagrove about coming on the Nigel Havers Life. She played his wife in *Hold The Dream*. Said Sue: 'Jenny would like her dog, Tasha, to be on the show.'

She knows the reaction this will get from Malcolm. 'No, no,' he grimaces. 'You know what they always do. . . .'

I talk him round when I suggest a gimmick entrance. Instead of giving Jenny the voice offstage, we give it to the dog. On the show, after a clip of *Hold The Dream* Michael says, 'A glamorous star with you there. You may recognise this voice, too . . .' And I scripted:

This Is Your Life

Michael took a trip to Dublin's oldest pub when Keith Floyd suddenly switched his plans . . .

. . . and Michael joined him at the bar.

Gary Glitter salutes his fans.

We gave Jenny Seagrove's dog the off-stage 'voice' to surprise Nigel Havers . . .

. . . and Nigel gave Tasha a warm welcome.

TASHA (THE DOG) V/O
'WHOOF, WHOOF, WHOOF . . .'

It took a while to get the perfect recording, but Jenny was happy, and so was Tasha. And very well behaved, too, much to Malcolm's relief, if that's the right word.

While all this has been going on, film researcher Sue Tiplady will have been busy seeking and getting in clips which may be appropriate to our projected programmes. When she is confident she has got just about everything I may need to put in my script, she will say, 'Come on, Roy, we're going to the pictures', and we sit down in front of a TV screen by the big table to play the clips. I make my selection and, if necessary, write Michael a brief commentary to speak over the chosen film. We also make a note of all the 'out' lines: these will go in Michael's script, so he will know when each clip is finished.

Another important visual contribution to any Life is the still photographs. Researchers will have been going through many a family album tracing the pictorial history of our subjects. Nothing gets a giggle more than a baby snap.

So, with briefcase bulging with research notes and copies of family pictures, I head for the peace and quiet of my office at home. In fact the telephone never stops because the nature of the programme means you are working on quicksands. So-and-so has had to drop out of one show, someone else finds he or she can now make it at the last minute, and it all has to be scripted.

Dean Martin has decided he will film for us in Las Vegas for Engelbert Humperdinck. But only if I write something for him. I write in the manner of Dean's drunk act. The tag is that he just cannot get his tongue around the name. He takes a slurp from his glass and mutters darkly, 'You'll just have to change that name, boy.' It gets a big laugh from Engelbert on the show.

The first batch of scripts completed, a car takes them to Michael's Surrey home for him to read and add his own comments. As he and I are about the same age, and share a similar background and sense of humour, his changes tend to be minimal. He likes to contribute especially to the fun bits of the show.

How he stopped himself from 'corpsing' – laughing uncontrollably – during the Bernard Manning show I'll never know. It was laughs all the way. Comedians Jim Bowen and Dougie Brown just 'went', especially when Bernard's former sergeant major appeared. He was unintentionally funny, talking on and on about Bernard's army days – Bernard had accidentally bayoneted him – so that big Bernard could not get a word in. This was a novel experience for him, but eventually he looked at his watch and said, 'Have you finished? I'm going on holiday in June.'

When the scripts return from Michael's scrutiny, director Brian Klein then gets to work 'putting the cameras on' – noting which of the six studio cameras will take what shots and from which angles of the action on stage. One camera – known as a 'slave' – will remain on the subject throughout, so that not a single reaction is missed.

These are the scripts everyone will work from on the day of the show.

That day begins with a script conference round the table with Michael Aspel. I sit to his right and Malcolm to his left. On my right is the script secretary, ready to make any last minute changes. Brian Klein and his PA will be in the studio control room lining up his shots with the cameramen.

Also at our meeting are associate producer John Graham, the researcher responsible for that day's programme, and the floor manager, who has charge of everything that happens on the studio floor. This includes timing Michael's cues in and out of film inserts, and leads-in to the offstage voices.

We will now have been joined by a second director and PA who will film the pick-up. John Graham will be familiar with the location, and he and the unit director will talk Michael through every step. There is no room for error. Missing the pick-up would be like missing the finishing post at the Derby. We have only one shot at it, and it's got to count.

For the pick-up today, Michael is off to Twickenham Studios from where he hopes to bring back Nigel Havers. There has already been a hiccup. Nigel wanted to change the date of the screening of *Good Guys*. His partner told him this could not be done. But he didn't tell him why.

Before he changes from casual gear to smart suit, Michael 'walks through' a rehearsal, purely for his moves and cues into film, and for cameras. Everybody in the team not working on the next show stands in for the real guests who will fill the seats on the night.

We break for lunch in the huge Thames riverside dining room where the after-the-show party will be held. Usually, over lunch, unless there are pressing problems outstanding, we try to avoid in-depth discussion about that night's programme. The attitude is that if we are not fully prepared now we never will be.

We have plenty of other things to talk about. We are all film and television addicts, including Michael – he has been a movie buff since childhood, which seems to have been spent at the Granada, Tooting.

If it's not films, it's cars. Michael takes some gentle ribbing because of his penchant for seemingly changing his car every few weeks. In recent months he has had a Jaguar, an Alfa Romeo, a Jensen and now a restored Mercedes.

He leaves in a studio car for the pick-up, with Malcolm Morris and John Graham.

For the next two rehearsals, one without, the final one with the guests, I stand in for Michael, holding the Big Red Book, going through the whole programme. Brian Klein perfects his shots, and when the

Who's the comedian who can make the professionals fall about? Bernard Manning, pictured here with his former sergeant major from National Service days.

guests arrive to record their voices off and go through their entrances and exits, I discuss with them and the researcher any problems they may have in telling their particular contribution to the programme. It still surprises me how often show-business professionals are nervous under these circumstances.

While the guests go to make-up and to their dressing rooms to get changed, we wait in Room 226 for the call from the car-phone from John Graham that will tell us if we have a show or not. It's the nail-biting period of the day.

The phone rings. It's Johnny: 'We're on! Heading back now!'

In the Green Room the good news is relayed to the guests, who resume sipping their drinks without the anxiety. The guest of honour is led to a luxury, film-star-type trailer in the scene dock, so that there is no chance of him or her spotting any straying guests. Champagne is poured purely for purposes of relaxation.

In the studio control room Brian Klein calls, 'Quiet, please, everybody. And cue pick-up VT. . . .'

Then the moment of the pick-up is shown to the studio audience and to the guests on the programme. It is watched on a behind-the-scenes monitor screen by Michael and the subject.

The famous signature tune strikes up, the floor manager cues Michael, and, as the script states: 'Subject enters with Michael, greets, and sits.'

Another Life is underway. In half an hour subject, guests, Michael and ourselves will be celebrating at the party Thames always throw. The buffet is five-star, and guests can have the drink of their choice. A fleet of cars stands by to take them home. But that won't be until late . . . very late.

If this all sounds very extravagant, remember that no one gets paid for appearing on the Life, so the hospitality is one way of showing our appreciation. Even so, each show costs less to produce than the average sit-com.

Next day there are thank-you letters to be written, and photographs taken during the recording to be chosen and put in the Big Red Book, which is still in our possession. It will be sent, complete with a photographic record inside of the programme's big moments, and a cassette recording of the programme.

Then it's our turn to receive the thanks. 'Astonished', 'Still in a daze', 'So thrilled', 'The night of my life', are just some of the comments.

It really does make Life worthwhile.

Chapter Two
Birth of Life

How do you sit down and come up with the idea of *This Is Your Life*? It is the question the production team is most frequently asked.

The short answer is: you don't. Television's most enduring format was not really invented; it evolved from something quite different.

Let me take you back, as a Life script might say, to the NBC station in Hollywood, 27 April 1946, where a young radio producer/emcee is presenting an unusual act on his *Truth or Consequences* show, one of the top-rated prime-time radio network shows of all time.

He is Ralph Edwards, who started working as a radio announcer while in high school in Oakland, California. Following graduation from the University of California, Berkeley, as an English major, he attacked New York and quickly became one of the most in-demand network announcers ever – heard on over forty shows a week.

In 1940 Ralph Edwards created *Truth or Consequences*, an audience participation show with no limitations: zany stunts, fantastic contests, and many 'good gesture' acts.

During the Second World War he persuaded his listeners to purchase over half a billion dollars in war bonds, for which he was presented with a special General Eisenhower Award. After the war, Ralph Edwards went to the Veterans' Administration in Washington and asked if he could be of help . . . particularly to returning war-wounded.

General Omar Bradley had charge of the Veterans' Administration. He thought Edwards could be useful and put him in touch with a service psychologist at a Veterans' Hospital in Long Beach, California. Ralph, talking to me at his home in Beverly Hills, said, 'They told me wounded, paraplegic boys were often afraid to go home, fearful they wouldn't be accepted and properly cared for. I decided to devote a segment of *Truth or Consequences* to wounded service men, reuniting them with friends and getting them to talk about their past.'

They decided to present a young ex-marine, Lawrence Tranter of Murray, Utah, on *Truth or Consequences* and surprise him with a show of love and pride from all of his family and school pals, his boss at the drug store and his favourite teacher. 'This Is Your Life past,' said Ralph, 'now, what about the future?' Knowing that Tranter was interested in watchmaking, Ralph arranged for Lawrence Tranter to be trained at the Bulova School of Watchmaking with a promise to help him open a jewellery shop of his own in the city of his choosing. 'Training completed two years later, Tranter returned to the radio programme – his wheelchair pushed by a lovely girl with red tresses, his wife,' said Ralph.

As all of this unfolded, Ralph realised he had a great new show and *This Is Your Life* began on radio (NBC network) in 1948. (In the meantime, *Truth or Consequences* continued as a hit radio and television show for thirty-eight years.)

This Is Your Life ran on network radio (NBC) for two years before transferring to television (also NBC) in 1952. Ralph Edwards featured outstanding people, from stars like Laurel and Hardy and Bette Davis to a Chicago cab driver, a character who even had coffee in the back of his cab for his customers.

The cab driver's name was Eddie Hamilton, and on the day of the programme there was a 'leak' to a newspaper that he was to be the guest of honour. To make sure he never got a chance to see the newspaper, Ralph's team became his non-stop 'fares' for the day, until the last 'fare' asked to be taken to the Studebaker Theatre where Ralph was waiting with the book.

More recently, we had the same experience with comedian Ken Dodd. Tickled we weren't when a national newspaper gossip columnist revealed that Michael Aspel would surprise him that day. Luckily for us, Doddy – who works nights, of course – is a late sleeper. Even more fortunate, his managers were in discussion at the time with Thames TV executives about a variety 'special' from the London Palladium.

So a 'cordon' was thrown around Ken, who found himself involved in all-day meetings, with hardly a chance for a cup of coffee, let alone reading any newspapers.

He was astonished when Michael Aspel pounced, just outside the Palladium. Said the comedian: 'Michael, that really put the wind up me. I thought you were the VAT man.'

It was almost by accident that the Life came to British television. The year was 1955, and Eamonn Andrews was sent to San Francisco in his capacity as boxing commentator (for many, the best in the business). The fight was between US Champion Rocky Marciano and Britain's Don Cockell.

Eamonn was already a BBC Television star, as host of *What's My Line?* Now the BBC were seeking another show for him to present. Before Eamonn left for America, Ronnie Waldman, head of BBC Light Entertainment, took him on one side and said he had been hearing a great deal about a certain programme on NBC. 'Take a look at it and let me know what you think. It's called *This Is Your Life.*'

Eamonn once told me: 'Well, I had a look at it, saw an American named Ralph Edwards presenting it, and my first reaction was: this *is* television. I immediately cabled Ronnie Waldman and told him it was a programme I would very much like to do.'

In the rarefied atmosphere of the BBC's corridors of power in the mid-Fifties, the Life idea was greeted with something less than enthusiasm. Telerecordings of the American version were sent for. There was much executive hand-wringing. It simply wasn't 'a BBC programme'.

Whenever we discussed this crucial period – would the Life make it to British screens? – Eamonn always reckoned it was one American edition in particular which finally persuaded the BBC hierarchy to give it a trial run. It was a Life on the Hollywood film actor Victor McLaglen. His seven brothers, all as well built as the star himself, flew in from all parts of the world for the reunion, bringing tears to those famous craggy features. But they brought a smile to Eamonn's, because those touching scenes did the trick with the powers-that-were in the BBC.

So Eamonn and the Life got the green light, though caution was

Life creator Ralph Edwards pictured with Eamonn on a visit to London.

hardly thrown to the winds: the programme would be transmitted on a monthly basis. In the television business that usually means someone is ready for it to disappear quietly from the schedules without too many red faces.

Red faces were soon everywhere when the worst that could possibly happen to the first British programme happened in spades.

Ralph Edwards was to present the first programme. He and his director, Axel Gruenberg, a great bear of a man, but prone to tears when directing emotional moments, arrived in London. Pretty soon Axel had good reason for tears.

The Americans looked at a shortlist of likely candidates for this first programme. Soccer legend Stanley Matthews was chosen. Unfortunately, a national newspaper had also drawn up its own shortlist and hit on Matthews by a process of elimination. At least, that was their story. Others thought it might have been a tip-off. Either way, when the long-since-folded *Daily Sketch* broke the story, it was bad news indeed for the group meeting in Ralph Edwards's St James Court flat. Eamonn told me, 'I'll never forget that day. I just felt numb.'

On location for *Dad's Army,* Clive Dunn is 'taken prisoner' by Eamonn.

As well he might; all the research had been done, the script written, guests invited. Matthews himself was away fishing. Was

there a chance the news of the 'leak' wouldn't reach him?

It was explained to the American that that was much more likely back home, where most newspapers are local. In Britain, where many are national, it was highly improbable that Matthews would not be aware of the story.

Ralph said that sometimes, even though the person had been told, he could pull it off. Tom Sloan, the new head of BBC Light Entertainment, said, 'No, Mr Edwards, you've come all this way to show us how to do surprises – now, *surprise us.*'

There was no programme being lined up in reserve; the chances of *This Is Your Life* making British screens in just four days' time looked remote.

Eamonn left the room for a moment. By the time he returned Ralph, Axel and the group had made a decision – the first subject of the Life here would be Eamonn himself. But the name they gave Eamonn was that of former world light-heavyweight boxing champion Freddie Mills.

With his boxing connections, Eamonn knew Freddie well. As a 'cover', a sports special was fixed up. Freddie would be a member of the panel, with Eamonn in the chair. Eamonn was given responsibility for luring Freddie into what would turn out to be the Life set-up.

Meanwhile, behind Eamonn's back, researchers were ferreting into his own story. His wife Grainne had told him she had to see her doctor. Eamonn was puzzled when he rang the doctor's and she wasn't there. She had gone on to do some shopping, she explained.

Eamonn and Grainne entertained Freddie Mills to dinner at their flat.

'I worked very hard on Freddie,' said Eamonn, then: 'To give him his due, he worked very hard on me.'

Freddie accepted Eamonn's invitation to go along with him to see this new programme from America in the studio next door to where the sports special was happening. Ralph Edwards, as presenter, walked among the audience, sprinkled with names who might be likely subjects. He stopped at where Eamonn was sitting with Freddie Mills. But he handed the book to Eamonn.

'This Is Your Life . . . oh, blimey . . . Eamonn Andrews . . .' read Eamonn out loud.

'I was in a daze,' he told me later. He was in a greater daze when, twenty years later and in response to an endless stream of letters, we trapped him again, this time for Thames TV.

On that occasion, Eamonn wanted a moving story with which to close the season. He was delighted when we told him we had found just the person – a heroic English missionary, returning home after a lifetime in Africa.

What Eamonn didn't know was that this particular hero did not exist.

A totally fictitious script was written. Eamonn rang the Life office from his dressing room to complain it simply wasn't human enough. On the fifth floor the team were working on his own Life, not knowing he was in the building. He had a day off – but had called in to collect some mail from his dressing room. All the evidence was swept off the desks in case he popped in.

Our plan was simple. Eamonn would be invited to make a guest appearance at the Teddington Studios – ten miles from the Euston offices and studios where Life was based at the time – on the *David Nixon Show*. David, that great magician, was a good friend from the earliest days of *What's My Line?* at the BBC, and had been a Life subject himself.

In fact, on that pick-up Eamonn had thought it was the end of his own life – literally. The idea was a trick in which David's magic associate Ali Bongo climbed into a sack, and, hey presto, out of the same sack came magician's assistant Penny Meredith.

It being a Christmas Show, it was Santa's sack. Without giving away Magic Circle confidences, Eamonn switched places with Penny, for whom the sack had been a comfortable fit. Not so for Eamonn. Not only was he like a trussed chicken in there, but David Nixon decided he would ad-lib a bit (as he often did), with Eamonn rapidly running out of air. 'Had David not opened the sack when he did I think it would have exploded,' said Eamonn, who just about managed to summon the wind to say the four magic words.

They're on the march from *It Ain't Half Hot, Mum* to help Eamonn 'throw the book' at their sergeant major, Windsor Davies.

Now it was David's turn to get his own back. But how to trick Eamonn?

It was his routine to telephone his wife and family in Dublin from his dressing room, after presenting the *Today* programme most evenings. We arranged for there to be a 'fault' on the line, and the call had to go through the Thames Television switchboard. So it was switched to Grainne, safely across the Irish Sea at our Teddington studios. But when they spoke, in Eamonn's mind Grainne was in Dublin.

So, after David Nixon had sprung the big surprise on The Big Fella (as we called him), he really did think it magic when Grainne walked on to the set.

'A record flight by Aer Lingus,' said Eamonn drily after the programme.

From that first programme, Life never looked back – it went from strength to strength and was soon occupying a weekly prime-time slot. So few would have imagined then that Eamonn himself would do a runner from the comforting arms of Auntie BBC.

But he did. He was tempted to independent television, to weekend contractor ABC TV, where I was a young current affairs producer with a young family.

That was 1964. By 1968 I had a third child, a huge mortgage and no work. That's how the unthinkable came about; I brought *This Is Your Life* to ITV.

But let's go back to the summer of 1964. As usual, Eamonn had spent the winter presenting the runaway hits of Life, *What's My Line?* and *Crackerjack* (on which Michael Aspel was to replace him).

As can happen in any industry, the 'Young Lions' were moving in to positions of influence at the BBC, and one of them was Donald Baverstock, former editor of the *Tonight* programme, and newly appointed Deputy Controller of Programmes at the BBC. He decided to drop *What's My Line?*, unfortunately without consulting Eamonn, who had just turned down a quarter of a million dollars a year to front the programme in New York.

Next, Eamonn was told the BBC thought it was time to 'rest' *This Is Your Life*. The irony is that both programmes were given the boot by the Beeb because they had decided they needed new product to take on the challenge of ITV. On ITV both programmes subsequently brought huge ratings and advertising revenue.

So the BBC made Eamonn an offer he *could* refuse. What they didn't know was that Eamonn had been approached by a former BBC programme director, who had worked with him on *What's My Line?*, about joining ITV. This was Brian Tesler, then Programme Controller of ABC Television, and now Deputy Chairman of London Weekend Television.

ABC had been told to pull their socks up on sports coverage. *World of Sport* was created, and who better to front it than Eamonn Andrews, for many years respected host of BBC radio's Saturday afternoon *Sports Report*?

But it was the promise of a Sunday job that hooked Eamonn. This was to be his own Sunday night chat show – Britain's first – with big name guests from all over the world.

'Live From London,' boomed the voice, *'The Eamonn Andrews Show* . . . and in tonight's show. . . .'

I was asked to leave my producer's job in Manchester to work on it, and what a great 'crack', as Eamonn might say, it really was. For four years, I met, entertained and wrote for the world's biggest stars, from Bing Crosby to Raquel Welch. Her manager told me that on the show she would be wearing 'not so much a mini-skirt, more a Band Aid'.

My home was still in the North, but in 1968 my wife and I decided it was time to move south with our three children, the last just twelve months old.

That was the year the government decided to reallocate the ITV broadcasting franchises.

I was at Eamonn's riverside home in Chiswick, along with Brian Tesler, waiting for the call which would tell us the result. ABC had lost. There would be a 'forced marriage' with London contractor Rediffusion. The result would be Thames Television, which became the weekday contractor for London for the next twenty-three years. Although I have always been freelance, I had had a contract with ABC since the late 1950s. And that contract ceased to exist when Thames Television was born.

So there we were, in the winter of 1968, myself, my wife Patti and our three children, sitting in the kitchen of our newly purchased home in Richmond, Surrey, with Dad out of work for the first time in his life.

Life was re-born at that very moment.

I was in a situation which certainly galvanised the mind. I had two points of television logic and experience on which to work. The first was that Thames Television, the new company, were left with Eamonn Andrews – the star whose poaching from the BBC ABC had trumpeted – without a network show. So desperate were they, they dispatched a senior executive to cull the vast television ocean of America in the hope of finding a species as rare as *This Is Your Life*.

At my home just over the footbridge across the Thames from the Teddington studios, my mind went back to the days of the Life I had watched back in the North. It had been compulsive viewing for anyone with a TV set.

Like every programme then, it was in black and white.

And that led to my second idea. At long last, colour television was to be launched in November 1969. After scribbling down ideas all day, after supper I turned to Patti and said, 'Would you watch a programme called "This Is Your Colourful Life"?' She agreed instantly that to bring back Eamonn fronting that marvellous TV vehicle was a great idea. But 'colourful life'?

I explained that it might have more chance of getting past the powers-that-be if it appeared to be launched in tandem with a massive marketing campaign to persuade people to ditch their old black and white sets and dash out and buy or hire the new colour TVs.
Hard to imagine now, but 'who needs a colour TV?' was a common expression. Rather like only a few short years ago when people were saying, 'But who wants satellite TV?'

It was one of those ideas I had nearly talked myself out of by next morning. I could hear all the executive arguments. At the launch of a brand new ITV company, Thames Television, with a franchise to broadcast to the capital, and to the network, five days a week, was this all they could come up with? A rehash of a programme the dull old Auntie BBC had taken off the air back in 1964?

I tested the water with Eamonn, who took the idea to Brian Tesler. Brian had given me my first break in television, in 1958, selecting me from a shortlist of experienced journalists to be producer of ABC TV's regional flagship current affairs programme *ABC of the North*. He it was who brought me to London to work on the late night Sunday chat show, and at his behest, I had returned north for a brief spell, to be editor of ABC's news and current affairs. I had not let him down.

Eamonn rang to arrange to meet me in my local pub in Richmond. When I walked in, just after opening time, he was already there, wearing that famous lop-sided grin.

'Brian will give us a pilot and six shows after if he likes it,' smiled Eamonn. He had even more to smile about. Unknown to me he had let his first-option rights to present the programme in England lapse. In the intervening few days he had flown to Los Angeles to meet up with Ralph Edwards and ensure those rights were once again secured.

Six programmes have now become over six hundred.

But who was to be the all-important first? Not necessarily the first programme viewers would see, but the show we recorded as the 'pilot', the try-out show to impress the top brass?

No one had any idea who the very first ITV subject to be transmitted on the network would be (I had a good idea, but kept it under wraps for reasons to be explained).

Eamonn, in his early BBC years, had had the advantage of carrying on Ralph Edwards's tradition (based on original inspiration) of bringing about a reunion of war veterans, not only with their families and friends but with their courageous wartime comrades. We were now two decades on. But Eamonn, rightly, insisted on looking for a first subject to record whose story was one of determined triumph over inconceivable odds.

My mind went back to the very title of this chapter: *Birth of Life*. To the blank, wheelchair-bound hopelessness of that very first subject of the Life on radio in 1946: paraplegic war veteran Lawrence Tranter.

Where was the story which encapsulated every ingredient of the original *This Is Your Life*?

For this try-out pilot programme in the harsh, commercial, realistic world of ITV, there was no room for a 'leak' or 'runner'. This was real Life.

Truly I forget the many names that were pitched, most of whom Eamonn had 'done' years ago at the BBC. I thought long and hard and went back to the fundamentals of the programme which had once held the nation's viewers spellbound. I tried to remember stories I had covered in my newspaper days in the north. Was there something there I was overlooking since my transition to the glamorous world of television and show business?

Indeed there was. The first subject of *This Is Your Life* on Thames Television was – literally – staring me in the face.

And from a wheelchair.

His name was Harry Driver. With his writing partner Vince Powell he created such television comedy gems as *For the Love of Ada* and *Nearest and Dearest* (for which I was later to co-write both TV and film). Vince still turns in great popular comedy such as *Ne'er The Twain*. He and Harry had been a semi-pro double act in the northern clubs. Then Harry, married with two children, was taken ill. Polio was diagnosed. He was confined to an iron lung.

A working-class northerner of great pride, he was determined to remain the family breadwinner. If he could not perform comedy, he would write it. If he could not sell his written comedy, he would write drama.

But how? His paralysis meant he could not even use his fingers, but in his mouth he could hold a knitting needle. With that knitting needle he could tap the keys of a portable electric typewriter.

As a young journalist in Manchester, I wrote an article about Harry.

With his partner, he had persevered, against all odds, to write some of the most successful comedies on British television, including one which took the nation by storm: *Love Thy Neighbour*, the first white-family-next-door-to-black-family comedy.

I had worked with Harry and Vince when an original script I had co-written for Hylda Baker (about a northern pub landlady, based on my own mother) was, for want of a better word 'fused' into *Nearest and Dearest*. I'll never forget Hylda, at a swish West End restaurant, telling the wine waiter how much she liked the wine. 'This sparkling Bordeaux, where does it come from?'

Anyway, the idea of a man in a wheelchair with a great Northern sense of humour became the first try-out subject of Thames Television's recording of *This Is Your life*.

The newly built studios at Euston Road were not ready, so we recorded the programme at the Burlington Hotel in the West End. It was a huge success. What's more, it was in colour.

My concept of 'This Is Your *Colourful* Life' had been dropped, without any argument from me; after all, the message had got through.

We had a start.

But Eamonn, as he did to the very end, still harked back to the days of live television. He loved the Harry Driver Life, but he didn't want to come back on air, on ITV, with a recorded programme.

At our meeting the next day he thumped the table: 'That was good, very good. But I want our first transmission on the ITV network to be *live.*'

But who? And how? Scanning the *Evening Standard* I spotted a London Palladium advertisement announcing that Des O'Connor was opening there in the week of our first broadcast.

Not for the first – or the last – time did Eamonn mutter: 'But is he big enough?' I convinced him we should do the Life on Des with a ploy Eamonn seized on – he would walk on stage at the Palladium and we would do the programme right there and then, live from that world-famous theatre.

But the Curse of the First Life struck again; this time not a leak to the press, but a far more bizarre situation.

Everything was fixed with the Palladium management for the evening of 19 November 1969. Guests who would appear on the show had assembled at Thames Television HQ. They were ushered into a luxury coach to be taken to the theatre.

At that very moment Des O'Connor was strolling from his dressing room and heading towards the stage door to take a breath of the evening air before going on stage.

A set of traffic lights, less than a hundred yards away, turned to red. A coach stopped. Our coach.

Des blinked. Did he recognise a familiar face or two? Or was it a trick of the imagination? Before he could get a closer look, the lights changed and the coach drove off.

On board was every single surprise guest. Fortunately we remained oblivious to the incident until after the show, by which time it had been confirmed to Des that he hadn't been hallucinating.

Frankie Howerd could just about manage 'Oh, missus!' when Eamonn collared him.

It wasn't long before the Life was hitting Number One in the ratings. Our promise of a 'pilot' and six shows was to become one of the longest runners on television.

Eamonn presented the show for eighteen years on Thames Television. I also acted as his consultant in the highly successful revival of *What's My Line?*, again for Thames. Yet sometimes I wondered if he wasn't still, at heart, a BBC man. Had the BBC axe not been poised over the Line and the Life I doubt if Eamonn would have 'defected'. Ironically, on his first-ever *Eamonn Andrews Show* for ITV, his trousers were held up by a pair of grey braces – stamped 'Property of the BBC'. But he wasn't any more; nor was he ever again.

As we took our places around the Life conference table one morning in 1986, during the BBC's celebrations of fifty years of television, Eamonn slipped a note to me. It was handwritten in the green ink that was his trademark. 'Roy, could you write a piece along these lines and place it, say, with the *Sunday Times?'*

I showed the note to no one, but I kept it. It began: 'Is somebody trying to tell us something? In the BBC's recent nostalgia splurge, who appeared more often than anyone else? Eamonn Andrews.

'We saw him on *Crackerjack*, on *What's My Line?*, and a *This Is Your Life* saluting Harry Secombe. Even David Frost did an impression of him. Then bang up-to-date 1986-style Ludovic Kennedy on *Did You See?* did a sparkling in-depth mini documentary on his current series. To crown it all, Robert Robinson featured him on Tuesday night in *The Magic Rectangle* – an anatomy of the television personality in which many BBC star names were featured. Yet when BBC Chief Bill Cotton chose a name he picked Eamonn. "Make no mistake," he said, "Eamonn Andrews is a very clever man. A very clever man." '

Eamonn's note then added: 'Hasn't anybody told them he signed up with Thames TV (then ABC TV) in 1964?'

So what, through me, was Eamonn trying to tell the BBC? That his contract was coming up for renewal (which it was)? I don't know. I never got around to writing the piece – I was far too busy with Eamonn's scripts – and he never mentioned the subject again.

In fact, his new contract for a further three years with Thames was agreed the following year, but by that time Eamonn's health had begun to deteriorate rapidly.

But his almost youthful enthusiasm for the programme remained. To surprise conductor Sir Georg Solti, I suggested he disguise himself as a Royal Opera House 'flunkey', complete with white wig, gaiters and buckled shoes. Eamonn, despite looking thin and gaunt, was game. When the car taking him to the Opera House in Covent Garden got stuck in a West End traffic jam, he wanted to dash from the car to the nearest tube station – still dressed as a flunkey. Now that really would have stopped the traffic!

Eamonn's wife Grainne, by the way, hated the disguises we dreamed up for Eamonn for the pick-up. She told me they made her cringe. Apart from that one reservation, though, she had been a wonderful, star-deflating ally of mine from the very early days of my starting to work with Eamonn.

The first time I delivered a script to Eamonn at their home beside the river in Chiswick, I wore a pair of very tight black trousers, mohair and silk, my first piece of reckless personal spending after signing my new contract.

Introduced to Grainne, I froze. In those days there was no question she could have stepped in as Elizabeth Taylor's double. A stunning woman, with a tinkling laugh and those Irish eyes.

I dropped the script. When I bent down to pick it up, the new trousers, with a noise that seemed to come from the soundtrack of a 'Carry On' film, split right down my backside. I paused in mid pick-up; my blushes were in technicolor. Eamonn just looked at me. Grainne burst into a peal of infectious laughter which, in seconds, had us all holding our sides. Or, in my case, my back sides.

We fast-forward to November 1987. Though we had only just started to record a new season of twenty-six programmes, Grainne had persuaded Eamonn to take a short, health-boosting break in Lanzarote to celebrate their thirty-sixth wedding anniversary.

This was to be immediately after we had surprised former Wales and British Lions scrum-half Cliff Morgan, now head of Outside Broadcasts at the BBC, at the Hilton Hotel in Park Lane, venue for a BBC Sport celebration dinner.

But Eamonn was having severe respiratory problems and he was rushed to the private Cromwell Road hospital. He insisted he would do the show.

'Only from a wheelchair,' said a nurse.

We postponed the programme. Nevertheless, Eamonn still sent for scripts to read in his hospital bed. With Grainne, he even watched that week's edition of the Life.

It was Irish comedian Jimmy Cricket, the last Life Eamonn would ever see. He could afford a special chuckle, because we nearly lost that show. In the middle of Oxford Circus the day before the programme, Jimmy accidentally bumped into our surprise fly-in from Australia. I broke the news to Eamonn in the office at Thames Studios at Teddington. He shook his head in disbelief.

'A ten million to one chance,' he sighed. 'It could only happen to an Irishman. What do we do?' I invented an excuse for the visitor to have been there without contacting him. 'Jesus, Mary, and Joseph,' muttered Eamonn.

Whispered our Catholic production secretary: 'For a Catholic, that's serious.'

In the Cromwell Hospital he saw his final credit roll: 'This Is Your Life. Presented by Eamonn Andrews'. Grainne kissed him on the cheek and left him to sleep.

My own sleep was broken at 3 a.m. on 5 November 1987, to tell me the Big Fella would never wake up.

Another call. A car was on its way from the studios of TV-AM for me to pay tribute to Eamonn. I was in a total daze. After the TV appearance, the car took me to Teddington Studios. Everyone who had ever worked with Eamonn was in a state of shock.

Terry Wogan came in to present a Thames tribute that night, during which we re-ran the Thames *This Is Your Life* on Eamonn.

It was difficult to come to terms with the fact that his life was over.

The official cause of death was 'progressive deterioration of the heart muscle'. Grainne told me at the family funeral in Portmarnock: 'I think it was more a case of a broken heart.'

She would not be drawn, but I believe she was referring to four years of financial turmoil and unsuccessful business ventures taking their toll. She also blamed that for the death of her father, Lorcan. 'His spirit was broken,' she said.

Within eighteen months, Grainne Andrews had passed away herself. Cancer was the official cause. Personally, when she was laid to rest by Eamonn's side in the hillside cemetery at Portmarnock, I thought there were two broken hearts.

For they had always beaten as one.

Chapter Three
New Lease of Life

In those hours, days, then weeks after Eamonn's death, I was often interviewed on television, on radio or in the press about him, a man who had truly been a broadcasting legend. The burning question was always the same: does his passing away mean the death of Life?

To be honest, I thought it did. Having worked with Eamonn for twenty-four years, going back to the time of his departure from the BBC, I thought ITV would kill off the Life.

My wife, Patti, questioned this. She reminded me that I had worked behind the scenes to ensure the continued success of the programme when many people thought it had outlived its welcome, and indeed its supply of subjects, its lifeblood. She also pointed out that I had never subscribed to this view, always believing firmly that *This Is Your Life* was and remains a self-regenerating concept. Stars, legends, heroes and heroines of one decade make way for those of the next. And the Life should be there to honour them.

Had not Life's creator, Ralph Edwards himself, been so taken with the massive popular success of the programme in the UK that he had brought it back to American screens for another successful run? And was Life not also a hit in Australia, New Zealand, Spain, Holland and Germany?

I sat down in my study and thought about what my wife had said. Next day, I rang producer Malcolm Morris. He was thinking along the same lines.

Meanwhile, we were only one month into a projected twenty-six-week season. Thames Television took the decision to repeat some Eamonn 'classic' Lives, plus the few programmes he had recorded just before his death. Then, at a tasteful interval after Eamonn's memorial service, at which there was a 'Who's Who' turn-out of the biggest names in the nation, from show business to politics, sports to the arts, Thames made it clear the company would like to keep the Life alive.

But this would not be until the following autumn season, starting in September 1988. That was many months away. After the shock of Eamonn's death started to subside, the nation had a new guessing game.

From schoolroom to bar room, factory floor to the City, building site to Women's Institute and around every television set in the land, just about everybody *knew* who would replace Eamonn, whose hands would turn the pages of the Big Red Book. Our telephones were red hot with suggestions, and not only from show-business agents and managers. Viewers, too, felt they had the one and only name. One or two 'names' even rang to suggest that they were the one to replace the Big Fella, among them several former subjects.

One lobby was for choosing a female host and I must confess I was not averse to this. Gloria Hunniford was on my shortlist. Naturally, the name of Terry Wogan came high on anybody's list. He had not hesitated to come along to the studios of the 'opposition' to present the tribute to Eamonn on the day of his death, and he had delivered, as usual, an impeccable, professional appearance. After that, we thought Terry would be favourite. Of course, he was still very much a BBC man, and under contract. But then, so had Eamonn been until he decided to quit and join ITV.

The guesswork continued. Michael Parkinson said he would not want the job, and suggested Frank Bough. Noel Edmonds, Leslie Crowther and Russell Harty (who was to die in June) were also tipped to be among the runners heading for the finishing post. Derek Jameson, who was presenting *Headliners*, hinted to me he would like to be in the frame.

I recalled once asking Eamonn if he had ever thought of who might step into his shoes. He grinned and said, 'Mike Yarwood?' He had always thought Mike's impression of him was brilliant.

How Eamonn's successor was finally found was worthy of a Life surprise pick-up at its best.

The scene was Twickenham, headquarters of the Rugby Football Union. February 1988, and the crowds were gathering for the England–Wales international.

Michael Aspel is a keen rugby fan and a self-adopted Welshman. His broadcasting career began in Cardiff, so his Welsh accent is impeccable and also hilarious.

Another Welsh supporter in the crowd that day was John Howard Davies, the former child actor (he was Oliver in the 1948 film of *Oliver Twist*) who became an award-winning director/producer at the BBC with comedies such as *The Good Life*.

He had joined Thames Television as Head of Light Entertainment. If Thames were to continue with a new series of *This Is Your Life* in the autumn, it would be his responsibility to choose the new presenter, Eamonn's successor as custodian of that famous Big Red Book.

Like thousands of others that day, Michael had brought a picnic lunch in the boot of his car. He was about to tuck in when who should spot him but John Howard Davies.

Casually, John said to Michael, 'Love to have a chat with you sometime.'

Michael knew exactly what he meant. The plot thickened.

Of course, the name of Michael Aspel had been mentioned in the course of our discussions, but was it a real possibility? After all, he was under contract to London Weekend Television for his chat show. It was very unusual for one company to release a contract artiste to another company, even within the ITV network.

But a cloak-and-dagger operation of *This Is Your Life*-style secrecy was under way. John Howard Davies let producer Malcolm Morris in on the secret, and Michael's agent was contacted. Talks went on at Michael's home in Esher. Eventually a 'package' was agreed by all concerned, including, of course, London Weekend. It meant Michael would continue to present *Aspel and Company* at the weekend as well as twenty-six Wednesday night Lives.

The official announcement came in March, five months after Eamonn's death. How much money would the 'package' be worth to Michael? With a verbal body-swerve that would have lit up Twickenham, Michael told the assembled press, 'A great deal less than you are going to print.'

When we were introduced, Michael told me, 'My great fear is the subjects will look at the book and say, "Oh, thank you, Eamonn." '

His fears proved groundless when he sprang his first surprise. Mind you, international rock star Phil Collins could have been forgiven for not recognising the man who confronted him in Covent Garden as anyone from television.

We persuaded the normally immaculate Michael to become a Covent Garden busker – unshaven, shabbily dressed, and wearing a wig of long, greasy hair. We also persuaded some big stars – Bob Geldof, Midge Ure and Howard Jones – to become buskers for the afternoon, so that the scruffy Michael could hide behind them. They were also part of our insurance: we had been tipped off that Phil Collins might do a runner if he saw the Big Red Book, so we hoped his pals from the rock scene would stop him!

Phil was taken to Covent Garden for an interview with an American television company about his latest film, *Buster*, based on the Great Train Robbery. That was our white lie.

When our own director and his production assistant arrived in Covent Garden to supervise the hoped-for pick-up, a scruffy, bearded figure shuffled towards them.

'Hello,' he growled.

They looked at each other. Surely no one they knew?

'Gotcha!' beamed Michael. They simply hadn't recognised him.

Michael hitches a lift with *Heartbeat*'s PC Nick Rowan (Nick Berry) on the North Yorkshire moors. They were on their way to 'book' Sergeant Oscar Blaketon, actor Derek Fowlds.

And if they were surprised, Phil Collins was absolutely stunned when the scruffy old busker produced the Big Red Book – for his first time – from under his tatty anorak. Phil was so taken aback he looked as though he couldn't have done a runner if he had tried.

To everyone's relief – especially Michael's – try he didn't, and it was the new lease of Life that was up and running.

But all the pre-pick-up activity in Covent Garden – where so many media firms have their headquarters – had led to a press tip-off. Michael as a busker was irresistible to Fleet Street, and our pick-up made page one pictures just about everywhere next day.

So it looked as though the viewers would now know the identity of Michael Aspel's first *This Is Your Life* subject. This we could not allow; it would dampen the big surprise element. Of course, the Phil Collins programme would be transmitted later in the series – it was a wonderful Life – but someone else would have to be chosen for Michael's début with the Big Red Book.

At that time, Hollywood and Broadway legend Mickey Rooney was opening in the West End with his American hit musical *Sugar Babies*. Nothing could have been sweeter for us than when we got the nod to mount a Life on Mickey. Researchers set out to find Mickey's children from all nine of his marriages. They flew in to London on the night, 11 October 1988, and followed Michael Aspel on stage at the Savoy Theatre at the curtain call for *Sugar Babies*.

By this time, Mickey Rooney's story had reached the proportions of the most far-fetched musical script.

Sugar Babies was based on burlesque – a saucy American form of revue – and couldn't have been more appropriate for Mickey, because his mother was a burlesque chorus girl and his Edinburgh-born father the 'top banana' (the show's main attraction). When his parents' marriage broke up, the young Mickey moved with Mum to Los Angeles. There he made fifteen films in four years as the all-American youngster Andy Hardy.

He also made *National Velvet* with Elizabeth Taylor, who wrote from her sickbed a letter for Michael Aspel to read on the programme.

Michael had a surprise for ringmaster Norman Barrett at Blackpool's Tower Circus, but comedian Bernie Clifton had a surprise of his own. He made an appearance as the 'Red Shadow', singing 'My Desert is Calling' – then cooled things down with an unscripted blast of dry ice. What's that on his shoulder? His 'weeping cat'. Said Bernie: 'It's an emotional night for me and the cat.'

Wrote Elizabeth: '*National Velvet* will always be one of my favourite films because I worked with one of the dearest, warmest and most giving human beings – you. All my love, Elizabeth.'

Ann Rutherford, his screen girlfriend in the Andy Hardy films, flew in, as did Donald O'Connor, legendary star of great movie musicals and Mickey's mate for forty years. We showed film of the two of them at Judy Garland's fifteenth birthday party in 1937.

We brought back memories of the film he made with Spencer Tracy fifty years before: *Boys' Town*, based on a true story of a priest who started the 'town' in Nebraska. We filmed there to show its work now.

Vic Damone, George Peppard and Anthony Quinn all added their tributes to the much-married Mickey, who said his marriage certificate should be made out 'To Whom It May Concern'.

But what was it that made this story compete with any flight of Hollywood fancy?

Virtually 'born in a trunk' youngster finds Hollywood stardom. His name is known the world over. His career goes into decline. By the late Sixties he is down to his last hundred dollars. Then an old Hollywood actor pal, who has become a producer and theatre owner in Miami, gets a play he wants to put on and immediately thinks of his mate Mickey Rooney. He finds him, now nearly down to his last buck.

The play is about alimony. 'I know all about that,' says Mickey.

The old pal is Eddie Bracken. The play is a triumph for Mickey. A New York producer is in the first night audience. In his briefcase is the script for *Sugar Babies*. It runs on Broadway for seven years. With Mickey Rooney.

You couldn't write it.

By the moment Michael presented Mickey with the book, we knew we had a great show. But would the critics think the same? And would our loyal viewers?

Today's critic Daphne Lockyer summed it up: 'So great was he (Mickey) to behold I actually forgot it was Aspel's performance I was meant to be reviewing. But, then, it's really a compliment to Aspel if I say that I barely noticed him at all. It shows he is doing his job.'

She went on: 'It was Eamonn Andrews's skill as well never to steal the limelight, but to train it on whoever appeared on his show. And Aspel has quite brilliantly taken over that mantle.'

Others echoed that view. And when the letters started to come in from the viewers, it was clear that John Howard Davies had done a perfect tackle in the Twickenham car park.

So, the transition from Eamonn to Michael had been made. But I have to say it was not without a great deal of head-banging or, rather, typewriter-banging on my part.

When I sat down to write the first scripts for Michael, it was Eamonn's voice I still had in my head. After twenty-four years, what else? I had consciously to remind myself of Michael's very special style. 'Laid back' is what many critics like to call it. Myself, I think it is 'quirky', a quirk being defined by the *Concise Oxford Dictionary* as 'trick of action or behaviour; twist or flourish in drawing or writing'.

Well, one of Michael's earliest ambitions was to be a cartoonist, and

I had to bring that 'quirky' concept to the page. Once it was there, he built on it.

On the Mickey Rooney show, introducing our emotional closing guest (for Eamonn, a moment of deep sincerity and drum-rolls, and he would demand it was written as such) Michael said, 'Yes, it's Mickey and Donald' – bringing on Donald O'Connor, flown in from Hollywood. 'Sounds like something out of Walt Disney,' beamed Aspel.

Wrote one critic: 'Tears of laughter or tears of sentiment – by this stage I can tell you I barely knew.'

I was to enjoy many tears of laughter working with Michael on those early programmes. Five successful years later, I still do.

I'm often asked what the two presenters of *This Is Your Life* have in common.

In the best possible way, if any two men could claim to be in touch with the so-called 'common man or woman', they are Eamonn Andrews and Michael Aspel.

Both were born into working-class families. Eamonn's father was a carpenter, Michael's a commissionaire. Both had an early interest in drama, Eamonn in amateur dramatics, Michael totally absorbed by the cinema.

They had educations of a similar kind – of the old grammar school variety, Eamonn at Synge Street Christian Brothers' School in Dublin, Michael at Emmanuel School in Wandsworth, where he was born.

And both started their working lives in jobs far removed from the glamorous world of broadcasting. Eamonn became an insurance company clerk. Michael worked first as a tea-boy in the office of a publishing company, then, after National Service in the army in Germany, as a bed salesman at a department store in Cardiff.

Both were frustrated actors. Eamonn even wrote plays for himself to be in. In Cardiff, Michael joined a local amateur dramatic company.

And both cut their broadcasting teeth in radio.

Eamonn, a successful amateur boxer, started to do freelance night work as a commentator for Dublin's commercial radio station. So keen was he, he once handed over his broadcasting position to climb into the ring, win the next fight, then resume commentary at the ringside on the next, still in his dressing gown.

Michael, eleven years younger, got his first job in radio via the amateur dramatic society, when the local BBC station in Cardiff wanted someone who could 'do voices'.

He was, and still is, excellent with accents and caricature voices, so he got the job in a children's adventure serial playing a number of different roles, including, as Eamonn put it on Michael's Life, Cardiff's James Bond of the early Fifties. The serial was called *Counterspy*, and Michael was the dashing hero, James 'Rocky' Mountain.

One day Michael asked the department store for time off so he could complete an episode. He was refused, but went along to the studio anyway. He got the boot from the bed department.

But a new dawn was breaking for the youthful Aspel. He started doing stints as an announcer – just as Eamonn had moved on from boxing commentaries to fronting a live theatre quiz show, later taken on tour in the UK by the bandleader Joe Loss. Long before *This Is Your Life*, Michael had followed Eamonn on BBC Radio's *Family Favourites*, then on BBC TV's *Crackerjack*.

Most amazing of all is that Michael, a car buff, wanted to buy Eamonn's twenty-year-old Mercedes after his death. In the event he didn't – it went for auction in Dublin – but Michael bided his time until he found a similar model and bought that.

Eamonn always suffered from nerves before a show, and so does Michael. During my years on *This Is Your Life* I have worked with the biggest names in the business, and I know that insecurity is the name of the game. All are convinced that one day someone will tap them on the shoulder and say, in Eamonn's case, 'Hey, you, back to that gas-lit flat in Synge Street your dad had for eighteen bob a week.' Or, in Michael's, 'Hey, you, back to Wandsworth, telly's not for the likes of you!'

In a curious way, both Eamonn and Michael found a totally uncharted path to success. But no one can take away their absolute determination to go for goal the moment they had got the pass. Neither are the types to boot doors open; but once in . . . tenacity is the word.

But what would they really, truly, have liked to do?

Eamonn once told me his ultimate ambition was to be a black-hat 'baddie', like Jack Palance in *Shane* (one of Michael's favourite films). But he would like to write the part for himself, because, even towards the end of his life, he still saw himself as potential novelist and playwright. He was putting off those jobs for his retirement, he told me. Once I offered to write his life story.

'Roy, I couldn't let you do that. You'd tell the truth.' He puffed on his Havana, and grinned the famous grin.

And Michael? He would love to knock off a few thousand words before lunch as a best-selling novelist between acting stints, preferably in the role of a rogue English lord, the black sheep of the family, who arrives in the Wild West.

In real life, he did get to act several times, once in a touring version

Michael Aspel was the recipient of the book this time. He is pictured with his actress wife Elizabeth Power, destined to find fame in *EastEnders* as Christine Hewitt.

of Noël Coward's *Private Lives* – in which he met his wife Lizzie, now Christine Hewitt in *EastEnders*. They had not been married long when Eamonn walked on the set of Michael's popular game show *Give Us A Clue* – with the Big Red Book.

'Truly a strange and amazing experience,' Michael told me. 'But I'm delighted Eamonn gave me that Life experience, because now I know what might be going through the minds of the people I surprise.'

It must work. In the preview of the evening's viewing on 17 April 1991, the *Daily Mirror* noted: 'For those of us who can still remember the way Eamonn Andrews presented this show with a cheeky twinkle, it has taken some time (since November 1988) to be convinced that anyone else could really do the job. . . . But Michael Aspel has made it his own, bringing professionalism combined with a charming lightness of touch. It can't be easy to suddenly whip out that famous Big Red Book, tell unsuspecting victims that their whole lives are about to pass before them, and then go on to keep the whole thing bubbling with just the right amounts of humour and nostalgia.'

The programme continues in America, where the national cable channel, American Movie Classics, is currently playing some of Ralph Edwards's vintage Lives – the subjects read like a list of names from Hollywood's Avenue of Stars. And in the summer of 1992 there was a special presentation at the Museum of Television and Radio in New York of an hour-long video covering the career of Ralph Edwards in production and broadcasting.

Yes. The Life has had a new lease of life.

Chapter Four
Life and Legends

With the select team assigned to work on the Life of Earl Mountbatten of Burma, I reported to a top-secret address in an anonymous Knightsbridge mews. Waiting for us was Lord Brabourne, Lord Louis's son-in-law and former wartime ADC.

The meeting was the first result of 'feelers' we had put out about the possibility of presenting the book to Lord Louis in the Jubilee Year of HM the Queen. Eight months of blood, sweat and tears were to elapse before that actually happened on 26 April 1977.

In the foyer of the Euston studios of Thames TV, Eamonn springs his surprise on Lord Louis Mountbatten — aided by the war hero's former ADC and son-in-law, Lord Brabourne, on Mountbatten's right.

On that day in 1976 we had to persuade Lord Brabourne to be our co-conspirator on the Life of his father-in-law. Born in 1900, the sixty-third year of the reign of his great-grandmother, Queen Victoria, Lord Louis had helped to shape the century's history. His mother, daughter of Queen Victoria's second daughter, Alice, was also named Victoria.

Veteran of two world wars and last Viceroy of India, his story was the very stuff of Life. Lord Brabourne listened to our early plans and promised he would consult his wife, Patricia, Lord Louis's daughter, and her younger sister, Lady Pamela Hicks.

That meeting had taken place just before Christmas. We were invited back to the same secret address early in the New Year.

This time Lord Mountbatten's daughters were there too. They poured tea and went around the room with sandwiches. As we chatted, their enthusiasm for the project started to mount.

Getting the go-ahead was one thing, but pinning down the globetrotting Lord Louis was another. How could we be sure he would definitely be in London to keep an appointment? It would have to be something special. It was Lady Pamela who came up with the answer.

April 26 was her birthday, and her father would definitely keep that date free to join whatever celebration was planned. One idea they had talked about was a treat for his grandchildren – a showing of some of the episodes of the 1967 television series of Mountbatten's *Life and Times*. Some of the grandchildren had been too young to watch it at the time.

The natural venue would be the viewing theatre at the studios of Thames Television, where the film was in the vaults. But when the family party arrived, who would be waiting in the foyer but Eamonn Andrews with the Big Red Book. Rarely have I seen Eamonn so nervous as he was that night, and with good reason. When he stepped forward with the book Mountbatten snapped, 'What do you mean?' Then he saw the beaming faces of the dozen members of his family, and himself flashed a smile which meant we could up anchor and sail away with our show.

But it was a programme – watched by twenty million viewers – which nearly did not happen. We had more than 180 guests arriving from all over the world, including Bob Hope, Danny Kaye, Dame Vera Lynn and Jackie Coogan. And a work-to-rule threat at Heathrow looked likely to throw airline schedules into chaos.

Worse still, four days before our programme, Mountbatten himself was enjoying a family holiday in the Bahamas. It was a relief to know that Lord Brabourne was with him, because, as a successful film producer, he was well acquainted with the vagaries and unpredictability of our business. It helped cool the panic factor.

There were sighs of relief all round when the airport dispute was solved and our guests started to arrive, among them Captain Charles Drake. He had started as a 'snotty' – naval slang for midshipman – with Mountbatten, who served in the First World War at sixteen. Captain Drake told how 'Dickie' Mountbatten had asked the First Lord of the Admiralty, on an inspection, if they could have their supper sardine ration increased from two to three. The then First Lord was Winston Churchill. The ration wasn't increased.

We showed film shot by another legend, Charlie Chaplin, of the Mountbattens' honeymoon in Hollywood in 1922. Sir Charles, who was not well enough to travel from Switzerland, sent a photograph

53

of himself with Lord Louis. The caption read, 'Breaking the news to Lord Mountbatten that he is no actor.'

Then he added, 'But a great military commander and peacetime administrator. Hollywood's loss was the world's gain.'

More archive film showed him with his cousin David, Prince of Wales, later King Edward VIII and later still Duke of Windsor, getting the crossing-the-Equator 'ducking'.

Former Hong Kong Governor Sir Robert Neville told of a polo goal scored by Lord Louis, which was 'unique in the annals of the game'. The ball had whizzed past him and was caught 'in the fundament' by Mountbatten's pony. Lord Louis rode over the goal-line, the pony lifted its tail, dropped the ball and a goal was allowed.

It was the turn of Lord Brabourne to be surprised by Michael Aspel at the banquet to celebrate five hundred Life programmes made by Thames.

A moving moment came with the arrival of survivors of the destroyer HMS *Kelly*, who had presented its torn and bullet-riddled flag to their skipper. Noël Coward had based his film *In Which We Serve* on their exploits, giving a break to two young hopefuls who also came on the show – Sir Bernard Miles (later Lord Miles) and Sir John Mills.

On 23 May 1941, the *Kelly* was attacked by twenty-four enemy divebombers and rolled over completely. A survivor, Fred Garner, turned to the first other member of the crew he spotted in the water and said, 'Funny how scum always rises to the top.' Then he realised it was his skipper, Lord Louis.

Lastly came a few survivors of the Japanese POW camps, freed by Mountbatten's South-East Asia campaign. When he visited the notorious Changi gaol, the prisoners, though starving and in rags, had formed a guard of honour for him. They were the 'forgotten army' Mountbatten had refused to forget. And all felt a part of the title he chose: Earl Mountbatten of Burma.

In the build-up to Christmas 1978, as I drove to the studios, inevitably Bing Crosby sang *White Christmas* on the car radio; but it was a black Christmas I was dreaming of – in the shape of three-times World Heavyweight Champion Muhammad Ali. On Christmas Day television I wanted to flatten the BBC opposition with the man who, at the time, was World Champion Personality.

The very mention of his name at the production conference meant that Eamonn would, from then on, hear no other. To the former Amateur Middleweight Champion of Ireland, Ali was a god-like figure; a fighter whose lightning intelligence was not merely confined to the ring. Not for nothing was he known as 'The Louisville Lip'.

Surrounded by the ladies in his Life, ring legend Muhammad Ali.

As Eamonn recalled to his cost. More than a decade before, after Ali had fought our own Henry Cooper, he made his first British TV appearance on Eamonn's late-night chat show. It was also the first appearance since he had announced his change of name, for religious reasons, from Cassius Marcellus Clay to Muhammad Ali.

He told Eamonn that if anyone in the USA still called him Cassius he said only one thing, 'You know my name, fella. . . .' It was stated quietly, but with enough menace to scare off a bar room of brawlers.

Said Eamonn: 'Fair enough, but let's talk about the fight last night, Cassius.'

Diminutive Dudley Moore threw himself out of the way of an imaginary punch at Eamonn. Noël Coward masterfully avoided choking. There was a slight movement of Ali's left shoulder, though he continued to stare in front of him.

'Muhammad,' he growled.

By Christmas 1978 the whole world knew his name. But, in fight-game parlance, how were we to land the 'sucker punch' on Ali with our Life 'hit'? For a start, we had to get him from America, where he was in constant demand for public appearances, often on the move from Louisville, Kentucky. And always with his wife, Veronica.

She, by the way, told us that when they were first introduced the Louisville Lip had gone very quiet. Later, when she knew him better, she asked him why. The World Heavyweight Champion three times over told her, 'Because I was scared stiff of you!'

Our first move was to send senior researcher Maurice Leonard (these days Michael Barrymore's producer) to stalk Ali throughout his American travels, grabbing any of Veronica's free time to get the much-needed personal background on the most public of sportsmen. On one such secret visit, an Ali 'minder' stepped from the bushes, stole up on Maurice from behind, and stuck a pistol in his ribs. Maurice protested he was expected by Veronica – which she confirmed – but on no account must the World Champion find out.

'The minder thought the worst,' said Maurice.

His telephone calls back to base confirmed we had the potential for a great Christmas Day programme. But the problem remained – how to get him to the New London Theatre for our recording date of 19 December – and the surprise Eamonn planned?

That was when we enlisted the willing services of ITV boxing commentator Reg Gutteridge. The ruse was that, for Ali's millions of British fans, Reg wanted to do a 'your life so far' interview, with film clips. For this, of course, Ali demanded a fee (fighters need to look to their old age) and this was agreed.

Ali flew in and was brought to the 'studio' for the arranged interview. But when he walked in through the side door of the New London Theatre auditorium the audience erupted. Eamonn could hardly get out those famous words above the uproar.

'My thanks to our good pal Reg Gutteridge for getting you here for that interview you knew about, but, in fact, if you'll step this way I'm going to do my best to knock you out with some great surprises,' boomed Eamonn above the din, this time getting the name right.

And surprises there were in plenty. Even his old mum and dad, though separated, had got back together to fly over for the occasion. His mother, Odessa, told us how Ali – then Cassius – had demonstrated his boxing prowess when only eighteen months old. Swinging his arms, as babies do, he'd knocked out one of her teeth.

But his affection for his mother was plain to see. He called her 'Bird' – 'because she's got a little nose just like a bird.'

We had filmed down Dixie Highway in Louisville, at Waddell's Barber Shop, where his Aunt Eva still did the hair-cutting. We flew her in to tell us how the future World Champ 'bawled the place down' when he was brought in for a haircut as a little boy.

And millions heard how Ali only became a fighter because someone stole a brand new bicycle his father had bought him. He reported it to the police and told the cop that if he ever caught the thief, 'I'm gonna whop him!'

The cop, Joe Martin, told the twelve-year-old Ali, 'You'd better learn to fight first.' Martin, later Louisville Police Chief, ran a gym in his spare time. His youngsters appeared on local TV in *Champions of Tomorrow* – never more true than when the young Cassius Clay made his first TV appearance.

Maurice Leonard actually found the first man to come out fighting against Ali. Ronnie O'Keefe was working on the production line at the Ford plant just outside Louisville. We flew him in for a twenty-four years' surprise.

Ali never did get the bike back, but he gained so much confidence at Joe Martin's gym that when he heard international fight trainer Angelo Dundee was in town he rang his hotel room from the front lobby.

What happened next was straight out of *Rocky*, or any Hollywood boxing movie you've ever seen. Angelo Dundee answered his hotel room phone.

The kid in the foyer spoke urgently: 'I gotta talk to you, mister. I gotta talk to you on account of I am gonna be the Heavyweight Champion of the World.'

Said Angelo: 'Son, if you're gonna be the future Heavyweight

Champion of the World, I guess you'd just better come on up.'

What a partnership that turned out to be, though Angelo reckoned it cost him a fortune when young Ali was shadow-boxing. He had this tendency to whack the gym doors off their hinges.

The young Cassius Clay won the boxing gold medal at the 1960 Olympics in Rome. But that almost didn't happen, because he was scared. Not scared of opponents, but scared of flying. We flew in his opponent in the final from Poland, 'Ziggi' Pietrzykowski.

Viewers also heard how Ali 'nicked' his penchant for personal publicity from an American wrestler called 'Gorgeous George'. He always told anyone who would listen that he was 'the greatest and the prettiest'.

Cornerman Drew 'Bundini' Brown was the man who invented 'He floats like a butterfly and stings like a bee.' And when Henry Cooper came on, Ali shaped up as he was reminded of Henry's punch that floored him. Ali himself had to confess it was a belter.

For me, the great moment was when 'Smokin' Joe Frazier agreed to fly over. Ali had been out of boxing for three years when he was sent to interview Joe for a book. Ali had been 'exiled' from the ring for refusing to fight in Vietnam on religious grounds, and at the time of this interview he was on the brink of his fighter's licence being restored.

He was so much looking forward to meeting Joe in the ring that on a drive from Philadelphia to New York he told Joe he'd written a poem about him:

> *Joe's gonna come out smokin',*
> *And I ain't gonna be jokin',*
> *I'll be peckin' and pokin',*
> *Pouring water on his smokin';*
> *This might shock and amaze ya*
> *But I'll retire Joe Frazier.*

Joe listened politely, then said, 'I think I'll stop the car and we'll go up that alleyway over there and sort it out here and now!' But they decided to save it for the ring.

From Hollywood, Anthony Quinn, a legend himself, told about stepping into the ring with Ali for the movie *Requiem for a Heavyweight*.

And that is what it very nearly was when we went over to Las Vegas to hear from Ali's boyhood hero – the 'Brown Bomber' himself, Joe Louis. Confined to a wheelchair, all he could manage was a very moving, 'Hi, Muhammad.'

Now, because of Parkinson's Disease, the great Muhammad himself has slurred speech, his voice often inaudible. But whoever can forget him floating like a butterfly and stinging like a bee? The Louisville Lip, punching his way into the Hall of Fame. Truly a legend.

Reach For The Sky was the film of the best-selling book based on the life of Group Captain Sir Douglas Bader CBE, DSO, DFC, a true story beyond the reach of any writer's pure invention. Said Eamonn Andrews outside New Zealand House just before the pick-up: 'Tonight, I hope to pay tribute to one of the greatest romantic heroes this country has known, this century or any other.'

It was Tuesday 2 March 1982, and sixteen floors above where Eamonn waited for the lift to the Martini Terrace, many famous names had gathered to witness Sir Douglas hand over a cheque for £50,000 to Action Research for the Crippled Child. All had been involved with SPARKS, the star-studded fund-raising organisation.

Few could be more qualified to hand over that cheque than the pilot who, with artificial limbs, became one of – in Churchill's immortal description – 'the Few'. The few to whom so many owed so much in the Battle of Britain.

'This story defies fiction,' said Eamonn, and it did. Our cameras saw the cheque handed over, then Eamonn made his way through the celebrity crowd to produce the book.

Researcher on the programme was John Graham, now associate producer, who discovered that Bader was such a brilliant sportsman he had been selected from the RAF rugby union team for the full England squad – until a fateful day, 14 December 1931.

The young pilot was visiting an aero club near Reading. He went for a 'spin' and crash-landed. His legs were mangled. His log-book read, 'Bad show.'

Laddie Lucas, his fighter-pilot pal who married the sister of Bader's wife Joan, told me he later questioned Bader on what had happened.

'Just made a balls of it, old boy. That's all there was to it.'

Kenneth More was the perfect casting to play Bader in the film *Reach For The Sky*. They became firm friends. Alas, on the night we surprised Sir Douglas, Kenneth was not well enough to join us. He was, in fact, as we learned later, suffering from Parkinson's Disease and did not have long to live.

His wife, actress Angela Douglas, came to the Royalty Theatre from where we presented the programme, with a moving message from Kenneth More: 'Your inspiration and courage is, quite rightly, a legend. It was with me all through the film and is with me still.' At that time, the Parkinson's still a secret, not many realised the profundity of that simple message.

Even without legs, Bader was not to be put off his sport, taking up golf and getting down to a handicap of just four; he could justly claim to top the crack of the late Sammy Davis Junior who, when asked his handicap, replied, 'I'm a one-eyed Jewish negro, what more do you want?' At least Sammy had legs.

Douglas Bader's accident meant he had to be retired from the RAF, but when Hitler invaded Poland he was among the first to volunteer to get back into the cockpit of a Hurricane or a Spitfire.

He proved to the RAF powers-that-be that he could still fly and, after Dunkirk, was appointed Squadron Leader at 242 Squadron at Coltishall, East Anglia. France had fallen. 'The Few' took to the skies and the Battle of Britain began. In one dog-fight a bullet ripped through Bader's Hurricane instrument panel, tearing away a cloth chewing-gum bag strung around his neck.

Air Marshal Sir Denis Crowley-Milling (then a humble pilot) told the packed Royalty Theatre (and twenty million viewers) about Bader going to the pictures on a rare night off. In the darkness, he stumbled on a step and called to an astonished usherette, 'I've damaged my

Douglas Bader won many battle decorations and honours, but this was the most unusual: on a visit to Alberta he had been made an honorary chief by a local tribe. Chief Jim Shot Both Sides and wife Roseleen told viewers that to them he was Chief Morning Bird Bader.

blasted leg. Fetch me a screwdriver.' He got it, fixed the joint in his artificial knee-cap, and said to the open-mouthed usherette, 'Thank you very much.'

By 1941 he was flying two sorties a day, alongside heroes such as Air-Vice-Marshal 'Johnnie' Johnson, later a Life subject.

Bader's luck could not hold out much longer and, when the rear half of his Spitfire was torn away in mid-combat collision, he thought this must be the end. Not so. As he attempted to bale out, his leg was trapped in the fuselage and ripped away. The irony was that had it not been an artificial limb, Bader would have hurtled to certain death in the crashing Spitfire.

He landed safely, and was captured by the Germans. The Commander of the famous JG 26 Fighter Wing was so impressed with this daredevil RAF pilot with no legs that he offered him a close look at the plane he'd been firing at, the Messerschmidt 109. That same Commander, General Adolph Galland, flew in to tell us that Bader's first request was to take the 109 for a spin around the airfield. 'It was clear what was in *his* mind,' smiled the German air ace.

When in 1945, General Galland was himself taken prisoner, Bader gave him a box of cigars. 'A formidable enemy, but even better friend,' said the man who had survived many a dog-fight with Douglas Bader.

It was Galland who agreed to a request from Bader that a new pair of artificial limbs be dropped by parachute to him. Equipped with new 'legs' and knowing he was due to be transferred to Colditz, Bader escaped from the hospital wing of the POW camp. We flew in the French nurse who helped him – and many others – in that escape. Like the elderly woman – ninety-eight when we did the programme, but still able to film for us – who hid Bader and others, she was discovered and sent to a concentration camp.

Sir Douglas greeted the nurse, Lucille Glaneux, with gratitude and affection the years had not diminished. Proudly she wore her French Resistance medals, including the Croix de Guerre for 'supreme bravery'.

Our audience rose to its feet in tumultuous applause, and not a few tears.

Bader was recaptured and tried tunnelling out of the next prison camp by hiding the soil in his artificial limbs. Then, when he was trying to escape, with others, through the wire, a German guard smashed the butt of his rifle down on the foot of the nearest would-be escapee. He could not understand it when Bader burst out laughing. It was his foot.

He tried to get out of Colditz with a party of laundry workers, but failed when a guard tapped his legs and was greeted with a hollow 'clunk'.

Sir John Mills told us how Bader became the only man to stand before the Queen to be knighted. And the Queen Mother sent a letter to be read out on the programme, thanking Sir Douglas for his 'courage in war and inspiration in peace'.

When the band of the Royal Air Force entered from the rear of the stalls to march down the aisles playing the famous 'March Past', there was not, as we say, a dry eye in the house.

Or the nation.

A telephone call wiped the smiles from our faces as we prepared to pounce on the legendary British-born comedian, Bob Hope.

It was from his wife, Dolores. We had flown her in, with their four children. And daughter Linda was the subject of the call.

She had visited a West End hairdressing salon where she had bumped into, of all people, a Hollywood friend – Frank Sinatra's daughter, Tina. A newspaper photographer was there to picture Tina. Now, right out of the blue, he had the chance to photograph the daughters of the two international stars together. Only after he had gone did it dawn on Linda that if her father saw that picture published he would know she was in London, and would want to know why.

No wonder we weren't smiling. We decided there was only one thing to do – take the newspaper into our confidence, with the promise of exclusive coverage on the night in return for publication of the photo being delayed until after the programme.

Another argument was simply why spoil the surprise for millions of viewers – and newspaper readers – for the sake of a headline? I have always thought that counter-productive.

The paper agreed, so we were able to go ahead with our surprise, but not without more behind-the-scene jitters. The great comedian had been booked for a non-existent interview on the *Today* programme at the Euston Road studios of Thames Television, where we planned to surprise him, on 17 November 1970. But he was detained at, of all places, the BBC. He was not aware, of course, that we were running to a very tight schedule because we had outside broadcast cameras in Regents Park, at the residence of the American Ambassador to Britain, Walter Annenberg.

The idea was for the ambassador to make a live contribution to our programme, congratulating Bob Hope on being voted 'America's most prized ambassador of goodwill' by the American Congress.

Mr Annenberg was about to host a banquet, with guests including members of the Royal Family, so by running late at our end we were now sorely trying his goodwill.

The situation was not helped by a member of the outside broadcast team accidentally leaning his chair against an extremely valuable painting, setting off the alarm system: the resultant security alert just added to our problems.

What is more, we were detaining one of Mr Annenberg's VIP guests – Lord Louis Mountbatten. He kept consulting his watch as I made small talk with him in the Green Room. It was clear if something did not happen soon the Admiral of the Fleet would be full steam out of the place.

At last, Bob sauntered into the studio foyer with that familiar casual air. Eamonn shed the panic of the last hour and feigned a similarly casual air as he approached to tell Bob it wasn't going to be an interview after all, but *This Is Your Life*.

Back in the Green Room Lord Louis, a stickler for military punctuality, was by this time champing at the bit. Quickly, he was taken backstage for his surprise walk-on. So keen was he to get on – and off – that he popped his head around the door at the back of the set. The audience spotted him, but Bob did not. The stage manager had to restrain him. Then on he came to thank Bob Hope for his ceaseless charity work, and one legend was clearly much flattered by the presence of another.

This time it looks as if the laugh is on Bob Hope when Lord Louis Mountbatten pops in.

Quite a few more legendary faces were on that programme, including Dorothy Lamour and Bing Crosby, Gregory Peck, Arnold Palmer, Sammy Davis Junior and John Wayne.

Mr Annenberg said his few words and the outside broadcast team cleared their lights, cameras and cables away in the nick of time, just as the banquet guests were arriving – including Lord Louis, punctual to the second.

If anyone could be said to have lived a second life it has to be the world's greatest football manager, Sir Matt Busby.

That he survived when a plane carrying Manchester United back from a European Cup game in Belgrade crashed on take-off from Munich in 1958, has been described as a miracle. Twenty-three people were killed, including eight of his famous 'Busby Babes'.

The disaster came just four weeks after he had been presented with the Big Red Book. But as the 1971 season came to a close I read on the sports pages that Sir Matt was about to retire after twenty-five years as Manchester United's team manager.

At the production meeting that morning I couldn't wait for the right moment to suggest, 'Why not do Sir Matt a second time?' Not everyone was quite so enthusiastic; after all, presenting the book for a second time had never been done before.

But, with a strong element of Northern football fans on my team, the idea simply would not go away. Had Sir Matt not been given the last rites after the Munich air disaster? Surely it could be said, in all honesty, 'Sir Matt Busby, This Is Your Second Life'? What is more, he had lived to build a Manchester United side which went on to achieve even greater glory, becoming the first English club to win the European Cup.

One immediate snag was that United would not be at home at Old Trafford on the day of the programme – for the last game of the season, and Sir Matt's last as manager, their fixture list took them to Maine Road, 'away' to rivals Manchester City.

But Matt, who started his working life down the pits in Scotland, had once been a City player. The manager was his old pal Joe Mercer, who would agree to a special presentation on the pitch before the kick-off.

Assigned to the project was researcher Jack Crawshaw, later a Life producer, who was born within a crowd's roar of Old Trafford, and who had delivered such a great job on our live transmission of the Life of United star Bobby Charlton.

Sir Matt had given Jack every assistance possible on that story in the first season of the Life at Thames. Now, on a day he knew Matt would be out at lunch with the club chairman, Jack drove up to Manchester for a meeting with Lady Busby at their home.

But Jack was driving the same car he owned when he worked on

Bobby's Life. It would be instantly recognisable if Matt arrived back home too early. Jack thought he had given himself enough time for the interview with Lady Busby, closed the front door behind him and climbed in his car to make his get-away.

It wouldn't start. He pushed the car around a corner so Matt would not spot it, and found himself in the very road where Joe Mercer lived. He left the car in the charge of Joe's wife, Nora, who was obviously in on our secret, and called a taxi.

So Jack left Manchester without the man they called 'the Father of Football' realising that back in London a book had been ordered with his name on it.

Came 5 May 1971, and a crowd of fifty thousand packed Maine Road. In the centre circle we had arranged for a table to be set up, and on it were two boxes. In one was an inscribed clock for Matt. In the other was the Big Red Book. Over the PA system Joe Mercer announced to the derby-game crowd what was about to happen: the presentation to Sir Matt, reminding City supporters that Matt had played for the club in the 1933 Cup Final.

Eamonn Andrews had been hidden in the locker room. But it was the Life team who were threatened with a 'booking'. We almost got the final whistle before we had kicked off. At the last minute the police at the ground decided that special permission should have been sought for this presentation in front of rival supporters. They did not want to take responsibility for a possible pitch invasion.

Back at the Piccadilly Hotel we had guests flown in from all over the world, including the Real Madrid star Sir Matt rated 'the greatest player I have ever seen', Alfredo di Stefano. Waiting in the tunnel at Maine Road we had George Best and Bobby Charlton. And disaster was staring us in the face.

It was Joe Mercer who saved the day, as he'd done so often in his playing days. He told the police, after our team had made every effort to contact the Chief Constable, that he would take full responsibility on his own shoulders.

It was agreed. Out on the pitch, with the two rival Manchester teams gathered, and fifty thousand people calling Sir Matt's name, Joe Mercer announced that a friend of Matt's was there to make the presentation.

Out came Eamonn Andrews. He presented the inscribed clock, then for the second box. Inside was the Big Red Book.

It was *This Is Your Life* for the second time – for the first time.

We made the programme in the ballroom of the Piccadilly Hotel, and as the story reached its emotional 'second life' climax, Sir Matt's own words were quoted: 'I will never forget the man who saved my life. The fact that I am here today is due to his skill.'

He was referring to the Munich surgeon who brought him back from the last rites, Professor Georg Maurer. When Professor Maurer walked on at the close and Sir Matt flung his arms around his shoulders, no further words were needed.

'There's a legendary name on this book,' Michael Aspel told the immaculately dressed, perfectly groomed man who walked through the front doors of Teddington Studios. 'Yours.'

Some of us had waited years for the moment when Douglas Fairbanks Junior – screen heart-throb, war hero and honorary knight – would see his name on the Big Red Book. We had planned to surprise him in New York and most recently in Hollywood, but keeping pace with the daily schedule of the eighty-year-old who looked sixty proved too much even for the Life team. No sooner had a venue been set up, than it was altered.

Until Thursday 7 December 1989. We knew that – other things being equal – he planned to be in London, his second home, for the occasion of his eightieth birthday. But how to pin him down for a Life?

The very name of Fairbanks is redolent of the whole story of the movies. Douglas Junior's mother, Ann Beth, was divorced from the world's most famous swashbuckling silent movie star, Douglas Fairbanks Senior, when their son was only nine. The sweetheart of the silents, Mary Pickford, became his stepmother.

And it was the silent movies that came to our rescue. We enlisted the aid of *Thames Silents* expert Kevin Brownlow, and booked him as the interviewer for a special 'look back' with Douglas.

Waiting to greet him for this 'extra' birthday party were many of his London friends, and from New York Leatrice Fountain, the daughter of another legend from silent days, John Gilbert.

Greeting him from Hollywood were a couple of great 'talkies', Bob Hope and Brooke Shields, and his family came in from New York, Miami and London, three daughters and eight grandchildren.

The love of his life, his wife Mary Lou, had sadly died. He had married her after divorcing Joan Crawford, whom he married when he was only nineteen. It lasted three years.

The photographs and film clips from the archive were a treasure-trove for any cinemagoer. We saw Douglas, aged six, with his father on the set of D. W. Griffith's classic *Intolerance*, and again in *Half Breed*.

But he had come up the hard way, starting as studio tea-boy, and making his first film, *Stephen Steps Out*, at just fourteen.

Then came the moment when Hollywood panicked; the invention of the 'talkies'. He made the transition, and his greatest competitor was the man known as 'America's Boyfriend', Charles 'Buddy' Rogers. Five years older than Douglas, he was to marry Mary Pickford after she and Douglas Senior divorced. We flew him in, an amazing eighty-five, to remind us, 'So, America's Boyfriend married the World's Sweetheart.'

The nostalgia-fest had only just begun as we proceeded to remind Douglas, and his many fans, of his hits of the Thirties: *Little Caesar* with Edward G. Robinson, *Catherine the Great* with Joan Gardner, *Moonlight is Silver* with Gertrude Lawrence, and we showed the famous sword fight with Ronald Colman in *The Prisoner of Zenda*.

When his best pal David Niven (we heard from Niven's son, James) became among the very first of the Hollywood Brits to volunteer at the outbreak of war, Douglas Fairbanks Junior threw himself into the war effort in the USA. His support for Britain was unstinting, organising war relief funds and voluntary hospitals. In 1942 he shed the role of screen hero to take on the real-life role of a naval officer, seeing early action on minesweeper patrol in the North Atlantic.

Later, he was involved in the invasions of Sicily, Italy and southern France, which resulted in a Silver Star, to which the Légion d'Honneur, the Croix de Guerre with palm, and Britain's Distinguished Service Cross were later added.

And on 28 March 1949, the former silent movie star was made a Knight Commander of the British Empire 'for services to Anglo-American relations'.

After the war he went into television (he had already made more than seventy-five films) and some of his British stars joined our celebrations, including Greta Gynt, Muriel Pavlow, Margaretta Scott, Robert Beatty and Christopher Lee. And from Ronald Reagan and Prince and Princess Michael of Kent came special birthday greetings.

Dinah Sheridan, Belinda Carroll and Michael Howarth recalled their West End stage appearance with him. The play was *The Pleasure of his Company* and, on the occasion of his eightieth birthday, very appropriate it was.

Chapter Five
Variety: The Spice of Life

'Bring Me Sunshine,' sang Morecambe and Wise at the close of every show in a decade of making audiences roll in the aisles at Teddington Studios. And that was the number that boomed out when Ernie Wise walked into Studio Two on Boxing Day 1990, believing that Thames Television had lined up a retrospective interview about those unforgettable Christmas shows he and his late partner Eric Morecambe had appeared in.

He could be forgiven for feeling a little puzzled. He told us later: had that really been his father-in-law coming out of the gents? (Ernie, knowing the studios like the back of his hand, had slipped Life's 'minders' to pop to the loo on the ground floor, only a few feet from where our surprises were hidden.)

If he was puzzled then, he was totally thrown when he walked into the studio to be greeted by a celebrity 'chorus line' with top hats and canes, among them Jilly Cooper, Gemma Craven, June Whitfield and Lionel Blair.

Before he had time to recover, an Oscar-winning actress told how the former Yorkshire working-men's clubs boy clog dancer had influenced her career with one of the 'plays wot he wrote'. She was Glenda Jackson MP.

We showed the hilarious sketch in which she played Cleopatra. She had agreed to that appearance in the wake of some heavy stage roles. Seen in a new light as a talented comedy actress, she was cast in the hit Hollywood movie *A Touch of Class* with George Segal – and that role won her her second Oscar.

An appearance with Morecambe and Wise influenced the life of newscaster Angela Rippon, too. We sprang her from her famous 'leg-show' song-and-dance routine. 'Before that, everybody thought the BBC used to roll me around on casters,' said Angela.

Sir Robin Day recalled his 1975 Christmas Show with the pair. 'It had always been my ambition to be a great music hall comedian like, say, Des O'Connor,' said the political pundit.

Eric's widow, Joan, made an appearance and told us how she had first met Eric when they were both in a show at the Edinburgh Empire. He always said the theatre should have a plaque outside: 'Eric Morecambe Fell Here.'

Ernie made a guest appearance on another Life, on 3 March 1992, after we had surprised Irish tenor Josef Locke, for nineteen years 'king' of Blackpool's 'Golden Mile'.

The Princess of Wales had to be in on our secret because the pick-up was on stage at the Odeon, Marble Arch, at the Royal Charity Film Première in aid of Turning Point, the charity which works to help people overcome drug, alcohol and mental health problems, of which she is patron.

The princess smiled warmly and joined in the applause when Michael Aspel walked on with the Big Red Book. Michael had been concerned about Josef's likely reaction because of his unpredictable reputation.

'He's a volatile character and very much his own man,' Michael told the viewers, pre-empting the distinct possibility that the Irishman would fly straight back to Dublin.

In the event he sat benignly throughout, taking the occasional sip from a pint of Guinness. Ernie Wise told how Josef had got Morecambe and Wise on to the Moss Empire circuit – second on the bill to his top – for thirty-five pounds a week.

And a wave of Blackpool nostalgia washed over millions of viewers as more stars of variety, Albert Saveen and Daisy May, Russ Conway and Ruby Murray came on, topped by the Beverley Sisters bringing pink champagne.

Josef Locke's recording of 'Hear My Song' – the title song of the film based on his life – went straight into the pop charts after a gap of forty years.

For the Life team, Sean Connery had always proved more elusive than his 007 James Bond character. He is an actor who has always jealously guarded his privacy, as is his right. This does not necessarily mean that one day we might not prove more successful than SMERSH.

Amazingly, when his agents were approached about a possible appearance on the Life of Oldham-born comedy actor and writer Eric Sykes, there was only a slight delay before a call saying that Mr Connery would appear live on the tribute from our television theatre. What's more, he arrived early when he heard Zsa Zsa Gabor was on the show – he wanted to meet her for the first time. The embrace in the Green Room would have done justice to a Bond movie.

About his long-time golfing partner Eric, Connery said he had enjoyed some of the best times in his life in Eric's company: 'Generous, just, talented, passionate and the best of men.'

This Is Your Life

Having just met the Princess of Wales . . .

. . . singer Josef Locke relaxes on set with a pint of Guinness.

Two of the many former guest stars on *The Morecambe and Wise Show* who recalled their appearances for Ernie Wise's Life — Angela Rippon and Robin Day.

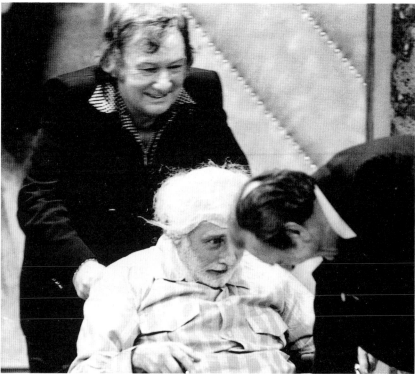

Quite a line-up for Eric Sykes:
Johnny Speight and Spike
Milligan . . .

Connery joined a comedy Hall of Fame on that show: Jimmy Edwards, Harry Secombe, Spike Milligan, Max Bygraves, Terry-Thomas and Tommy Cooper. Spike had to dab away tears of laughter as Tommy entered carrying a plank (he had appeared with Eric in *The Plank* on TV) and, despite the suspicion of a libation or three, proceeded to take over the show.

. . . Tommy Cooper . . .

72

. . . Zsa Zsa Gabor . . .

. . . and Sean Connery.

Once Tommy had the audience in the palm of his hand, he couldn't stop, and overran his allotted spot so much that Eamonn Andrews gave up the ghost and, for the first time ever, took a seat with the rest of the guests to crease up laughing with them.

Even Bob Monkhouse, master of the fast patter, was lost for words when surprised by the Big Red Book.

Among the great ad-libbers falling about at Tommy that night was Frankie Howerd, like the mad magician himself a great clown.

We had surprised Frankie three years before. Again the Life cross-fertilised, with Eric Sykes appearing, along with Cilla Black, Dora Bryan, Barbara Kelly and many more, including Peter Cook.

Peter it was who came to Frankie's professional rescue in 1962. Frankie had hit such a low he was actually thinking of quitting the business. Then Peter Cook booked him for The Establishment Club, where he was 'rediscovered'. And how – he was booked for a spot on television's first satire programme, *That Was The Week That Was*, fronted by a youthful David Frost, and that led to Frankie playing the lead in the West End in *A Funny Thing Happened on the Way to the Forum*.

Not bad for the young man who, just out of the army, had failed his audition for the Royal Academy of Dramatic Art. An actor of no mean standing told viewers that he had been so impressed with Frankie's performance in *Forum* he had gone backstage to congratulate him. The actor was Richard Burton.

Ronnie Corbett was involved in some comedy acting with Ronnie Barker when the Life struck. It was March 1970, and the two Ronnies were on the David Frost programme. The Life had done so well in the

TV ratings that we invented a sketch in which Ronnie Corbett played a character obsessed with the idea that Eamonn Andrews would one day knock on his door holding the Big Red Book.

With the collaboration of Ronnie Barker and David Frost we came up with a pay-off for the sketch – Frost would arrive with Eamonn; fade out. End of sketch.

What Ronnie Corbett didn't know was that it would be the start of his real-life *This Is Your Life*. He sat down and covered his face in disbelief when it dawned on him that the whole sketch had been a double bluff.

Be-feathered Danny La Rue was in full flight on stage just before Eamonn pounced.

Another pick-up we did in front of a TV audience was Jimmy Tarbuck, then presenting *Live From Her Majesty's* in February 1983.

His daughter Liza, who went on to television success herself in the sitcom *Watching*, told us how her proud father had gone to see her in a Shakespeare production at the National Youth Theatre. He told her afterwards how brilliant she had been, when Liza knew for a fact he'd snoozed throughout.

Cilla Black and her husband and manager, Bobby Willis, once saved Jimmy's early career – by hurling insults at him. In his early days in the Liverpool clubs in the Sixties, Jimmy used to entertain in between the pop groups. He had to put up with a lot of banter from the crowds, and got so used to 'fielding' the insults – getting big laughs by turning the insult on the heckler – that he was lost without them. So one night when the audience was far too polite Cilla and Bobby came to Jimmy's rescue with some choice cat-calling.

Michael Parkinson told us Jimmy had once listed for him what would have been his all-time great Liverpool team had they all been contemporaries. We got that fantasy team together. It included Kenny Dalglish, Graham Souness and Ian St John, now of 'Saint and Greavsie' fame. And Tarby said of his boyhood soccer hero Billy Liddell, 'I really loved that man.'

Two more of his heroes made his night: golfing legend Henry Cotton and Jimmy's favourite comedian, Bob Hope.

Michael Parkinson also featured strongly in the Life we did on Billy Connolly. At the height of his chat-show fame, Parky had been visiting Scotland and someone had handed to him a recording made by a local Glasgow comedy hopeful. By the time he got back to London, a non-stop busy Parkinson forgot all about the record. His son Andrew picked it up and listened to it. He told his father this was exactly the kind of 'unknown' guest he should book for his show. Michael listened to the record, laughed a lot and booked 'The Big Yin', who never looked back.

There's a five-star welcome from the Life audience for this popular comedian. Freddie Starr was christened Frederick Fowell, but soon changed it because his mates kept calling him 'Foul Freddie'. When he joined a young people's road show he invented one of his best loved characters and became 'Freddie the Teddy', the famous teddy boy.

We travelled to Sheffield to surprise home-town girl Marti Caine. She was in the city centre interviewing women on the subject of men for Yorkshire Television when a coach rolled up. On board was a party of family and friends. And we learned from them that slim-line Marti had once come third in the Junior Miss Great Britain contest – when she had a forty-inch bust.

She was christened Lynne Denise Shepherd and, no, she didn't steal her name from Michael Caine. She was glancing through a gardening catalogue and stole it from 'tomato cane'.

On a live link from London, Sacha Distel paid Marti his compliments. He knew what the show was all about because we had surprised him back in 1971 when he flew in from Paris to top the bill at the Talk of the Town.

Sacha's parents were Russian immigrants: his father had fought with the French Resistance and his mother was sent to a concentration camp. At a monastery in wartime Paris Sacha's life, and the lives of many Jewish children, had been saved by a French priest. Discovered, the priest had been sent to the notorious Dachau concentration camp.

Père Domaigne was his name. We found him, and brought the two together for the first time in thirty years.

'Once she packed saucepans at a Cardiff factory; tonight she's packed the Royal Albert Hall,' said a nervous Michael Aspel, backstage at that venerable venue.

Packed was right – five and a half thousand fans were there on the night of 10 December 1992 to hear Shirley Bassey in concert.

The finale was not what she expected. She got the deafening standing ovation she deserved. But as Michael stepped onstage behind her, the international singing star was puzzled by the sudden increase even in *that* decibel count.

Then she saw Michael. Her first instinct was to back off. The audience willed her back to Michael. With all the drama we expect of her, she succumbed. The vast audience was in raptures.

And so was Shirley when, safely back at the Teddington Studios, in front of a somewhat smaller, though no less vociferous, audience, she got her first surprise. We had flown in her sister, Grace, who went to live in America forty-five years ago, for a tear-stained reunion. And that was only the start.

She told us how Shirley's first audiences were the neighbours back in Tiger Bay. If Shirley was mopping the doorstep or beating the

Shirley Bassey gets a surprise on-stage at the Royal Albert Hall.

carpets, they would yell, 'Come on Shirley, give us a song.' She never needed asking twice.

Hard to believe, looking at the glamorous woman in the guest-of-honour seat, she was celebrating forty years at the top.

As Elizabeth Taylor wrote, asking Michael to read her letter, Shirley is 'undeniably one of the greatest singers of our time'.

Not bad for the youngest of seven children of a Nigerian seaman and a Yorkshire mother who divorced when Shirley was only two. Her life has not been without tragedy, especially the deaths of her first husband and her daughter. Little wonder the roller-coaster drama of her life comes through in her passionate delivery of her songs.

Outside the Embassy Club in Manchester, Michael Aspel thought he was taking his own life into his hands.

'Why do I feel like a kamikaze pilot?' he asked. Very likely because he was about to walk onstage straight into the firing line of the comedian who machine-gun fires his put-downs: Bernard Manning.

In fact, Bernard has fired insult lines at so many of his fellow comics we wondered if anyone would come on the programme – always provided Michael got to him in the first place.

The audiences at his club, used to his colourful language, were also used to him paying off his act with a particularly personal brand of expletive, after which he would comment something along the lines of, 'So after that they won't be coming for me with that bloody Big Red Book tonight!'

Actually, he didn't say those words the night Michael walked in. He had to admit that for the first time he was speechless.

The whole show remained totally good humoured, and clean . . . well . . . we did have to tidy it up a little bit in the edit. But with his ninety-year-old mum there, Bernard was on his best behaviour. She used to be on the till at the club, and told us how Bernard had always said if the lights ever went out to throw her body over it.

He may well have expected to trade insults with the best when Jim Davidson made a surprise appearance. Instead, the big man almost melted when Jim said, 'Bernard is the best stand-up comedian in Britain today, and possibly of all time.'

Actress Mollie Sugden came to the studios to take part in a children's programme, but was met by three people to whom she'd played 'mum' — Nerys Hughes, Jack Smethurst and John Alderton. And Eamonn was there with the book.

Seven years before we had launched a friendly 'invasion' of Jim Davidson's home in Sunningdale. Through his living-room window he saw thirty Royal Irish Rangers, with pipers, marching up the drive.

Jim had travelled to the world's trouble-spots to entertain them and other regiments, including two visits to the Falklands. They loved the idea of being 'in' on entertaining Jim, and sat on set throughout the programme, during which we learned that his family all called him Cameron – his second name.

He had failed an audition for *Opportunity Knocks*, but reached the All Winners Final of *New Faces* in 1976. Danny La Rue was there to tell us he gave Jim a maximum of one hundred points.

'You can't do that,' Danny was told. 'Nobody's been given a hundred points before.'

Said Dan: 'In that case I'll give him a hundred and twenty-five!'

Jim's older brother Bill told us how Jim had come by his 'Nick-Nick' catchphrase. Bill himself had been in the police for ten years. And that was how Jim came across the 'talking brooch' expression – from the radio on the police lapels.

Jim Davidson enters the Life theatre to be greeted by the Royal Irish Rangers who had just knocked on his door.

The Life of Rolf Harris produced one of our most extraordinary fly-ins. He had a special pal back in Australia, an aborigine called David Blanasai. But when we tried to contact him, somewhere out of Darwin, we were told he had 'gone walkabout'.

That meant he was on a self-survival trip into the bush, and that's a lot of miles of the Northern Territory. It became a search worthy of Crocodile Dundee, as his pals and the police – on our behalf – got on to his trail. And found him.

Trouble was, his friends told us, he had no clothes suitable for an English winter. We cabled the money to kit him out and when he flew in he looked as though he might be a member of the Australian touring team. But, having flown ten thousand miles, David wanted to appear on British television in more traditional garb – which turned out to be a huge, feathered head-dress and bamboo skirt. He requested water from one of our young ladies, who politely enquired if he would prefer a gin and tonic. But he wanted the water to mix with the clay which was smeared over his half-naked body to complete the outfit.

Only one thing was needed to complete the ensemble before he walked out on to the set – his didgeridoo, the aboriginal wind instrument Rolf had introduced to us Poms. At the end of the show, Rolf took over the instrument and played us out.

A very smart Nora Batty (Kathy Staff) on her special night in 1984.

The didgeridoo sounds not unlike something the Goons might have invented, but military music was more appropriate when the late Peter Sellers, wearing a German SS uniform, complete with helmet and dark glasses, joined us to surprise Spike Milligan.

As it turned out, Spike surprised us. It was April 1973 and we were waiting for him, with Sellers, at the De La Warr Pavilion in Bexhill, scene of a reunion with his former comrades in the 56th Regiment of the Royal Artillery. That's where he had joined up as Gunner Milligan.

Knowing Spike's unpredictability, we had a researcher follow his car all the way from London. Spike got suspicious and reported his follower to the police, who stopped the unfortunate researcher and detained him for questioning. A phone call from the 'nick' cleared him.

Peter Sellers howled with laughter when I told him about this predicament. 'Don't worry,' he said, 'Spike wouldn't miss this reunion for anything.'

He was right, and when Sellers marched on in his Nazi outfit even Spike was taken aback. But only momentarily. Spike shook the proffered hand of the 'SS man' – then instantly dropped his trousers. His Royal Artillery pals roared.

Spike had first met another Goon while on active service in Italy – Sir Harry Secombe CBE, whose Life Michael Aspel presented in February 1990. Spike was on parade for that.

Les Dawson was the 'dame' in *Dick Whittington* when Michael Aspel walked onstage at the Theatre Royal, Plymouth, in December 1992. When Les spotted him, he said, 'As it's you, I'll do it.' Sadly Les, who had been voted Variety Entertainer of the Year and had just become a proud father again at the time of our show, died of a heart attack on 10 June 1993. A favourite line of Les's had been, 'One day I'll die standing behind a brewery with an eclair in one hand and a pint in the other.' Even death didn't escape the Dawson treatment.

So, too, were Sir Geraint Evans and Dame Kiri Te Kanawa (both former Life subjects). They smiled when Harry's brother, Fred, who had become a vicar, told us how Harry, as a youngster, had been too shy to sing in front of an audience. So he used to sing in the family home's outside loo – but with the door open.

The former Goon was knighted in 1981 for charitable services – he has raised more than three million pounds for war widows and orphans.

As 'The Forces' Sweetheart' herself, Dame Vera Lynn, put it on the night, 'Harry is one of the biggest hearted people in show business. I cannot think of anyone more loved.'

Les Dawson's lugubrious features have brightened many a Royal Variety occasion. But when we surprised him onstage at his 1992 Christmas panto in Plymouth, it was the Duke of Edinburgh who had the last word: and I do mean word.

Researcher Mandy Nixon (daughter of the late star magician David) discovered Les and the Duke had an on-going dispute centred on – of all things – the correct method of cooking a black pudding. Lancashire-born Les was adamant: the only way to serve that county's delicacy is *boiled*. His Highness totally disagreed. He sent us a letter, on Buckingham Palace notepaper, and requested that Michael read it on the programme.

It contained one word: *'Fried!'* Signed, Philip.

Sadly, Les died of a heart attack on 10 June 1993. Michael Aspel had known him since *Crackerjack* days in 1968. In a tribute Michael wrote, 'There was an honesty in his work that reflected his way of life. He was an unsentimental man, except where his family was concerned – and that, in the end, meant more to him than anything else.'

Chapter Six
Life's Heroes and Heroines

How do names totally unknown to the general public find their way on to the front cover of the Big Red Book?

First clues that 'unknown' lives may be worth further enquiry may come in letters from viewers who believe a certain person they know would be worthy of a tribute. Other clues may come from close scrutiny by the Life team of the Honours Lists, especially deep down in the small print. A paragraph in a newspaper, perhaps detailing a dramatic rescue, will leap out at one of us. TV and radio news bulletins can have the researchers reaching for pencil and paper to scribble down an incident or a name.

A letter suggesting the name of Father Michael Doheny, who had been involved in rescue missions in the most desperate places in the world, led to some of the most complex 'pick-up' arrangements the Life has ever known.

Our enquiries showed that Father Michael had a younger brother, Father Kevin Doheny, whose work risking his own life, particularly during the appalling carnage of the civil war in Nigeria, made a gripping story equally worth telling.

The result was a double bluff which, for weeks on end, had everyone working on the Life not knowing their right hand from their left. The daring plan was to tell Father Michael we would be presenting the book to Father Kevin, and vice versa. Both men, quite selflessly, thought the other brother more than worthy of such a tribute. We got their wholehearted co-operation in piecing together the other's story.

On the evening of Tuesday 9 October 1984, some latecomers joining the audience at the Royalty Theatre in London's West End thought they were there for a programme about the charity Concern, which supported the work of both priests.

Then out stepped Eamonn Andrews, who went first to Father Kevin, to say, 'You know why I'm here, don't you?' He beamed and nodded: 'I certainly do.'

Next, Eamonn went to Father Michael and said, 'And you know why I'm here, too?' He nodded agreement. 'I do.'

Then Eamonn told them he had 'a double confession' to make. 'This Is Your Lives,' he said, and led the totally bemused pair up onstage to take their seats as guests of honour.

Millions of viewers heard how the two brothers had spent over three decades putting their lives in jeopardy to bring medicine, food and hope to refugees, many disabled through famine, pestilence and front-line warfare.

Father Michael had a close shave with death flying in urgent supplies in Biafra. The landing strip, a rough track in the jungle, was blacked out to avoid bombing raids, and his pilot narrowly missed crashing into a tree. Danish volunteer pilot Captain Gunnar Østergaard was there to tell the story. It had been fifteen years since last they met.

ITN war reporter Michael Nicholson, himself a later Life subject, told how Father Kevin was so close to the front line in Biafra that he could not go forward and his retreat was cut off. He made his own canoe to escape and return with medical supplies for the stricken township.

Author Frederick Forsyth, then an agency reporter, told of the priests unloading supplies from a truck by paraffin lamp, constantly dive-bombed by flies. After every expletive came the words, 'Forgive me, Lord.'

They were tending wounded after a bombing attack when Group Captain Leonard Cheshire, VC, of 'Dambusters' fame, and his wife Lady Ryder visited them.

The brothers had worked in Bangladesh, Tanzania, Thailand, Uganda and in Ethiopia during the 1972 famine which, Jonathan Dimbleby told the viewers, they had helped bring to world attention.

Martin Sheen, Glenda Jackson, Senator Edward Kennedy and Mother Teresa added their tributes.

At the party afterwards the two brothers who, in their lifetime, had just about seen it all, still could not believe they had been taken in by our double bluff.

But they were delighted they had.

Announcements of the imminent fiftieth 'birthday' of Oxfam did not go unnoticed in the Life office, and we started to look for someone whose life had been devoted to that organisation.

All signs pointed towards Oxfam's world-ranging troubleshooter Jim Howard. He had flown on mercy missions to scenes of indescribable horror, often in the immediate aftermath of war. He had fought famine and disease in Honduras, the Andes, Somalia, Sudan, Iraq and, in Cambodia, was one of the first eye-witnesses of the infamous 'Killing Fields', the legacy of Pol Pot's Khmer Rouge.

Award-winning journalist John Pilger told us how this qualified water engineer – a first priority when disaster strikes – 'came in to Phnom Penh like a one-man cavalry to sort things out.'

He could not have achieved so much without the help of a young student who spoke English. Finding her was not easy. Eventually we discovered she had moved on to study in Moscow. Then we found she'd returned home to Cambodia. But she did not have a visa to leave Cambodia for England. Programme co-ordinator Mandy Lee fixed it at the last minute, and Sopheak Neary flew in from Phnom Penh as our final surprise for Jim Howard.

He had arrived at Teddington Studios with a whole party of friends and colleagues from Oxfam, expecting to see a programme about the fiftieth birthday celebrations. Instead, it proved to be *his* party when Michael Aspel strolled in to Studio Two with the Big Red Book.

A jungle clearing in the African bush was the scene of the pick-up for East Africa's 'Flying Doctor', Dr Michael Wood, in March 1972. Women and children of the Masai tribe anxiously waited for his arrival, and so did Eamonn Andrews and our crew.

Dr Wood had performed an amazing eleven thousand operations in his career. He had qualified as a surgeon at the outbreak of war and quickly became accustomed to dealing with emergencies. Later he was inspired by Albert Schweitzer to form the Flying Doctor service. He had flown his light aircraft over a territory equal in size to Western Europe.

On this particular day his schedule would take him to a village outside Nairobi. The natives were summoned from the bush by drumbeat. Many walked miles to attend the Flying Doctor's mobile surgery.

A sudden cloudburst drenched everybody. Then, as the sky cleared, there was Dr Wood's small aircraft coming in to land. As he stepped from the plane, safari-suited Eamonn was there with the Big Red Book.

It took a while for it to sink in with the doctor that we wanted to fly him from Nairobi to London there and then, a four-thousand-mile hop, where all our surprises were waiting. When he realised we had arranged for another of his team to stand in for him at his mobile surgery he was happy to join us – with someone else at the plane's controls.

David Ellaway is the kind of ambulanceman you might see arriving at the scene of a minor road accident. But this member of the Gloucestershire Ambulance Service is also rather special, as we discovered.

He is one of a handful of Red Cross volunteers trained to be rushed to the scene wherever international disaster strikes.

David had put his own life at risk many times when the Life surprised him on 10 September 1985. He had put his special medical skills to use on the Caribbean island of St Vincent after a volcano erupted. He had been in the thick of sniper-ridden activity on the border of Pakistan and Afghanistan, helping with the vast refugee problem in the wake of the Soviet invasion. He had witnessed the horrors of famine in Ethiopia, and again in the Sudan.

There he wrote a poem, 'The Beja Boy is Dying':

> *The Beja boy is dying, that's what they said to me,*
> *And they took me by the hand and led me there to see,*
> *To where he sat on a seat of mat, still and very cold,*
> *At just one year, the wizened face of a man so very old.*

No ordinary ambulanceman.

Millions who were enthralled by the wartime behind-enemy-lines series *Wish Me Luck* had no idea it was based on the real-life exploits of a war-widowed mother who happened to speak fluent French.

She was eighty-year-old Yvonne Cormeau MBE, Légion d'Honneur, Croix de Guerre. The Gestapo had always failed to surprise her. We had a more pleasant surprise.

Jane Asher was one of the stars of *Wish Me Luck*, and she accompanied Michael Aspel to the studios of London Weekend Television for a cast 'photo-call' to which Yvonne had been invited.

All were conspirators in on our Life top secret. We took her into surprised, but delighted, custody.

'I won't cry, you know. We were trained not to,' she told Michael.

Daughter of a Belgian diplomat father and a Scots-born mother, Yvonne had been widowed early in the war and volunteered for Britain's 'secret army' – the Special Operations Executive. The legendary 'spymaster' Colonel Maurice Buckmaster, chief of the French section of the SOE trained her and gave her the codename 'Annette' (ours was 'Luck').

She was parachuted into France on the night of 23 August 1943, and told she could expect no mercy if caught. Colonel Buckmaster told us Yvonne had transmitted 389 and received no fewer than six hundred vital messages behind enemy lines 'under circumstances of extreme danger'.

The occupying forces sometimes suspected areas from which she may be operating. Once they were almost within knocking-on-the-door distance. But they ruled out the village because it had no electricity or running water. They did not believe an English *woman* would choose such a place to hide. With no chance of a bath?

Our final surprise was the arrival of the daughters of the French Resistance hero who had hidden Yvonne – and her give-away parachute

– on the night she was dropped behind enemy lines. Their father had perished in a concentration camp, but Simone and Paulette Bouchou were there to greet Yvonne. Oh . . . she *did* shed a tear.

Few 'unsung' heroines were brought to our notice more frequently than 'Sister Mac' – so many people wrote to tell us about this star of the world-beating nursing team at Great Ormond Street Hospital, internationally famous for its treatment of desperately ill children.

On Friday 31 January 1986, there was a children's party in one of the wards. Eamonn Andrews donned a party head – Disney character Pluto – to attend, and surprise Sister June McElnea, MBE.

As he said, he was seeking a little lady with a big heart. At eighteen, when she wanted to become a trainee nurse, she stood just 4 ft 11 in, and the minimum height requirement was precisely five foot.

She went for her interview wearing the highest of high heels and a hat that looked like a chimney. She got the job and went on to become a nursing sister at Great Ormond Street whose very personality turned tears to smiles among the children whose lives were constantly in the balance.

Cricket commentator Brian Johnston and his wife Pauline came to tell us how 'Sister Mac' had kept up their spirits for twelve years of care of their daughter, Joanna. Joanna came, too.

Sister Mac had her own hero, cricketer Ian Botham. We made sure he was able to have a word from the West Indies, where he was on tour. For good measure, David Gower, then the England captain, introduced the whole of the team to wave their greetings to a remarkable woman whose true height might have meant she did not measure up to the job.

Grateful children, and their parents, testified how she had seen them through unimaginable crises. One mother, Ann Towse, had sent Sister Mac a Christmas card that year, recalling the period when her young son, then aged four, was in Great Ormond Street, and the doctor had said, 'We can do no more for David.'

The card said, 'You were close by and ready to help. David will be twenty-one next birthday. How wonderful to have known a real saint.'

Aged twenty-three and about to qualify as a nurse, Margaret Price, MBE, also had hopes of swimming the English Channel, when she was knocked down by a car on a zebra crossing. She was paralysed from the chest down, but on 26 February 1981, Life's viewers heard how she inspired others by turning tragedy into triumph.

It was the 'International Year Of Disabled People' and we surprised her at the headquarters of the Sports Council in the Brompton Road. She had gained no fewer than nine medals in the Olympics for the Disabled.

Joining in our tribute that day were Olympic Silver Medallist Alan Pascoe, Gold Medallists David Wilkie and Sharron Davies, England ladies cricket captain Rachel Heyhoe Flint, West Ham and England's Trevor Brooking, and athletics star Sebastian Coe.

Four of Margaret's world records were for swimming. Former Wales and British Lions captain Cliff Morgan told how he once dived in the pool for a practice swim with her and had to gasp, 'Margaret! Bloody slow down! I can't keep up with you!'

Appropriately, it was Christmas 1980 when we surprised Joan Wells, described by Eamonn Andrews as 'someone who has given her heartfelt best all her life and has received no public thanks, nor does she expect any.'

Over a period of twenty-seven years this Chester housewife had opened the doors of her home to more than 150 foster children, some orphaned, others from broken homes.

From all over the country they came for the Life reunion, including one young man who had spent his childhood shuttled from one home to another until he went to live with Joan and her husband Ron.

Reaching twenty-one, he went to see a solicitor to change his name legally to theirs, and became Paul Wells.

A letter from one of her foster children put us on the trail of another special foster mother, Kitty Wilson from Saffron Walden.

At one time she was caring for as many as twenty-seven children. She was invited to London, at our suggestion, by one of her foster daughters for a special Mothers' Day treat.

A crowd of her foster family was at Liverpool Street Station for her first surprise. There were more to come, including a former US Army sergeant, Walter Rogers, who forty years ago had delivered a sleigh filled with teddy bears to Kitty's home: they were presents to the children from GIs at the nearby base who were missing being with their own families that Christmas.

Said Walter: 'The spirit of Christmas is a year-round way of life for Kitty.'

Hanging on a wall in the Life office is a framed certificate from the Royal National Lifeboat Institution which states: 'The Committee of

Management Desire to Record their Warm Thanks to This Is Your Life for helping the Lifeboat Service in the field of Public Relations.'

From the youngest, then only twenty-four years old, Brian Bevan, to the oldest, seventy-nine-year-old 'Skipper' Jack Woodhouse, the pleasure has been all ours in saluting the courage and daring of Britain's lifeboat crews.

When we surprised Brian Bevan on 13 March 1980, he had already won a clutch of awards never before equalled in the service which has recorded so many distinguished acts of bravery. The young cox of Humberside's Spurn Point had won the RNLI's bronze, silver and gold medals for gallantry at sea.

A relief crew stood in that night so he could be joined in London by his own much-decorated crew.

Jim Davidson helped Michael be a 'stowaway' to surprise Britain's oldest serving lifeboatman, 'Skipper' Jack Woodhouse.

We heard how he earned his gold medal by racing the lifeboat into a trough between two waves in storm-lashed seas so that a ship's skipper could make a desperate last leap for life before his coaster rolled over and sank. The secret of Brian's earrings also came out – there is an old belief among fishermen that having your ears pierced results in better eyesight.

What Brian had in common with Britain's oldest lifeboatman was that neither could swim.

We went to Caister on the Norfolk coast to smuggle Michael Aspel aboard the new lifeboat on a freezing January day in 1991. John Woodhouse, known as 'Skipper' since he found a cap with the words 'Skip-Jack' on it when he was only seven, was about to take a practice launch with the rest of the crew.

This included a rather unusual member – comedian Jim Davidson. When appearing in summer season at nearby Great Yarmouth, Jim carries a bleeper ready for call-out. He has a very genuine commitment to the lifeboats: he bought the Caister in-shore lifeboat out of his own pocket.

'Skipper's' family tradition with the Caister boat went back to his grandfather, one of eight crewmen who perished on a rescue mission in 1901. When 'Skipper' started in the service fifty years before our programme, the boat had to be rowed.

Jim Davidson, smuggling Michael Aspel aboard, reminded him of the crew's motto: 'Caister men never turn back.' Said Michael: 'Let's hope my lunch doesn't.'

It didn't, and Michael popped from below to surprise 'Skipper' on deck.

We heard how, at seventy-four, he had survived an operation for cancer, when it was suggested he might never go to sea again.

'Why?' enquired the droll old sea-dog. 'Is the sea going to dry up?'

Richard Evans, cox of the Moelfre boat in Anglesey, had just retired when we surprised him in 1970: at the time he was the only living holder of two gold medals for bravery.

Matthew Lethbridge BEM, cox of the St Mary's boat in the Isles of Scilly, had three silver medals and had been part of a string of international headline-making missions, including the *Torrey Canyon* disaster, the Fastnet race and the BA helicopter crash in July 1983, in which twenty people died. Survivors said it was 'a miracle' when Matt Lethbridge steered his boat through swirling fog to rescue them from the freezing water. Said one of his admiring crew: 'It was as though Matt had some sort of built-in radar system.'

Alf Pavey was very helpful getting together a Life on his cousin and deputy cox Vic Pitman, who had just been awarded a silver medal for saving the lives of seven people from a sinking yacht off the coast of Weymouth.

Alf, the regular cox, had been on holiday. But he had a record of more than four hundred turn-outs, saving three hundred lives. Everyone agreed he deserved our tribute, and Vic was the first to co-operate.

But we carried on seeking Alf's co-operation on a Life on his cousin. Eamonn Andrews was waiting in the boat-house when the crew came in.

When Alf realised our double bluff he let out a roar that could have been heard the length of the coast, and flung his white cox's cap to the floor.

A signed, framed picture of the Weymouth boat hangs on the wall of the Life office, a memento of that February day in 1977.

A bluff of a different kind surprised RAF helicopter winchman Robert Pountney of 202 Squadron Search and Rescue from RAF Lossiemouth, on the east coast of Scotland. He had turned out for a routine practice mission to rescue a climber who had fallen on to a ledge halfway down the cliff face at Clashnach Cove.

But the 'injured' man in the rock-climbing gear turned out to be Michael Aspel, with the Big Red Book hidden under his climber's jacket.

Virtually the whole of RAF Lossiemouth headed for the vast hangar from where we broadcast the programme on 2 October 1990.

Bob's most dramatic mission came on the night of 6 July 1988, when the 'scramble' bell rang. It was the first indication that the oil-rig platform Piper Alpha was ablaze.

Winchman Bob Pountney and his crew flew to the rig, 120 miles north-east of Aberdeen. The inferno below was the scene of the worst oil-platform disaster anywhere in the world. Three times he was winched down to the deck of the rescue support ship to haul badly burned stretcher cases to the helicopter.

Sadly, one died, but the other two survived to join us on the programme, and to thank our guest of honour and his crew.

Petty Officer Larry Slater of the Air Sea Rescue flew more than 160 missions, saving thirty-six lives, including that of pop star Simon Le Bon, and earning the George Medal for bravery.

The Le Bon rescue was his second mission of the day from Coldrose in Cornwall. Simon's yacht, *Drum*, had upturned off Land's End. Inside the boat, six people, including the pop star, were trapped in an air pocket. Larry Slater repeatedly dived into the air pocket, finding his way through a mass of wreckage and ropes to rescue all six people.

Dr Anthony Jones is a mountain rescue expert whose bravery and skill have saved hundreds of lives in many parts of the world. On

18 October 1992 he was on home territory with the Ogwen Valley Rescue Team, taking part in a practice operation in Snowdonia.

He had no idea that the helicopter swooping through a valley between snow-capped mountains had Michael Aspel as a passenger. And a question occupying our thoughts was: would Dr Jones recognise Michael, and would he know our programme? For this Doctor of Marine Biology at the University of North Wales, Bangor, spends all his spare time on the mountains; he doesn't even possess a TV set.

Said Michael: 'It's possible he might not know just who, or what, I'm about.'

Whether he did or not, encouraged by the rescue team, he was whisked to our studio in Manchester, where we had assembled many people who had reason to thank Dr Jones for their lives.

And the granite-faced man in the kilt – he is of Scots ancestry – melted a little when we flew in his sister, Marianne, from Cape Town.

Viewers also learned a well-kept secret. In 1983, Dr Jones had been made an honorary member of the US Air Force Pararescue Team. Senior Master Sergeant Jim Meulchi told us that meant having two green feet tattooed on his backside. In return, Dr Jones insisted the Americans should have the logo of the Ogwen Valley team tattooed on the other cheek.

'And you'll just have to take my word for it,' smiled the master sergeant.

A flight to Dacca in Bangladesh ten years ago changed the life of British Airways stewardess Pat Kerr – and the lives of thousands of underprivileged and abandoned children in the poorest of Third World countries.

Unknown to Pat, director Brian Klein and researcher Sue Green, with a film crew, captured the scenes which motivated her in giving up the high life to bring a new life to the children of Dacca.

We recreated her privileged view, as a BA stewardess, from the luxury of the five-star Sonargar Hotel. From its air-conditioned rooms she could see the sharply contrasting scenes of grinding poverty, especially the plight of the children.

On that trip, Pat Kerr made a decision. On her return, she requested a long period of unpaid leave. Next time she arrived in Dacca, it was not as a crisply uniformed stewardess – just a dedicated young woman, heading for a run-down building in a back alley, home for 150 children.

It was the start of a seven-year struggle to build a children's village. Back at British Airways, with the support of then Chairman Lord King,

This Is Your Life

RAF helicopter winchman Robert Pountney heads for the rescue of a 'fallen climber' . . .

. . . he lands at Clashnach Cove on the east coast of Scotland . . .

. . . he reaches the 'climber' . . .

. . . who happens to be lying on a Big Red Book.

she turned that orphanage nightmare into a dream of the future – and that dream into reality. She received all manner of support from her colleagues, who formed the BA Staff Dacca Orphanage project.

She was signing copies of her book *Down To Earth* for her colleagues at Heathrow on 29 September 1992, when Michael Aspel dropped in with another book with her name on it.

She was so stunned she protested, 'No, no, no. . . .' But a little gentle persuasion got her safely to our guest-of-honour seat in the studio. On our big screen, six hundred children back in Dacca greeted her with a wave and the name they call her: 'Pat Mummy'.

Former stewardess Pat Kerr was signing copies of her book for BA colleagues when Michael arrived with a book of his own.

Chapter Seven
Hollywood Life

When the Life team descends on Hollywood and sets up office in a hotel suite, the scene takes on the frenetic activity, and uncertainty, of a film set. But no one could write the script.

Programme co-ordinator Mandy Lee will have flown in the team under the strictest secrecy. The hotel pool may look inviting, but researchers have to plunge into the telephones. From then on there are yelps of success and deep groans of disappointment as guests agree to appear – or drop out.

'We'll have to get a crew to film Charlton Heston – he can't make it live.'

Then: 'But Burt Lancaster's with us.'

'Got Bo Derek!' yells someone else. 'She'll join us at Dudley's restaurant for the pick-up.'

Chevy Chase, Robin Williams and Bob Hope are added to the list.

For the Life of Alice Faye, legendary star of the halcyon days of Hollywood musicals, we assembled a guest list to make any Hollywood mogul envious.

At Metromedia, 5746 Sunset Boulevard, on Wednesday 5 December 1984, a fleet of stretch limousines ferried in Alice's star friends and colleagues from more than eighty films.

She had agreed to an interview about her career for a British television 'cinema' programme. But the night before we had a secret meeting at the Hyatt on Sunset with her husband of forty-three years, Phil Harris – remember his hit recording of 'The Poker Game'? – to finalise details. Our advance party of researchers had been in constant contact – whenever Alice herself was out of town. Fortunately for us she was doing a good deal of travelling promoting a cosmetics product.

Phil was to accompany her to the studio for the 'interview'.

The 'pick-up' went smoothly. Eamonn Andrews had been hiding in wait as Alice Faye stepped from her limousine with a chuckling Phil Harris (he and Eamonn had met when Phil topped the bill at the London Palladium).

By the time the limousine drew up at the studio, we had hidden behind the set Fred MacMurray and his wife June Haver, Rudy Vallee, Senator George Murphy, Cesar Romero, John Payne, Mary Martin, Ruby Keeler, Pat Boone and Bob and Dolores Hope. We were also ready to roll with tributes from Benny Goodman, Don Ameche,

Anthony Quinn and Ginger Rogers. Names who had packed cinemas the world over in the late Thirties and throughout the Forties into the Fifties.

But we hardly had a packed studio. In fact, the four hundred audience seats were empty with twenty minutes to go.

Due to a mix-up, a studio audience had not been booked to see a line-up of talent Sam Goldwyn would have died for. And in Los Angeles, in the evening, you can't simply rush out and haul people in off the streets, because no one is on the streets – except in cars.

So we grabbed every chauffeur of every stretch limo we could find and rushed them to audience seats. Then we dashed around every occupied office at Metromedia trying to fill more seats; wild-eyed and demented we must have looked as the clock ticked towards our allocated recording time.

Even with audience ranks swelled by our own production team, barely a tenth of the seating was filled. But what a noisy lot we were! When it came to laughs and applause we did our utmost to sound like four hundred. At the end of an hour we were hoarse, and constantly applauding hands hurt.

But when we returned to Britain with the recording, we had so many letters, it seemed that sixteen million people thoroughly enjoyed the story of the girl from New York's 'Hell's Kitchen' who had successfully auditioned for the famous Ziegfeld Follies but had to be dropped when they discovered she was still only thirteen.

In New York in her teens she had met a struggling young musician with whom she was to appear in the 1940 movie *Little Old New York*. His name: Fred MacMurray.

And, for the singing star of scores of films, we had found her first-ever appearance on celluloid – which she had never seen before. It had been shot at a garden party at the home of Rudy Vallee, the Sinatra of his time.

Alice was delighted with our final, and very British, surprise. In an RAF camp on a sweltering outpost of the North-West Frontier of India on 5 June 1937, a group of British airmen, Alice Faye fans all, held an 'Alice Faye Dinner' and sang her big hit, 'You'll Never Know Just How Much I Love You'. We flew in the man who organised that dinner, Wing Commander Rex Wigfall, to meet his screen heroine and present her with the menu he had kept for nearly fifty years.

Hollywood 'sex thimble' Dudley Moore couldn't have been more surprised when former World Light Heavyweight Champion Archie Moore walked on the Life set at ABC studios in Hollywood in 1987.

In fact, when Eamonn Andrews suggested his name you could have put us all down for the count. When I went to talk over my script with Eamonn in his suite at the Beverly Wilshire, he couldn't wait to tell me his 'great, great idea'.

This, it turned out, was to set our researchers to finding any British expatriates with the name of Moore, and put them in the audience, so Eamonn could finish by saying, 'And one other very special member of the Moore clan whom you've also never met but who, at one time, conquered England as you've conquered America . . . yes, for ten years Light Heavyweight Champion of the World, the great Archie Moore.'

The quizzical expressions on the faces of the team at this suggestion could not dampen Eamonn's enthusiasm. We all knew he would seize any opportunity to get a fighter on any programme.

Expatriate Moores were thin on the ground, and the great Archie himself was hardly high profile now. Two Moores were found and brought, puzzled, to the studio. Eamonn beamed with pleasure when told we had located Archie, and he would be joining us.

Said Eamonn on the programme: 'Archie, great to have you with us.'

Replied Archie: 'And great for me to know I am a long lost relation of the great Dudley Moore.' (He wasn't.)

Whereupon the ex-prizefighter picked up the former Oxford music scholar and said, 'No wonder they call you "Cuddly Dudley".'

Eamonn: 'Thank you, the great Archie Moore.'

What really puzzled us was that this programme – unlike some, when we discover subjects may not be quite as popular as their public image – was choc-a-bloc with star names. Archie, we didn't need.

Traffic-stopping Bo Derek, Dudley's co-star in *10*, was at the pick-up. Dudley, as he often did, was tickling the ivories at his restaurant in Market Street, Venice Beach, not knowing we had hidden Bo, and Eamonn, in the kitchen staff loo. Keeping watch from one of the tables was Dudley's glamorous actress wife, Brogan Lane.

A Hollywood actress who shall remain nameless asked if anyone had any 'coke' and looked on in astonishment when Eamonn, ever the gentleman, leapt to his feet to bring her a coca-cola from the bar.

'Not *that* coke, silly,' said she, whereupon Eamonn produced a diet coke.

We even had a special chauffeur – Ted Ross, from Dudley's *Arthur* films. Somehow we had all convinced ourselves he was the same 'chauffeur' who had appeared with Paul Hogan in *Crocodile Dundee*. Only when he flew in first class from New York to stay at the Beverly Wilshire – all at our expense – did we discover he had been nowhere near that film. Alas, word did not reach Eamonn on this, so that when Ted Ross turned up for rehearsal, Eamonn greeted the bemused actor with, 'Love your performance in *Crocodile Dundee.*' When the sturdily built Mr Ross snarled at Eamonn, 'The next guy who says that . . .', we headed for the Hollywood hills.

Our grand finale was lost when Blake Edwards phoned to say he and his wife, Julie Andrews, would not be with us. Julie had hurt her back.

It was time to call on old pals, and I came up with an idea for Bob Hope which Eamonn loved. Fortunately, so did Bob. 'A kinda cute little gag,' said the great comedian.

Bob walked on with a golf club. 'I command you to kneel,' said Bob, tapping the club on Dudley's shoulders. 'On behalf of Prime Minister Margaret Thatcher, President Reagan and a lot of other comedians, I dub you Sir Dudley of Dagenham.'

He topped a line-up which included (as well as Archie Moore) Joan Rivers, Robin Williams, Chevy Chase, members of the Los Angeles Philharmonic (Dudley had played the Hollywood Bowl), Henry Mancini, Sammy Cahn, John Dankworth and Cleo Lane. Dudley joined Sammy, Johnny and Cleo in a jam session on set.

Zsa Zsa Gabor greets her favourite Arab stallion.

The mansion at One Thousand and One Bel Air Road was once owned by Elvis Presley, has a nightclub on the roof and had a Hollywood legend by the pool having tea on the afternoon of Sunday 19 November 1989.

'She's a lady who's created more worldwide headlines than anybody even in *this* town,' said Michael Aspel, before a nervous knock on the door.

He added he hoped she was in receptive mood because 'this lady packs a punch'.

Courtroom pictures of her and the Beverly Hills cop she was said to have slapped had just been flashed around the world. Who else but Zsa Zsa Gabor? Our worry was that by the time of the programme she would be serving a few days' gaol sentence for slapping burly officer Paul Kramer, who had booked her for driving with an out-of-date licence. But all was well.

Associate producer John Graham had the star's husband, Prince Frederick von Anhalt of Saxony, on his side. John was in the Gabor Rolls-Royce with the prince when they spotted Officer Kramer signing autographs in Rodeo Drive, the most expensive shopping street in the world.

And John got the best hotel service of his life when he had lunch with Zsa Zsa's daughter, Francesca, at the Beverly Hilton. Her father was Conrad Hilton.

Mother Jolie and older sister Magda, with long-time family friend, former 'Tarzan' John Frederick, were there. But younger sister Eva refused to come; she and Zsa Zsa, who had arrived in America together from Budapest in 1940, were having a spat.

Someone else who wasn't there was Officer Kramer. I had the idea that we could finish the show with him coming on to bury the hatchet. But the Beverly Hills police department buried the idea.

For a character like Zsa Zsa, we needed an 'impact' ending. In 1984, at the opening ceremony of the Los Angeles Olympic Games, she had ridden her world champion white Arab stallion Silver Fox. We managed to smuggle Silver Fox into the studios, and I waited backstage with a pretty young lady researcher. When the horse heard the name of Zsa Zsa the result was physically apparent and increasing by the second.

The wide-eyed researcher mused, 'Is that the effect she's always had on men?'

We surprised William Shatner, Captain Kirk, on the 'flight deck' of
the Starship Enterprise at Universal Studios, and he and Michael Aspel
were 'beamed' – using special effects – from there to the studios.

Actress Heather Locklear, Shatner's blonde, glamorous partner
in *T. J. Hooker* (and 'Sammy Jo' in *Dynasty*) nearly didn't make it.
Being on location, she had recorded a message, but a young lady
visiting one of the team drove off with the tape in the boot of
her car. It began a 'calling-all-cars' search worthy of T. J. Hooker
himself.

But Mr Spock, alias Leonard Nimoy, was there, minus his Vulcan
ears, and we closed the show by 'beaming' up Bill's twenty-month-old
grandson, Grant.

Thursday 16 November 1989 saw the Life in the newly restored
art deco surroundings of the St James Club on Sunset Boulevard –
a building once home from home to the stars of the Thirties – to
surprise a devastating young English actress who had first caused a
sensation with Marlon Brando in *The Nightcomers* and was now Sable
Colby in *Dynasty*: Stephanie Beacham.

Charlton Heston – her screen husband in *The Colbys* – caused a few
heart tremors among the team when he telephoned to say, sadly, he
could not make the studio 'live' because he was on location that night.
His schedule, suddenly, had been switched – a frequent occurrence in
Tinsel Town. But he would film a message for Stephanie for us from
his home before he left.

We had a wonderful line-up of guests greeting Stephanie in London –
Susan Hampshire, Nyree Dawn Porter, Robert Powell, Susannah York
and the whole of the cast of the hit TV programme *Tenko*.

But for the actress who had flown to Hollywood 'with one change
of underwear in her bag' to seize the chance to play Sable Colby, we
really needed a big Hollywood name to finish the proceedings.

We set out in pursuit of the diffident star with whom she had just
made *Napoleon and Josephine*, Anthony Perkins of *Psycho* fame. Due
to a misunderstanding, when he arrived he was under the impression
he would be 'live' with Charlton Heston. Our young lady researcher,
however, convinced him he should appear, which he did, much to
Stephanie's appreciation. I warned our researcher to avoid stepping
under the shower that night. . . .

We had visited *Dynasty* two years before, in February 1987, in search
of the heart-throb British actor, then playing Ben Carrington, Christopher
Cazenove.

This Is Your Life

At Universal Studios, Hollywood, on the set of *Star Trek*, Captain Kirk (William Shatner) gets an out-of-this-world surprise.

I had flown in with then associate producer Brian Klein (now a producer/director) as the advance party. On the plane we had talked about an absolute 'grabber' of a pick-up if we could open with Joan Collins about to descend the famous Carrington mansion staircase, not with Blake Carrington (John Forsyth) but with Eamonn.

Eamonn had still to arrive in Hollywood, but we were convinced he would go with the idea, so we approached Joan Collins who, great professional that she is, loved it.

But just before Eamonn flew in, there was a snag. Joan had to fly to Europe to film just twenty-four hours before our glamorous pick-up. Then I snapped my fingers (a habit that gets to you in Hollywood) and announced an idea that could still save it.

Brian and I were waiting for Eamonn when he and Grainne arrived at the third floor suite at the Beverly Wilshire. Grainne slept off the jet lag, but Eamonn poured us drinks. I outlined the plan agreed with Joan Collins. It is a technique used every day in this town. We shoot the scene at the top of the Carrington staircase with Eamonn and Joan Collins. We film the walk down, and at the door to the kitchen Joan says to Eamonn, 'He's in there, Eamonn, having breakfast with his daughter (that is his screen daughter, the stunning Terri Garber). Fingers crossed, good luck.'

Joan then flies off to her location, and Eamonn returns next day to do the actual 'hit'. Brian Klein and I sit back with our martinis in the plush surroundings, convinced we have solved the problem.

Eamonn sinks his martini. He shakes his head.

'What time must we shoot this?'

We tell him it will be early. About 8 a.m. Another shake of the head.

'I can't appear with Joan Collins looking like this,' he says. Clearly, he is convinced a few hours' sleep will not improve his condition.

Then, suddenly, he says, 'Look, I know you've been knocking your brains out to make this idea work, but I can't do it because it would be a lie. We would be cheating the viewers.' He leaves us to finish our drinks and goes to bed.

So Eamonn appeared at the top of the staircase by himself. When we arrived to film Joan Collins, as planned, the first thing she said was, 'Where's Eamonn?' and we offered some 'not very well' excuse. And Joan did her bit without him.

But John Forsyth and Linda Evans were there to point him in the right direction, and stars Heather Locklear, Gordon Thompson, Jack Coleman and Terri Garber were on set, joined by Dian Cannon and Angharad Rees, former *Poldark* star and Christopher's wife.

It was Angharad who insisted we fly in actress Marsha Fitzalan (Rik Mayall's wife in television's hit comedy series *The New Statesman*). The reason was that when Christopher and Angharad were going through a crisis in their marriage, Marsha rang to invite him out to dinner 'to the noisiest restaurant in Clapham High Street'. The purpose of the dinner was to let Christopher know that Angharad 'still loved him dearly'. Alas, the reunion was not to last; they separated, permanently, in the summer of 1992.

Hollywood legend Burt Lancaster, with whom he'd filmed *Zulu Dawn* in the African bush, gave Christopher the final accolade.

Sometimes the opportunity to spring a Hollywood Life surprise in London cannot be resisted, such as when we knew Joan Collins would be flying in to celebrate the eightieth birthday of her father, Joe, former agent and partner of Lew Grade.

Joe was in on our secret, of course, and we asked him which of Joan's fifty films was her favourite. Immediately he said, *The Girl on the Red Velvet Swing* – the story of legendary New York Edwardian chorus girl Evelyn Nesbitt. This was possibly because Joan's grandmother, Hattie, had herself been a chorus girl – with 'the Cape Girls' in South Africa. We flew in her Hollywood co-star, Farley Granger, who had found fame in Alfred Hitchcock's *Rope* and *Strangers on a Train*.

Joe Collins told us he was against his daughter becoming an actress – as an agent he had seen too many disappointments and pitfalls. Joan told him she was going to audition for the Royal Academy of Dramatic

Art. So convinced was Joe that she didn't stand a chance, he told her he would agree to her acting ambitions if she got in. Joan passed her RADA audition.

Fellow student David McCallum arrived for a fencing class with her. Miss Collins entered wearing a leotard. The young Mr McCallum had a distinct problem with his sword.

Joan Collins greets the nursing staff who cared for her daughter after a serious road accident.

Gregory Peck and Robert Wagner added their tributes from Hollywood.

For all that tough Alexis image in *Dynasty*, Joan was visibly moved by the arrival of singing star Roger Whittaker.

When her daughter, Katy, then aged ten, had been in a car accident and was in a critical condition, Joan was in Paris on business. With her daughter's life touch and go, she could not get a flight out for eight hours. It was 2 a.m. Joe Collins rang family friend Roger, who owns his own plane, and within the hour he was flying to Paris to bring Joan to her daughter's hospital bedside. Joan lived in a caravan in the hospital grounds for six weeks until she was sure Katy would pull round.

Quite a few more 'Brits' who have made it in Hollywood have featured in a London surprise. At the New London Theatre on 20 February 1980, Stewart Granger walked into our trap, met by former British leading ladies Margaret Lockwood, Jean Kent and Moira Lister.

Maurice Denham, with whom he started at Hull Rep, was there, with Glynis Johns, Peter Bull and Dame Flora Robson. Dame Flora told us she had been out and bought a new dress because she knew she would be seeing him again and 'that's the effect he always had on us girls'. She was seventy-seven at the time and had toured with Stewart and Jack Hawkins in 1937.

Everyone on the show called Stewart Granger 'Jimmy', and for an interesting reason. Born in London on 6 May 1913, son of an army major, he was named after his father, James Stewart. Unfortunately, when he decided to become a film actor there was another James Stewart around. That's when he became Stewart Granger.

His daughter Lindsay told how he got hold of a piece of historic Hollywood. On a visit to Los Angeles, her father had taken her to see the famous MGM lion, which roared at the start of every MGM film, and was called Leo. When the lion died, the studio presented the skin to Stewart Granger.

Wilfrid Hyde-White, son of a Gloucestershire clergyman, had his lucky break in films in 1936 with Charles Laughton in *Rembrandt*. He attained international stardom with Rex Harrison and Audrey Hepburn in the film of *My Fair Lady* – and he was no stranger to the famous Ascot racecourse scene.

He loved to go racing and was very superstitious. At Ascot he always went through the same ritual, doffing his topper and bowing solemnly three times to the weather vanes, for luck.

Our pick-up was, naturally, at Newmarket, and in our studio he was joined by Ballard Berkeley, Faith Brook, Peter Sellers, Sidney Tafler, Frankie Vaughan, Coral Browne, Trevor Howard and best friend (and racegoer) Robert Morley. Asked the secret of Wilfrid's success, Morley replied, 'He's never made the mistake of taking acting seriously, dear boy.'

Hollywood really was in London the night we surprised Peter Ustinov in November 1977. He was playing Agatha Christie's Hercule Poirot in the movie *Death On The Nile*, and the whole cast came along to our studio.

And what a cast: Bette Davis, Mia Farrow, Maggie Smith, Jane Birkin, Angela Lansbury, Lois Chiles, Jon Finch, Olivia Hussey and Simon MacCorkindale.

Henry Fonda spoke to Peter from Hollywood, and Sir John Gielgud arrived to put the icing on a very rich cake. But the final scene went to Bette Davis. Displeased with the hub-bub at the play-back she turned

This Is Your Life

Peter Ustinov was filming at
Pinewood as Poirot when Eamonn
arrived undetected on the set of
Death on the Nile.

Bette Davis was there to greet
him . . .

. . . and so was this star-studded
cast.

from her front-row seat and silenced the room with an imperious glare of those famous eyes, followed by 'Ssshhhhussh!'

Horror film veteran Christopher Lee had just appeared in the Royal Film Première of *The Three Musketeers* when we 'ambushed' him in March, 1974.

Friends who hadn't found him quite so frightening in real life included Charlton Heston, Sammy Davis Junior, Trevor Howard and Joanna Lumley.

Peter Cushing told us about making *The Curse of Frankenstein* with Christopher as the monster and himself as the baron. Christopher kept giving Peter the giggles doing Bugs Bunny impressions while in costume as the monster.

Vincent Price related how a fellow passenger on his flight from Hollywood had asked, 'Are you Boris Karloff?'

Vincent: 'No, he's dead.'

Tried again: 'Are you Christopher Lee?'

Christopher Lee was looking slightly wary when horror film colleague Peter Cushing made his entrance. Christopher was famous as Count Dracula, but Peter told how he made him laugh with his impression of Bugs Bunny.

Vincent: 'Nope, I'm not him either.'

Passenger: 'Well, then, who the hell are you?'

Craggy-faced actor Harry Andrews had made *Solomon and Sheba* with Gina Lollobrigida, who flew in for his Life in February 1985. For effect, I suggested she make her entrance wearing Sheba's regal head-dress. This she did, but unfortunately the name of the costumier's was still sticking to the outside.

We went to Paris to surprise one of the most romantic stars of the last thirty years – Omar Sharif. Michael Aspel was waiting as he stepped out of the apartment block where he lives.

Then it was a flight back to London to hear from Sir David Lean, Rod Steiger, James Coburn and, of course, Peter O'Toole from *Lawrence of Arabia* and *Night of the Generals*.

When we filmed in Omar's home city of Cairo – where we heard he was such a good soccer player he could have played for his country – our camera crew got beaten up. The director had offended some religious fanatics by 'dirtying up' a traditional robe for a piece of 'character' filming.

We flew back to Hollywood to spring our surprise on 25 February 1993 on the great Ann Miller, she of the legendary legs which could 'machine-gun' tap at five hundred a minute. She had been booked for a celebrity interview at the studios of CBS in Television City. She did not know that Stage 42 was ours.

How about this for a story you could hardly invent? Her mother, Clara, takes the little Ann to dancing lessons in her home city of Houston, Texas, to strengthen her rickets-threatened legs. Those legs were to be insured by MGM for a million dollars – each.

Divorced, mother takes twelve-year-old Ann to Hollywood. She wins a talent contest. The result: a booking at the Bel Tabarin in San Francisco. Who should walk in one night but Lucille Ball? Who should be with her but an RKO movies talent scout?

But Ann was still only thirteen. Her mother quickly added five years to her daughter's age to make her more acceptable in an adult part, and the result was a starring role in *Life of the Party*.

What a party we had that night, with contributions from Mickey Rooney (with whom she co-starred in *Sugar Babies*), Cyd Charisse, Donald O'Connor, Esther Williams, Jane Powell, Debbie Reynolds and surprise guests Howard Keel and Kathryn Grayson from *Kiss Me Kate* – in which Ann performed the unforgettable 'Too Darn Hot' dance routine.

We finished with another dance routine from the 1937 film *Stage Door* in which she featured in a double act.

Her partner had been Ginger Rogers. Though confined to a wheelchair, Ginger was at *our* stage door to surprise her friend. She told us she had kept a couple of secrets about Ann during the making of that film: firstly, she knew Ann was really only fourteen and, secondly, she was wearing lower heels and a sawn-off topper so the difference in the height of the two twinkle-toes stars would not be apparent.

Ann Miller and Ginger Rogers, together on camera again, fifty-six years after *Stage Door*. The essence of This Is Your Life.

Chapter Eight
Life in Coronation Street

Alec Gilroy, landlord of the Rover's Return (actor Roy Barraclough) was enjoying a break in Marbella after a long stint of work on *Coronation Street* when he was summoned back to Manchester.

Executive producer Bill Podmore told him on the phone that two scenes he had shot with his new screen wife Bet (Julie Goodyear) had gone wrong technically. There was a fault on the tape. He would have to come back for one day only. Roy Barraclough was not pleased.

When he found out the real reason for his holiday being interrupted he was downright furious. The Life team was behind it all.

A combination of circumstances led to the plot to bring him back. On that date, 13 October 1987 – only three weeks before the death of Eamonn Andrews – we had intended surprising England striker Gary Lineker. Researchers had already been to Barcelona, for whom he was playing, to talk to his wife Michelle and to Gary's friend and then Barcelona manager, Terry Venables. Then Terry and Barcelona suddenly parted company, and Gary was in a rare off-form spell: he hadn't scored in eight games for the club. We decided to postpone.

Meanwhile, in Manchester, Roy Barraclough had 'married' Julie Goodyear, finished an exacting period of work, signed a new contract and, unknown to us at that time, planned to take off for a well-earned rest.

In London, we had planned an outside broadcast for Gary's Life and, consequently, had lost our studio availability there.

Following the Street wedding, Alec Gilroy was now a firm favourite with viewers. Bill Podmore was always a good friend of the Life. A telephone call confirmed he would help us again and, even better, Granada had a studio free that day.

Smiles all round among the team in London, as researchers set to work on Roy's story – and an excellent story it was, from holiday camp 'Bluecoat' to dramatic roles in rep, and his Ada to Les Dawson's Cissie in their hugely comic TV act.

Then the phone rang. It was Bill Podmore. There was a snag – our subject would be out of the country. There was no way we could stop him but, with Bill's co-operation, we could get him back for that one vital day.

Even that wasn't easy. There were no scheduled flights to Manchester. He would have to fly into Gatwick, where we would lay on a private plane. From Gatwick, Roy telephoned. He couldn't find the pilot.

Back in Manchester, we had hatched a pick-up plot which had Eamonn in the uniform of an AA patrolman with his head under the bonnet of Julie Goodyear's Rolls-Royce, conveniently 'broken down' on Roy's route by chauffeur-driven car from Manchester Airport to Granada.

Julie waved to the car, which stopped. Out stepped Roy and our 'AA patrolman' looked up from under the car bonnet, holding the Big Red Book.

Roy Barraclough was totally stunned.

'Tonight, *Coronation Street*'s Alec Gilroy, alias actor Roy Barraclough, This Is Your Life,' beamed Eamonn.

'Oh no it bloody isn't,' snorted the landlord of the Rover's, though viewers never heard that bit.

When Julie realised that Roy really was annoyed about his holiday being interrupted for his Life, she went to her dressing room for a weep.

But on screen it was all smiles and, afterwards, Roy told us he had enjoyed it; and the programme certainly got a great reaction when it went out. When he returned (again) from Marbella he telephoned our office to thank everyone involved. In fact, he said it was the most exciting part of his holiday (the weather had been terrible).

'Curly' from the Street (actor Kevin Kennedy) was a surprise guest on the Life of Kevin Lloyd – 'Tosh' Lines in *The Bill*. They had appeared together in *The Borgias*, and the head tucked under Curly's arm is the wax model of Kevin Lloyd's head made so it could be seen departing his shoulders when he was executed.

Real life produced a drama well up to *Coronation Street* standards on the evening of 7 October 1980, the occasion of the Life of Julie Goodyear, in those days the Street's Bet Lynch.

We knew she had a visit to London planned, so we organised a red-carpet welcome at Euston Station, with flowers, champagne and a brass band playing 'She's a Lassie from Lancashire'.

What happened next was not planned. Unknown to Julie, as soon as her train had pulled out of Manchester, Life associate producer John Graham arrived to catch the next train – in the company of the whole of the rest of the cast of Britain's most popular drama series. The plan was to walk Julie on set at the Royalty Theatre, then immediately 'spring' the surprise of all her friends and colleagues – whom she thought she'd left behind in Manchester – coming on behind her.

But a huge warehouse fire a mile out of Euston cut off the railway line's electricity supply, and the train carrying the Street cast screeched to a halt. Pausing only to give the steward £30 to give them anything they wanted (it *was* 1980), John leaped from the train to organise a rescue. We learned later that Liz Dawn, who plays Vera Duckworth, had caused consternation aboard the stranded train by asking for chips.

John found some senior BR officials and persuaded them to get out an old diesel engine. Back at the Royalty, because of the now hour-long delay, our 'warm-up' man was getting so desperate he was asking the audience if *they* knew any gags.

Relief all round when John eventually arrived with the cast and smuggled them into the theatre. The curtain went up on a show that turned out to be particularly popular, since Julie had recently come through a cancer operation.

She had been a secretary and Manchester fashion showroom model before getting an eight weeks' booking to appear in a small part in the Street. It was actress Pat Phoenix – Elsie Tanner – who thought Julie had great potential and put in a word for her at Oldham Rep, where she was taken on as assistant stage manager. When she returned to the Street, it was to stay.

Pat Phoenix was the Street's first Life subject. In the late afternoon of 15 November 1972, there was a knock on the door of Number 11, Elsie Tanner's Coronation Street address.

She had just played a scene with Len Fairclough (Peter Adamson) expressing annoyance that her screen husband (later her real-life husband, Alan Browning) was late and they were due to go to a party.

Eamonn goes to Coronation Street
to knock on Elsie Tanner's door,
to surprise that firm favourite, the
late Pat Phoenix . . .

. . . and whisk her off to a nearby
studio.

He came around the corner and Elsie slammed the door in his face. He banged on the door.

'Elsie, love, don't make matters worse. Get this flamin' door open.'

The door is flung open. Angrily Elsie blurts out, 'I treat myself to a new frock, new hairdo. . . .'

Then it dawned. Her 'husband' had swapped places with a stranger in the Street – Eamonn Andrews. He walked the still-stunned Pat to another Granada studio, from where we made the programme. By that time, Pat had already been a Street resident for twelve years. She was in the very first episode, on 9 December 1960.

Pat Pilkington was her real name and when she hit hard times as a struggling young actress in London, working on a market stall and sharing one pair of stockings with her flat mate, she decided to change her name.

Staring into the fire one night she said, 'I'm going to change my name to Phoenix. It's a bird that rises from the ashes.'

It was to prove prophetic. She went to Manchester to read for a part in a new six-week series called *Florizel Street*. When its creator, Tony Warren, heard her read his words, that was it. Said Tony: 'I knew I had found my Elsie Tanner.'

William Roache, in the role of Ken Barlow, was also in that very first episode. He had been Ken for a quarter of a century when the Life arrived in Coronation Street on 16 October 1985.

When he was demobbed from the Royal Welsh Fusiliers, he decided to become an actor and went around theatres looking for work. Perhaps he had been inspired by the enthusiastic write-up he had received in a Liverpool newspaper for a school production of *Macbeth*, in which he had played *Lady* Macbeth.

At the stage door of Nottingham Rep one evening, looking for work, he bumped into the unmissable figure of Brian Blessed, soon to be of *Z-Cars* fame, but at that time humble assistant stage manager.

Brian was able to offer Bill a role at the theatre – as stage carpenter. But when Bill got the chance of an audition at Oldham Rep, Brian coached him and his ambition to become an actor was achieved.

He was at Oldham Rep when Granada auditioned him for the Ken Barlow role, and at the time of writing he is the sole surviving member of that original cast.

Ken Barlow's 'Uncle Albert' Tatlock in those early days was played by a great character actor, Jack Howarth. Cast in the original six episodes, he told his wife it was 'some North Country thing about a corner shop'. Jack didn't think it would 'catch on'.

But he was still in it when Eamonn Andrews popped into the Rover's Return at opening time on 20 November 1974.

When Eamonn said, 'I'm taking you to London' Jack must have still been playing crusty old Albert, because he said with steely determination, 'Oh no, you're not, you know.'

It took a great deal of persuasion to get him to change his mind. Jack had spent four years in the First World War trenches in the Lancashire Fusiliers and if he wasn't for shifting, he wasn't for shifting.

He was delighted he surrendered that night, though, especially when he spotted old comrades in the front row of the audience and we played the regimental march.

In fact, afterwards, Jack and his wife, Betty, became such devoted fans of the programme they used to pop in to see us socially.

Rover's Return barmaid Betty Turpin – actress Betty Driver – had a night off from pulling pints when we surprised her on the evening of 21 January 1976. She was visiting London for a dog show.

But the newsvendor at Euston Station was Eamonn Andrews. And in the Big Red Book was a story which must have astonished her younger 'regulars'.

Betty had been a child star of the Thirties and a singing star of the Forties and Fifties. As a schoolgirl she had attended the same singing and dancing class as Beryl Reid.

Before Betty was even seventeen, the legendary showman C. B. Cochran had signed her for West End revues, and she appeared in the film *Penny Paradise* in 1938. For seven years, she was top vocalist with the famous Henry Hall Orchestra – he of 'Tonight is my guest night' fame. Though in poor health, Henry talked to Betty in our studio on a special telephone line.

Betty had been managing a real-life pub with her sister, Freda, when tempted back into the business via *Coronation Street*.

Behind the cantankerous character of Percy Sugden is a life of laughs. Actor Bill Waddington, like Betty Driver, had lived a full 'other life' before *Coronation Street*: he was a stand-up comedian of the old school.

Joe Loss and his Orchestra were the first surprise when he stepped off the train from Manchester one afternoon in September of 1986. 'Prickly' Percy could not believe his eyes, because he had shared many a variety bill with Joe Loss back in those immediate post-war years when variety was still packing them in.

Joe reminded Bill how the young comedian had actually got a few reluctant laughs when they played that 'graveyard' of English comedians, the Glasgow Empire. Joe had joshed, 'You were so good I reckon tomorrow night you could risk losing the Glasgow accent.'

The story Percy Sugden had been keeping under that famous flat cap started in Oldham, where he was born at the Clarence Hotel – his parents were the publicans – and started to learn violin at an early age. His sister, Connie, told everybody he was so bad even his pet dog put its paws over its ears. So he took up the ukulele.

This proved the chance to succeed for Bill. Called up during the war, he was taken up by army concert parties. He was in 'Stars in Battledress' at the Normandy landings in 1944, made his radio début in *Ack-Ack, Beer-Beer*, and became a stand-up comic immediately after the war.

He had shared variety bills with the best, including Frankie Laine, who greeted him from San Diego.

Oh, yes, and someone else. Back in the early Fifties, when he was billed at Manchester's Hulme Hippodrome as 'Witty Willie' he used to do a sketch with a certain comedienne.

Her name was Jill Summers – now his 'love interest' as Phyllis in *Coronation Street*.

The only sadness was that his wife of forty years, Lillian, a former singer and dancer, had died, so could not share his night.

Elizabeth Dawn – that great character Vera Duckworth – also proved to have a past in the entertainment business, starting as a club singer in her native Yorkshire between jobs in a toffee factory, as a shoe-shop assistant and in a real-life 'Mike Baldwin'-type clothing factory.

Michael Aspel came to give her the surprise of her life – Vera would giggle at that – in the Rover's Return as a result of a 'white lie' script I wrote to promote *Coronation Street* in Canada.

Vera was sitting at the bar and called out to husband Jack (Bill Tarmey) to take a telephone call. All went fine on the first 'take' but we needed another to be certain. This time the urbane Aspel, in cloth cap, took Jack's place.

For the first time in a long time, Liz Dawn was at a loss for words. And that is saying something of a lady whose husband, Don Ibbetson, told us his impression on first meeting her in a pub: 'I reckoned she'd been vaccinated with a gramophone needle.'

Julie Goodyear's hysterically funny contribution was memorable, even though she wasn't there in person. She was on holiday in Cyprus, where we had filmed her. When we saw the film, we howled, and so did Liz Dawn. Julie, typically mischievous, had surrounded herself by what could only be described as the local 'Chippendales'.

'Big lads, aren't they?' said Julie, dead-pan. Then she added, 'You know that bit at the end of *This Is Your Life* where they fly you in?' A slow-burn glance at her 'Chippendales'. 'Well, *I'm* not coming!'

But there were a few tears that weren't of laughter. This went back to a time when Liz had been asked for her autograph by a group of deaf people. She had been so touched that Father Terry O'Meara, who runs a deaf choir (they 'sing' the words in sign language), told us Liz was now fund-raiser in chief, and was even learning sign language herself.

Though Vera Duckworth worked for Mike Baldwin at his Coronation Street clothing factory, 'Mike' himself, actor Johnny Briggs, came from a very different background.

The Street's scotch-drinking Cockney is a born-and-bred Londoner, and that's where we surprised him, on 5 January 1983, in Covent Garden, where he was making a special presentation of a 'Sunshine Coach' on behalf of the Variety Club.

Pat Phoenix was Eamonn's co-conspirator at the Punch and Judy pub. Six-footer Eamonn tended to tower over the diminutive Johnny, but the actor was used to this. His lack of height hadn't prevented him getting his first real television break.

He had been to the Italia Conti Stage School, and gained experience in rep at Leicester and Nottingham when in 1964 he auditioned for the part of Detective Sergeant Russell in *No Hiding Place*, a huge hit at the time, and dominated by Superintendent Lockhart, played by Raymond Francis.

Raymond told us how Johnny wore 'lifts' in his shoes for his audition as the would-be policeman. The producers were impressed with his performance; so much so they asked if he could come back again, this time wearing 'lifts'. Double 'lifts' got him the part, and the show ran for six years.

A tribute far removed from a TV series came from Dirk Bogarde, who had appeared with Johnny in the 1962 film *HMS Defiant*, the story of an eighteenth-century man o' war. Dirk, playing an officer, had to sentence humble able-seaman Johnny to be lashed.

Vera Duckworth would have liked that.

However, Dirk Bogarde didn't very much like the idea of appearing on the Life. For some years he had made his home in the South of France, and had become an author (and much acclaimed, too). When researcher John Graham, now associate producer, thinking Nice would be nice, telephoned him, Dirk – very reluctantly – said he would film a few words to camera for us in Nice if the researcher could find the film and, more pertinently, the scene in it with Johnny Briggs and himself.

Coronation Street, not surprisingly, was not exactly big in Provence, so the star status of J. Briggs, Esq, had passed him by. Sadly, we were convinced that at the end of the telephone conversation, Dirk had delivered an urbane 'bonne chance'.

A few days later he answered the phone; a call from the same sun-seeking researcher who told the film star, 'Mr Bogarde? I've got some good news and some bad news. The good news is that me and the crew are about to board the plane to Nice, and the bad news is we found the film.' John Graham beamed.

Even the reluctant Dirk had to chuckle. What's more, he proved as good as his word and filmed for us. It was a highlight for Johnny Briggs on the night of his Life.

It was a full house in the 'Kabin' newsagents when Michael Aspel broke the news to Mavis Wilton (Thelma Barlow) that her name was on the book.

Mavis Wilton (Thelma Barlow) was busy at the till in the Kabin in Coronation Street and had her back to the door when a customer walked in, to buy an evening newspaper. The story was to make the front page next day, because the customer was Michael Aspel.

When she turned around, at a nudge from Rita Fairclough (Barbara Knox) so taken aback was she that Michael Aspel said later, 'I thought you were going to say "Ooh, I really don't know" ' – as Mavis would have done.

When the whole cast greeted this popular colleague in another studio at Granada, viewers might have been puzzled by a missing

Michael Aspel approaches the Rover's Return with Vera Duckworth (Elizabeth Dawn) . . .

. . . with a surprise for her 'husband' Jack, played by William Tarmey.

face – her Street husband, Derek Wilton, alias actor Peter Baldwin.

There was a reason: Peter had been Thelma's 'husband' in another time, at another place, namely the Bristol Old Vic in the Fifties in Congreve's *The Way of the World*. And on he came later.

Thelma had worked for a firm of auctioneers in Huddersfield and studied drama in the evenings at Huddersfield Technical College. She had gone on to work with Richard Briers in rep in Liverpool, and with Keith Barron at Bristol. Keith recalled her performance as a cub-mistress in Keith Waterhouse and Willis Hall's play *All Things Bright and Beautiful*. He reckoned the dithering character was the genesis of Mavis of the Street.

Two long-lost friends from the Street were resurrected, Valerie Barlow (Ann Reid) and Rene Bradshaw (Madge Hindle).

Mavis had first arrived in Coronation Street in 1971. When the characters there put down roots they seem to be immovable.

And so are the viewing millions in front of their TV screens.

The closing moments of *This Is Your Life* in Manchester on 22 October 1992 captured television history – the whole of the cast of Britain's most popular soap opera were fighting back real tears, and none too successfully.

The programme had started in jaunty style; Michael Aspel knocking on the door of Number Nine, Coronation Street. Vera Duckworth answered, and invited him in.

While Vera (Liz Dawn) 'got ready', Michael introduced our programme from the Duckworths' parlour. 'Here I am, chez Duckworth,' he said.

Then we saw Vera leading him down the street to the Rover's Return to surprise her screen husband, Jack – alias actor William Tarmey.

We had surprises not only for Bill, but for the viewers not aware of his real-life story in show business. For more than twenty years he played the clubs as a singer. Here we had the 'Sinatra of the Street'.

More than that, he had undergone life-saving heart surgery in 1987, taking four months out of the Street while his wife Alma ('Ally' to Bill and the family) nursed him back to health.

While she helped us with our surprise we became aware that Alma herself was fighting illness, an arthritic condition of the spine. She required hospital treatment while we were still working on the research.

His many friends in the cast were aware of this; viewers were not. There was, therefore, a double-edged impact when Michael Aspel revealed Bill had recorded a song, dedicated to his wife, before he went into hospital for heart surgery. The recording was to be given to her if he did not pull through. It was the song made famous by Bette Midler, 'You are the Wind Beneath my Wings'.

Instead of our closing music that night, Bill sang the song to Alma, his childhood sweetheart.

There wasn't a dry eye in the Street.

Chapter Nine
It's a Musical Life

Pop or opera, classical music or jazz, the Life has featured some great musical greats – and once stopped the traffic on Broadway itself.

Composer Jule Styne had come a long way from his humble origins at 228 Brick Lane, Bethnal Green, in London's East End where he was born in 1905.

Where Broadway meets Times Square there is a famous non-stop moving strip giving news flashes to that brash, noisy, teeming little bit of Manhattan. As Jule Styne reached that junction, walking down

Stopping the traffic in New York's Times Square to tell composer Jule Styne it's his Life . . .

. . . and Carol Channing is there to confirm it.

121

Broadway with a friend on the evening of 23 May 1978, the news flash read: 'Tonight, Jule Styne, This Is Your Life.' And from the bustling Broadway crowd, out stepped Eamonn Andrews. We had been in New York for a week, fixing that and many more surprises which we sprung on the astonished Jule at the studios of WNEW TV on East 67th Street.

We played some of his hit numbers: 'Three Coins in a Fountain', 'Everything's Coming Up Roses', 'Time After Time' and many more. Lyricist Sammy Cahn sang a new version for Jule: 'Time after time, I tell myself that I'm, so lucky to have met Jule Styne.'

Among the Broadway legends there to confirm that view were Carol Channing – for whom he wrote 'Diamonds are a Girl's Best Friend' – Dolores Gray, Alice Faye, Gene Autry in Hollywood, Tony Bennett in Las Vegas and the great man with whom Jule wrote the score for *Gypsy*, Stephen Sondheim.

Amazingly, the star Jule first rubbed shoulders with was turn-of-the-century music-hall headliner Sir Harry Lauder, back in the East End. Jule's father Isador was a great fan, and took the young Jule to see his idol at the local music hall. Jule dashed on to the stage, whereupon Sir Harry picked him up and had him join with him singing his hit number 'Daisy, Daisy'.

Jule emigrated with his family to Chicago in 1910. By the 'Roaring Twenties' he had his own band in the Chicago of Al Capone and the mobs.

He left for New York to become, at first, a vocal coach. Tony Martin was among his clients. And Jule had a huge hit with Judy Holliday in *Bells are Ringing*.

As Stephen Sondheim said on the programme, 'Several generations have danced and romanced to his music.'

The Bee Gees emigrated to Australia with their parents and found success. The family sailed there on August Bank Holiday 1958 on the £10 'assisted passage' scheme, brought in to encourage more British to settle in Australia. It more than paid for itself.

They were in the studio of DJ Steve Wright at Broadcasting House on the afternoon of 1 March 1991. On the turntable was their hit 'Got to get a Message to You'. What they didn't know was that Michael Aspel was on his way with our special message.

For weeks, John Graham had been travelling to the Florida homes of Barry Gibb and his brothers, twins Robin and Maurice, conducting top-secret interviews with their wives. It was a well-kept secret, too, because when Michael Aspel walked into that radio studio the boys were dumbfounded.

'Jesus, I don't believe it!' yelled one, and buried his head in his hands. 'Stitched up like kippers!' shrieked another. The studio crew and producers burst into spontaneous applause as Michael delivered the line: 'Tonight, the Bee Gees, This Is Your Life.'

Outside, our limousine waited, engine ticking over, to take them to the studios at Teddington. Normally, on this journey, subjects are treated to a glass or two of champagne, but the Bee Gees do not touch alcohol and settled for diet coke. Michael Aspel travels separately, and for a good reason. Making idle chat during the journey he could easily let slip a surprise we have in store.

Frankie Howerd looks ready to conduct the Bee Gees, Maurice, Robin and Barry Gibb.

The Bee Gees' story spanned three decades of pop music, and the star names giving their personal tributes to the boys, not only as performers, but as composers, included Kenny Rogers, Dionne Warwick, Neil Sedaka, Diana Ross and Barbra Streisand.

Researcher Sue Green had been trying for weeks to get past the security screen surrounding Michael Jackson. On the morning of the programme her home telephone rang. It was Michael Jackson. He wanted to record a greeting there and then on her answering machine – but Sue hadn't a clue how to set it. 'I'll call back,' said Jackson. Luckily he did – because shell-shocked Sue hadn't taken his number.

Sue had also flown to Las Vegas, where the boys' parents, Hughie (who has since died) and Barbara were living. They came over. And Hughie's offstage line got a huge laugh from his sons: 'Do you realise it's taken an English TV programme to get your mother off the slot machines in Las Vegas?'

Barbara told how the boys were singing in harmony when they were still at infant school in England. And when the family emigrated

123

they sang from the back of a lorry at Brisbane speedway track, where the crowd threw coins to them. Yet remarkably, the writers of hits like 'Massachusetts', 'Jive Talking', 'How to Mend a Broken Heart' and so many more cannot read music.

Susan George, a long-time family friend, very kindly praised the way the programme handled a tribute to the boys' late brother, Andy, who had died at the age of only thirty, three years before.

For our final surprise we flew in the Brisbane DJ who had first talent-spotted the boys at the speedway track. His name was Bill Gates, and it was he who gave them the name the Bee Gees.

Former Hot Gossip and Pan's People dancer Sarah Brightman had taken off in more ways than one when we set out to surprise the West End and Broadway musical star at RAF Wittering in Lincolnshire.

She'd been promised a 'flip' in a Harrier jump-jet as a thank you for a charity concert. As she roared round the skies she had no idea another aircraft was flying in the direction of the base, with a passenger list of surprises.

Her colleagues from the popular television dance groups were on board with Michael Aspel, ready to pounce when the Harrier landed.

Back at our studio were more surprises, including – from *Cats* – Bonnie Langford, Wayne Sleep, Paul Nicholas, Brian Blessed and choreographer Gillian Lynne.

Sarah had been acclaimed for her performance as Christine in *Phantom of the Opera*, composed by her then husband, Andrew Lloyd Webber, so she might have been forgiven for looking somewhat puzzled when he wasn't at the studio (apparently) that day in September, 1989.

We found Andrew in Hollywood, in Universal City, in the company of *ET*, *Indiana Jones*, and now *Jurassic Park* creator Steven Spielberg, no less. They were looking through scripts, they explained, which is why Andrew couldn't be in London.

In fact, it was a gag. As soon as we had recorded on videotape at Universal City, Andrew had caught a plane back to London and walked on to our set.

Andrew hadn't much cared for the catering arrangements, apparently, when we did his Life at the New London Theatre in 1980, and wanted to bring his own chef to Teddington. In the event, he was perfectly happy with the party afterwards, and so was everyone else.

Michael Crawford really did have to stay in Los Angeles – he was packing them in in *Phantom* – but he sent a contribution from there.

We had surprised Andrew with the cast of *Evita*, which included Elaine Paige, David Essex, John Turner, Stephanie Lawrence and Paul Nicholas.

As a child, Andrew had loved the music of Edmundo Ros, who rang from his home in Spain, delighted that Andrew's taste for Latin American music had come through in his latest hit musical.

Andrew also has a great love of pop/rock music. One of his favourite numbers is the Everly Brothers singing 'Bye, Bye, Love', and he couldn't have been more delighted when we flew Don Everly in from Nashville to surprise him.

Another young man with a classical music background revelled in pop stardom. Nigel Kennedy was 'the punk virtuoso of the violin' when he had a chart-topping hit with 'Four Seasons'. He was receiving a gold disc award at the Abbey Road studios of EMI when Michael walked in with the Big Red Book.

His mother had moved from Brighton to the West Midlands when Nigel was eight, and he had developed a life-long passion for Aston Villa. His girl friend, Brix E. Smith, told how she had spotted him wearing Villa boxer-shorts during a quick change at a concert at the Royal Albert Hall.

So we went over to Villa Park to see the whole team scraping away on violins. And the former child protégé – at seven he was at the Yehudi Menuhin School of Music – played the theme from *Match of the Day* to our audience on his priceless Stradivarius. It was much appreciated by England and Spurs striker Gary Lineker, who was there with his wife Michelle.

Yehudi Menuhin missed that particular contribution – he had to be in Pasadena, California, from where he greeted his former pupil.

Stephane Grappelli had visited the school when Nigel was there, and we had film of them playing jazz violin together.

Michael thought he had struck a mildly discordant note when he said, 'You pay the price of all the world travelling with the failure of your marriage.'

Said Nigel: 'Thank you, man. Brilliant.' Then, a few moments later, apparently just realising what Michael had said: 'What was that about my marriage again, mate?' But it was all good-natured ribbing.

'I wasn't going to mention it myself,' smiled Michael.

Nigel: 'It was written in, wasn't it?'

Before he found fame, when he was studying at New York's Juilliard

School, Nigel made ends meet by busking on Fifth Avenue, usually outside Tiffany's, where he sometimes found fifty-dollar bills dropped in his busker's violin case. Back in London, and buying his Stradivarius on the never-never, he tried busking in Covent Garden, but was stopped by a security man who said to the violin virtuoso, 'Can't busk here without a licence, mate.'

Cellist Julian Lloyd Webber told us Nigel's playing had moved him to tears. And to prove that Nigel's appeal really is 'across the board', we brought in pop stars Kate Bush, and Mark King and Mike Lindup of Level 42.

George Martin, the man who put the Beatles on the map, said Nigel 'was like a breath of fresh air'. George had conducted a concert Nigel did in aid of the Prince's Trust at the NEC in 1989.

Petula Clark has a cuddle for her son, Patrick Philips, then aged three, on the night of her Life in April 1975. On the right are Kathleen Harrison and Jack Warner, her 'parents' in the popular 'Huggett Family' films.

George himself was the subject of the Life on 30 January 1980. There were greetings from two of his protégés – Paul McCartney, arguably the world's most successful composer, and Cilla Black on a live link from the Wimbledon Theatre where she was appearing in *Aladdin*.

For many musicians, Gerry Marsden of Gerry and the Pacemakers, Billy J. Kramer and the Temperance Seven, George had been the musical genie. He had learned the piano from his uncle Cyril, who was there, at eighty-three, playing 'Tiger Rag'.

For the Life of Dame Kiri Te Kanawa, at the Royalty Theatre on 23 October 1981, Prince Charles wrote a letter to her to be read on the programme, with a hand-written PS. It said, 'I hope this isn't too much of a shock for you!'

The girl from New Zealand's quaintly named Poverty Bay had been personally chosen by Charles to sing at St Paul's Cathedral for his wedding to Lady Diana Spencer that same year, an occasion watched by eight hundred million television viewers in seventy-four countries.

The full letter from Charles read: 'I am writing to send my very best wishes to my favourite soprano and to say how much one of her greatest fans admires her glorious voice *and* her acting ability.'

We flew in Kiri's father, Tom (her mother had died nine years before) to tell how they had adopted Kiri when she was just five weeks old. Her Maori name 'Kiri' means 'bell' and 'Te Kanawa' 'chief kinsman to Tom'.

Another Dame, and another opera great, greeted her from Sydney: Dame Joan Sutherland.

Sir Harry Secombe came along to tell us how he had a bit of trouble pronouncing her name when she appeared as a guest on one of his own TV shows.

Dame Kiri told him, 'Don't bother. Just call me "Tin Knickers".'

We beat a path to the car park of the Royal Opera House in Covent Garden to spring the surprise on Sir Geraint Evans, son of a Welsh miner who had become one of the world's great opera stars.

Joseph Cooper, chairman of the TV quiz programme *Face the Music*, played for Geraint in the RAF during the war, when he auditioned for the British Forces Network.

A relieved Michael Aspel watches as George Shearing 'reads' the famous words — in braille.

Geraint became a regular broadcaster, which led to his having tuition at the Hamburg State Opera. Elisabeth Schwarzkopf, his legendary leading lady in *La Bohème* – his Covent Garden début – was not well enough on the night to get to the Zurich studio we had booked. But her telephone call from home delighted her former leading man.

So, too, did our live link to Wales, where the choir his father had once conducted gathered to sing for Sir Geraint: the Pontypridd Male Voice Choir, all sixty of them.

One of the most unusual pick-ups in the history of the Life was at Ronnie Scott's world famous Soho jazz club on 17 December 1991. Very unusual: the 'This Is Your Life' message on the Big Red Book was in braille.

This was so that blind jazz pianist George Shearing could trace the message when Ronnie Scott invited Michael Aspel on to the club stage.

Mel Torme, Peggy Lee, Henry Mancini, the King's Singers, John Dankworth and Stephane Grappelli paid their tributes to this Battersea coalman's son. Blind from birth, George had played his way from local pub pianist to international stardom.

Later in life, in 1952, inspired by his visits to Harlem listening to the music of Dizzy Gillespie and Charlie 'Bird' Parker, he sat down to write the jazz 'standard', 'Lullaby of Birdland'.

It took him just ten minutes.

Stephane Grappelli and John Dankworth led George to a piano to 'jam' us out with 'Birdland', Stephane on violin, John on sax, George at the piano. As they say in the business, the audience 'broke the furniture'.

Just as astonishing was the musical Life of Evelyn Glennie – who had been an acclaimed solo virtuoso percussionist on the concert platforms of the world by the time she was twenty-five.

Yet she is profoundly deaf.

This was a unique story of success against all the odds. Evelyn had made history by becoming the first full-time solo virtuoso percussionist ever. And as no fewer than six hundred instruments make up the modern percussion section, that's quite an achievement.

We hit the high road to her native Scotland to surprise her on 16 November 1990. She was at the Glencairn Primary School in Motherwell, presenting musical instruments on behalf of the Beethoven Fund for Deaf Children.

James Galway, Richard Stilgoe, Sir Georg Solti and Princess Michael of Kent were among those waiting to speak to her back at the studios of Scottish Television in Glasgow. What's more, astronomer Patrick Moore was there to re-create a duet of 'The Two Imps' he had played with her on the marimba at a literary dinner.

Confirmation of her international status came when she played Bartók's Sonata for Two Pianos and Percussion with American virtuoso Murray Perahia and Covent Garden maestro Sir Georg Solti, and we had film of this great performance.

What is Evelyn's secret? She 'feels' notes from vibrations – the lower the note, the deeper and stronger the vibration low in the body; the higher notes she detects on the higher body – face, hair, finger-tips.

Her mentor, the world's greatest living percussionist James Blades, then aged ninety, made the journey to Scotland to make a prediction: that Evelyn Glennie will end her days as Dame Evelyn.

Dublin-born Bob Geldof is the son of a chef on the *Queen Mary* and had a Belgian grandfather. An unlikely background for a knight. Bob was awarded an honorary knighthood for his work on 'Band Aid' – which culminated in the sell-out Wembley concert with all proceeds going to ease the consequences of the famine raging in Ethiopia.

With Midge Ure he had written 'Do They Know It's Christmas' – the best-selling record and video in aid of famine relief. Midge, and Bob's wife, Paula Yates, were our co-conspirators in getting him to our television theatre on 15 January 1985.

Paul Young and Spandau Ballet's Martin and Gary Kemp were there; Sting spoke from holiday in Antigua, and Kool and the Gang from New York.

Bob Geldof actually started his pop career as a band manager 'but edged closer to the microphone'. Then he changed the band's name to the Boomtown Rats. A fan of the legendary Woody Guthrie, he had read that was the name of Guthrie's boyhood New York street gang.

His first hit came in 1979 with 'I Don't Like Mondays' – which no doubt he didn't when he was a baker's roundsman – then in 1980 he appeared in Alan Parker's film *The Wall*. Alan was there to sing his praises as an actor.

All sang his praises as a man of concern and caring.

Probably the most unusual musical Life came when Michael Aspel and the team travelled north to Stockport, Cheshire, on 9 February 1993.

Percussionist Evelyn Glennie gets some assistance from a surprise guest – Patrick Moore. It was a star performance.

Our destination was St Winifred's School, and the name on the Big Red Book was that of the headmistress, a nun, Sister Aquinas. She was celebrating not only thirty years as headmistress, but twenty-five years of a succession of school choirs which have to be top of the playground pops.

In her study are gold and silver discs for backing on hits such as 'Matchstalk Men' and 'No One Quite Like Grandma'. Many deserving causes have benefited from concerts and royalties, from needy children to the elderly and handicapped. When Michael arrived, the latest choir was backing *Coronation Street*'s Jack Duckworth (William Tarmey) singing 'One Voice'.

It all started when a parent, who owned a recording studio, heard the choir and sent a recording to the television programme *Stars on Sunday*. The choirs of St Winifred's have been stars ever since, and from Stockholm Abba's Bjorn Ulvaeus sang their praises.

Sister Aquinas was born in Bridgwater, Somerset, and went to the convent school there. Because of the war, the convent's senior class had an unusual pupil – a boy. He left in 1946 and travelled the world working for the Foreign Service. They had not met for forty-seven years – until that night in Manchester when the Life surprised the musical nun with former classmate Michael Marshall.

Everyone agreed they had much to sing about that night.

Chapter Ten
This Sporting Life

Frank Bruno, George Best, Virginia Wade, Alex 'Hurricane' Higgins, Ian Botham, Nigel Mansell, Rory Underwood – all are sporting names instantly recognisable even to people who have never attended a sporting event in their lives. And all have been subjects of the Life.

Viewing figures prove that people never tire of stories of sporting achievement, particularly when someone wins against all the odds.

Opening the programme with soccer, Manchester United's Bobby Charlton was celebrating being Player of the Year, European Footballer of the Year, and receiving an OBE for services to the game when we surprised him at London's Sportsman's Club on 26 November 1969 – just three years after he had won a World Cup Winners' medal with an England team captained by Bobby Moore, whom we surprised a couple of years later. The programme, broadcast live from the club, was the second of Thames Television's Life transmissions.

Bobby had had a miraculous escape in the Munich air disaster twelve years before, escaping with hardly a scratch. He had just established a regular first team place and Sir Matt Busby said it must have taken 'a terrific effort of will' to go back on the field at Old Trafford 'with just about every familiar face now missing'.

In April 1958, two months after Munich, Bobby pulled on an England shirt for the first time and scored from a cross from legendary winger Tom Finney, also a Life subject.

Soccer ran in the Charlton family – his mother's cousin was Newcastle United and England star Jackie Milburn (who was himself surprised with the Big Red Book at the studios of Tyne Tees Television in Newcastle).

By the time we surprised Bobby's big brother, Jackie, Leeds United and England centre half, on 16 April 1973, they had become the first brothers to play together in an England side since Nottingham Forest's Frank and Fred Foreman back in 1899.

In 1967 Jackie had been voted Footballer of the Year, taking the title from Bobby. Leeds and Scotland star Billy Bremner said the only reason he got the Leeds captaincy was that Big Jack did not want to lead the team on to the pitch. He had a superstition that if he came out last he would play better.

The odds were stacked against us on 17 November 1971, the first show of the second series when 'We return to surprise one of the most talked about people in Britain,' said Eamonn Andrews.

What he might have added was, 'But will he show up?' – for the name on the book was that of Manchester United's George Best, probably the greatest individual player of his time. His pop star good looks made him as popular with the ladies as with the crowds on the terraces.

The great Bill Shankly compares hair styles with soccer legend Denis Law.

And team-mate George Best discovers even he can't body-swerve the book.

But even in those days he was not the greatest respecter of punctuality, and we intended going live with the programme. We had gone to great lengths to get George to make an appearance at a fashion show in London. To our relief, he showed up and was blocked by Eamonn's tackle.

The shipyard worker's son from Belfast was spotted by United 'scout' Bob Bishop who described the youngster as 'just over five feet tall and seven stones, wet through'.

He crossed the Irish Sea at fifteen to join United – wearing his first pair of long pants. Then he felt homesick and ran back to Belfast. He was coaxed back, made the first team at seventeen and, in 1966, after United's European Cup win over Benfica, in which Bobby Charlton scored two goals, he earned the title 'El Beatle'.

England's Kevin Keegan had just been voted European Footballer of the Year when we surprised him on 4 February 1979 – at the christening party for his daughter, Laura Jane. A huge christening cake, on a trolley, was pushed into the hotel reception by Liverpool and England team mates Emlyn Hughes, Phil Neal, Mick Channon, Ray Clemence, Phil Thompson, Ray Kennedy and Ian Callaghan. From inside the cake sprang Eamonn Andrews to surprise the proud father.

Kevin was playing for Hamburg by that time, and his team mate Horst Bertl explained that the supporters had christened Kevin 'Mächtig Maus' – 'Mighty Mouse'.

But who was the 'scout' who spotted him in the first place? The headmistress of his tiny primary school in Yorkshire, Sister Mary Oliver. She had written in the scrap of a lad's school report: 'Kevin's football must be encouraged.' After that, the other nuns called her 'STS' – 'Soccer Talent Spotter'.

Kevin's boyhood hero, Billy Wright – 106 caps for England and another Life subject, thanks to his wife Joy and sisters Teddy and Babs of the Beverley Sisters – was there. So was another former Life soccer subject, a legendary player and manager of Liverpool.

'Many people have helped me on my way, but only one person made me,' said Kevin. And on came Bill Shankly.

As with Kevin, a teacher figured strongly in the making of Manchester United and England captain Bryan Robson, surprised in a 'traffic jam' on 21 January 1985. On a business trip to London, his car was blocked by a lorry. The driver turned out to be his father, Brian, a professional long-distance lorry driver.

'Hello, son,' he said. 'I've a special delivery for you here.' He opened the rear-loading doors and out leapt all his United colleagues.

The teacher was sportsmaster Bill Chapman, who devised a special training programme for the skinny, undersized twelve-year-old, who went on to become Britain's number one footballer.

Boyhood heroes Bobby Charlton and Denis Law (another Life subject) were there, as was Bryan's Newcastle United favourite, Welsh international centre forward Wyn Davies.

Then England manager Bobby Robson (no relation) said he saw Bryan filling a crucial role in England's soccer future: an accurate prediction.

From soccer to the strawberries and cream of summer and the Centre Court at Wimbledon.

Virginia Wade had lost in no fewer than four Wimbledon semi-finals before winning the Ladies Championship against Bette Stove in HM the Queen's Jubilee Year, 1977. Rarely had the nation appreciated a sporting victory more deeply. 'Ginny' had been carried on a wave of emotional support.

But where was she? Where would she be next? Being a professional tennis player means living out of suitcases as well as tennis bags. By the time the Life was back on air for the 1977 season (ours, that is) we thought we had the elusive champion committed to New York. Researchers flew in to Manhattan to arrange a likely pick-up and the opportunity to present the programme in New York, where Virginia had many friends.

All was going so well that the senior researcher took an evening off to go to the movies, to see *Star Wars*. There were so many special effects noises going on during the film, it took her a while to realise one of the signals was coming from her own bleeper.

The call was to say that Virginia had suddenly decided to fly to London to receive an award at the National Sports Stadium at Crystal Palace (she had been voted Player of the Year and Sportswoman of the Year following her Wimbledon triumph).

So it was that Angela Rippon announced another award on the night of 7 December 1977 – the Big Red Book. And there was Eamonn Andrews at Crystal Palace.

Billie Jean King, six times Wimbledon Champion, added her tribute, as did Dan Maskell (another Life subject) when he quoted that favourite line of Kipling's inscribed above the entrance to the centre court: 'If you can meet with triumph and disaster and treat these two imposters just the same. . . .'

Said Dan: 'Virginia is the living proof.'

Angela Rippon helped Eamonn serve the book on Virginia Wade.

Michael greets a new, temporary receptionist at Thames TV – in fact the girlfriend of world snooker champion Stephen Hendry. . .

. . . and this was his reaction.

Half a century before, 1920s crowds had flocked to see Kitty Godfree play. Twice she was Wimbledon Champion, and won five Olympic Gold Medals.

A delightful ninety-one-year-old, she was actually cycling to her local supermarket in Richmond, Surrey, when Eamonn Andrews surprised her. (He had had to relearn to ride a bike in order to pull off this dangerous mission, and was nearly knocked spinning by an irate motorist who yelled, 'Why don't you learn to ride the damn thing?')

After that, all ran smoothly. On the evening of 15 September 1987, many tennis greats paid their respects to Kitty, among them Martina Navratilova, Chris Evert, Fred Perry, Angela Buxton, Christine Truman, Sue Barker, Angela Mortimer and, on a live link from Paris, her great contemporary Jean Boratra: they had been singles champions at Wimbledon in the same year – 1924.

Kitty's victim in her first Wimbledon final (1924), Helen Wills Moody, spoke to her from America, and her second, in 1926, Spain's Lili de Alvarez (now Contessa de la Valdemme) was there.

Kitty did not go home on her bicycle. Nor did Eamonn.

Seventy years separated Kitty Godfree and twenty-one-year-old world snooker champion Stephen Hendry, who walked into the foyer of Thames Television at Euston on 24 October 1990 and got the surprise of his life when the receptionist with the long blonde hair threw back her locks and smiled at the visitor. The 'receptionist' was his girlfriend, Mandy. He thought she was back in Scotland.

From behind a screen came fellow pros from the snooker circuit Joe Johnson, Mike Hallett, Doug Mountjoy, Terry Griffiths, Tony Meo and John Spencer. Alex Higgins, Willie Thorne and Cliff Thorburn added their greetings.

Stephen had just become snooker's youngest ever world champion, taking that record from Alex Higgins. In the final he had beaten his boyhood idol, Jimmy White. Jimmy was there to tell us that after playing against young Stephen once in Ireland he had given him an Irish pound note on which he had written: 'To the next Jimmy White. From Jimmy White.'

And Stephen was delighted to return the compliment when it was the turn of his hero to be surprised in February 1993, after he had just won the UK Championship.

Some letters asked how could we do a Life on someone so young? Our answer: he had just become the best in the world at what he does.

Incidentally, the programme was the highest rated of the season in terms of viewing figures.

Alex 'Hurricane' Higgins was the ripe old age of twenty-two when he became the youngest world champion, and he had just won the Benson and Hedges Masters against Terry Griffiths when we surprised him doing some trick shots with singer Joe Brown at the Pot Black Club on 2 November 1981.

He and Joe had just won a pro-celebrity tournament, and there was quite a turn-out of pros and celebs, including Steve Davis, John Virgo, John Spencer, Emlyn Hughes, Brian Close, David Watkins, Dave Lee Travis, Duggie Brown, Dickie Henderson, Frank Carson and the prettiest opponent he'd ever had at snooker, Suzi Quatro.

Son of a Belfast railway labourer, Alexander Gordon Higgins, known to his family as Sandy, often went without meals to save the threepence for the price of a game at his local billiard hall. He also collected potato peelings from neighbours to sell as pig food to raise the money to get on the tables.

He first crossed the water to become a stable-boy in the hope of being a jockey, but one night a snooker tournament in Bolton changed his life. Ten times world champion John Pulman was there to present the winning trophy and to take on all-comers. No one could beat him until 'this little kid from Belfast'.

There and then the former world champion told Alex, 'You've got to go professional.'

So the nation's jockeys were saved from the competitive instinct of 'the Hurricane'. But few in any sport could summon the sheer guts and determination of a National Hunt jockey whose story touched all hearts.

Monday 12 October 1981, saw the Life team smuggled into the pretty Cotswold village of Chipping Camden. Bob Champion was getting married at the parish church of St James. Guests included Terry Biddlecombe, John Francome, Richard Pitman, Fred Winter, Lord John Oaksey, John Rickman and Josh Gifford.

Wedding bells were ringing, confetti was being thrown, when an 'uninvited' guest, Eamonn Andrews, stepped forward outside the church. We recorded the programme in the wedding reception marquee.

That year, Bob Champion had not only won the Grand National, he had won a battle for life against cancer after being given just eight months to live.

Like something from a film script, his favourite horse, Aldaniti, had 'broken down' twice, having strained a tendon on the same foreleg on both occasions, and, like the jockey, seemed certain never to race again.

But in his hospital bed, fighting the cancer and undergoing the most painful treatments Bob Champion told trainer Josh Gifford, 'Never mind. Aldaniti and myself will just have to make our comeback together.'

From then on, his dream was to win the Grand National on his favourite horse. The odds against them doing it must have been incalculable.

But then so was the depth of bravery and determination of rider – and horse. They made it.

An unexpected guest popped out of the shadows at Bob Champion's wedding – Eamonn.

One of the most dramatic Grand Nationals of all time was featured on the Life on 13 November 1974.

It had happened eighteen years before. Jockey Dick Francis was in the lead, riding the Queen Mother's horse, Devon Loch, which collapsed just yards from the winning post.

It might have been a scene from one of Dick's subsequent best-selling thrillers. On the show, not only did Sir Gordon Richards pay his respects to a fellow pro but so too did fellow novelist Kingsley Amis, who said he had read every one of Dick's books.

We set up a deliberate mystery with Paul and Linda McCartney at the EMI studios in Abbey Road on Wednesday 6 November 1974, to surprise a young man who'd nothing to do with pop music. Fighting was the game for twenty-three-year-old John Conteh, the Liverpool-born son of a seaman from Sierra Leone, and he had punched his way to world fame while retaining the looks of a film star. He was the newly crowned Light Heavyweight Champion of the World, Britain's first for over a quarter of a century.

Fellow Liverpudlian Paul had been at the ringside with Linda. There was a picture of John on the front cover of Paul's latest hit album. Paul's telegram before the fight read, 'You made me Number One. Now you be Number One.'

After his victory, Paul and Linda lured John to the EMI studios to pose with Paul for a picture to be taken by Linda, a professional photographer.

What a line-up for the Life. The new glamour-boy champ, the ex-Beatle and his wife. Then, panic.

Eamonn briefs Paul and Linda McCartney on how we plan to surprise a new world champion . . .

. . . and John Conteh is caught off-guard for once.

The despatch rider taking the top-secret script to the programme's director skidded on the wet, wintry road and crashed. Bravely, he shook himself down and got on his bike, not realising that one large envelope still lay by the roadside. It contained the secrets of the Life.

More panic when a return to the scene of the accident revealed the envelope was missing. Luckily for us, the finder sent it on to the director's address, unopened. As it was marked 'Strictly Confidential', the temptation to open it must have been pressing, especially as it had the Thames Television logo on it.

We got our man at Abbey Road, thanks to Paul and Linda, and back at the studios Henry Cooper and eight more British champions were there to surprise John, plus an old friend, *Man at the Top* star Kenneth Haigh, and his New York model wife Myrna. Oh, yes, and John's nine brothers and sisters. His mum Rachel said she'd fought the championship herself that night. On Merseyside, at least, it was a knock-out.

British Heavyweight Champion Henry Cooper wouldn't have missed that night when Eamonn surprised John Conteh, for no one was more surprised than Henry when Eamonn feinted with the Big Red Book at the Euston Road Studios on 14 January 1970, during the first Thames series.

Henry's taxi pulled up and he walked into the foyer, expecting a sports programme about his career, especially his fights with Muhammad Ali.

Ali was on the satellite and ex-fighters such as Billy Walker and Joe Erskine who knew what it was like to step into the ring with Henry in his prime had their say before the bell. Even Ali had been saved by the bell once, when Henry Cooper knocked him to the canvas. But Henry has always maintained Ali was the greatest fighter of his era.

All who know him would maintain that Henry Cooper is the greatest gentleman fighter of his era.

The popularity of heavyweight Frank Bruno transcends the fight game. His 'Know what I mean, Harry?' in banter with commentator Harry Carpenter (another Life subject) has become a national catchphrase.

On 26 January 1993, he was with comedian Freddie Starr at the London headquarters of Central Television, watching a preview of Freddie's Easter 'special', which featured the two of them in a sketch. Frank wasn't aware Michael Aspel was 'on the bill'.

Frank's wife Laura and pretty daughters Nicola, ten, and Rachel, six, were waiting to surprise him, and so was Harry Carpenter.

ITV's boxing commentator Reg Gutteridge read a warm letter from Muhammad Ali.

There was a letter, too, from Prince Charles, thanking him for his work on behalf of the Prince's Trust, which helps deserving young people.

'I am sorry I can't be with you. It would give you a terrible shock and probably embarrass you dreadfully,' wrote Charles.

But the biggest surprise was the 'voice off' which said, 'I've got the belt you want, Frank, and one day I'll give you the chance to take it off me.'

The voice belonged to Britain's first World Heavyweight Champion this century – Lennox Lewis.

But Big Frank was floored in the last round by a little old lady – his eighty-four-year-old grandmother, Henrietta, our surprise fly-in from Kingston, Jamaica.

If there is a more testing moment in sport than pulling on the boxing gloves, then it must be putting on the crash-helmet in motor sport.

It is generally agreed the world's most dangerous sport is motorcycle racing. Barry Sheene was the master, world champion not once but twice in a death-defying sport which we illustrated with a piece of film at an exhibition of racing motorcycles in London.

Viewers saw Barry racing at 180 mph and surviving a crash at that speed at Daytona, Florida. Then Eamonn Andrews crashed through the screen on which the film was being shown – with the Big Red Book. It was 12 January 1978, and Barry had just been awarded an MBE.

In that Daytona crash he had sustained a broken thigh, wrist, forearm, collar bone, six broken ribs and compression fractures of the vertebrae. Seven weeks later, he was racing again. One of the all-time greats, Giacomo Agostini, came to tell us that when he witnessed the crash he had thought Barry Sheene was dead.

One of Barry's greatest fans joined us to celebrate the fact that the great motorcycle racer, whose father Frank had tuned motor-racing machines in Italy, was still alive: ex-Beatle George Harrison, making a rare TV appearance.

On four wheels, world champions Graham Hill and Jackie Stewart were recipients of the Big Red Book, and Graham was twenty-four before he even got behind the wheel of a car.

A more recent British World Champion is, of course, Nigel Mansell. We surprised Nigel not as he came off the racing track but as he came out of the air. He had been taking part (as a passenger) in an aerobatics display by the Red Arrows formation team at RAF Scampton in Lincolnshire, launching the twenty-fifth season of the Red Arrows. We flew him back to London by helicopter.

It was 15 December 1988, and his wife, Rosanne, told viewers how Nigel had won her while he was at the wheel of a clapped-out mini-van. He stopped to offer her a lift to the Midlands college where they were both studying.

Stirling Moss made a pit-stop to say hello, and viewers heard how in June 1977, at Brands Hatch, Nigel had broken his neck in two places. He was back driving within seven weeks.

Still not put off, in 1978 he sold everything, including his home, to raise the money to carry on racing. He even cleaned office windows.

There could be no greater illustration of Nigel's total determination than what happened at the Dallas Grand Prix in 1984. It was so hot, the sun melted the track surface. Cars broke down everywhere. The drive-shaft on his car snapped, losing the gears. Nigel got out and collapsed trying to push it to the finishing line. American driver Charles Wagner was in awe. 'The Churchillian spirit,' he said.

Nigel Mansell turned up again as Michael Aspel's 'chauffeur' to drop him at the Grosvenor House hotel in Park Lane on the evening of 6 December 1992. The occasion was the annual 'Autosport' dinner, and we had a surprise for a man who has been world champion first on two wheels, then on four – John Surtees.

We flew in Barry Sheene from his home in Brisbane. Former world champion on four wheels Jackie Stewart was also there.

And we had a greeting from Argentinian motor-racing legend Juan Fangio, who spoke to John in Italian, the language they learned when they both raced for Ferrari.

'Fiery Fred' Trueman is a cricketing legend.

When he popped into the Anchor Hotel at Southwark Bridge, just before flying out to Australia for commentating duties, on 31 October 1979, there was a new barman: Eamonn Andrews.

Even at birth, young Fred looked as though he might be capable of his 100 mph deliveries. The fourth of eight children of a Yorkshire miner, Fred weighed in at 14 lb 8 oz.

On his Test début against India in 1952, he took four wickets for no runs, and went on to become the first man in the history of the game to capture three hundred Test wickets. Legendary Australian batsman Neil Hawke was the three-hundredth victim. Said Neil: 'The only consolation was that it got me into the record books, too!'

We flew in an old pal and great rival, Australian fast bowler Keith Miller. Keith quoted a letter sent to Freddie from the great Herbert Sutcliffe, of Yorkshire and England, after Freddie had taken his 250th Test wicket. It read, 'In figures alone, this must make you the greatest bowler the world has ever seen.'

Freddie's first Yorkshire cap has a special resting place. It is buried with his proud father.

Another proud cricketing parent was the mother of the world's greatest all-rounder of his time, Sir Garfield Sobers. She was at the Garrison Racecourse in Bridgetown, Barbados, to see her son knighted by the Queen in 1975. It was the first ceremony of its kind to be held outside the British Isles.

Gary was celebrating his knighthood at the Barbados High Commission in London when we surprised him, and got an even bigger surprise when his mother, Thelma, walked in. She had boarded a plane for the first time in her life to take the nine-hour flight to London. She had always said, 'I don't want to travel to that cold country.'

Sir Gary himself flew in from Australia for our surprise on Ian Botham. He had been young Ian's boyhood hero and inspiration.

It was 4 October 1981, and that summer Ian Botham had vanquished the Australian tourists virtually single-handed. His century at Old Trafford had made him Britain's most popular sporting hero.

We surprised him, appropriately, at Lords, thanks to England team manager Raman Subba Row, captain Keith Fletcher and vice captain Bob Willis, who had assembled the team for a 'briefing' on the eve of their tour of India.

Former England skipper Brian Close greeted from Barbados, Dennis Lillee from Australia and Geoffrey Boycott from Hong Kong. Geoffrey had been the first to tag Ian 'Guy the Gorilla' – and sent him a present of a bunch of bananas and a couple of coconuts.

Ian's best pal from Somerset, probably the world's best batsman, Viv Richards, rang at the last moment to say his flight from Antigua had been cancelled. Hastily we arranged a live link so the two famous cricketing pals could talk to each other.

And the cricketing hero he had idolised as a boy, Sir Garfield Sobers, paid him this tribute: 'Today, Ian, I want to say *you* are the world's best all-rounder.'

Geoff Boycott had a word with Ian Botham from Hong Kong and reminded us of his nickname 'Guy the Gorilla' – then sent him this appropriate gift, a bunch of bananas.

Ian Botham spoke to Graham Gooch from location on Ian's charity fund-raising walk from Aberdeen to Ipswich, after we had surprised the England captain at the Excelsior Hotel at Heathrow with the Test side before flying out to Australia, on 17 October 1990. Aussie skipper Alan Border and bowler Jeff Thomson – a former Essex team mate – greeted from Australia.

That summer, Graham had slogged his way into the record books against the Indian tourists: *Sunday Express* sports columnist Norman Giller, who wrote the script (as he sometimes does), described him as 'the greatest scoring machine in the history of Test cricket'. Said manager Mickey Stewart: 'He helped pump back the pride into English cricket.'

Graham Gooch trained with West Ham and Ian Botham with Scunthorpe – once he actually got a first team game – but sporting legend Denis Compton played on the left wing for Arsenal and was a wartime international footballer as well as getting himself into cricket's record books with his run-making for Middlesex and England.

Denis thought he was coming to the studio for an *ITV Sport* interview with Nick Owen. Before the evening was out, some of the greatest names in cricket had been reunited with the 1950s 'glamour boy' of the game, whose advertisements for Brylcreem had made his face – and hair – among the most famous in the land.

Peter May, Alec Bedser, Trevor Bailey, Ted Dexter, Godfrey Evans and Sir Leonard Hutton all sang the sporting praises of the man known as 'Compo'.

Keith Miller let viewers in on a secret, explaining why he bowled the occasional 'bouncer' to his great pal. They used to bet on the same horses and if Keith got the message via a fielder that they had got a big winner, he signalled the news to Denis with a bouncer.

As South Africa returns to the world sporting stage, few stories could be more moving than that of Basil D'Oliveira, whom we surprised in the Long Room at Lords on 17 March 1971, on England's triumphant return from Australia after winning the Ashes for the first time in twelve years.

For the Cape Coloured South African, prevented by law from playing for his own country, it was a particularly personal triumph.

Years earlier, listening to the commentaries of John Arlott, Basil, a total stranger, had written to him for advice. It took two years but John, thanks to his cricketing contacts in the Central Lancashire League, got Basil taken on by the Middleton club. From there he went on to a glorious career with Worcestershire and England. Small wonder John was a little damp of eye that night.

Few British athletes return with Olympic golds, and we were quick to surprise Mary Peters on 24 January 1973, shortly after she came back from Munich. She had also just been awarded an MBE in the New Year's Honours list.

Two hundred and fifty million viewers had seen her not only win the gold medal but at the same time set a new world record for one of the toughest of athletics events, the Women's Pentathlon.

We hit the trail to Scotland to surprise another gold medal winner in the 1980 Moscow Olympics. Alan Wells – the 'Edinburgh Express' – had brought back Britain's first hundred metres gold for fifty-six years.

It was the high road again, this time to Dundee, on 29 November 1991, to the vast Caird Hall to celebrate a slip of a girl who had just won the 10,000 metres world championship in Tokyo and raced to victory in the New York Marathon. What's more, Elizabeth McColgan had just become a mother.

The audience in her home city – celebrating its eight-hundredth anniversary – gave her a standing ovation. Two members of the men's relay gold medal winning team greeted her from training camp. Kris Akabusi was Male Athletics Personality of the Year, and Roger Black Male Athlete of the Year. Liz McColgan had won the female equivalent of both titles. Baby daughter Eilish was there to share Mum's glory.

Olympic pentathlon gold medallist Daley Thompson was Michael Aspel's running mate when we travelled to Manchester to surprise another former gold medallist – and newly crowned javelin world champion.

Tessa Sanderson was giving an aerobics class at Ashton on Mersey High School, for the benefit of the cameras of Granada's *Good Morning* programme – or so she thought.

Daley Thompson was first to walk into the gym to tell her she had another surprise caller – Michael.

Born in Jamaica, Tessa's parents had gone on ahead to build a home for the family in Wednesfield, Staffordshire. When the time came for Tessa and her sister Pat to join them they had severe worries about the English weather. Pat told us they had heard it was so cold in England that if you touched your ears they would fall off. Their consolation was the discovery of the great British chip.

Olympic team manager Mary Peters, Tessa's own heroine, told us how, despite injury, Tessa had turned the tears of disappointment at the Moscow Olympics into tears of joy and triumph in Los Angeles.

There were a few more tears that night, too.

The glory days of British golf were celebrated on 5 February 1986 when we surprised Henry Cotton, three times British Open Champion.

We went to the Barbican for the International Golf Show where Henry was being awarded a gold medal for services to the game. Helping with our surprise, driving off an indoor tee, were Sandy Gall, Ted Dexter and Cliff Michelmore, and back at the studio some of the greatest names in the sport, including former Open Champions Max Faulkner and Fred Daly, the then reigning champion Sandy Lyle, plus Bernard Gallagher, Sam Torrance, Mark James and Jeremy Bennett, all former winners of Henry's 'Rookie of the Year' award.

Arnold Palmer and Sam Snead greeted from America, as did another old pro – Bob Hope.

Former Life subjects Peter Allis and Jimmy Tarbuck were there, and so was Britain's Ryder Cup captain Tony Jacklin.

Tony we surprised outside Buckingham Palace in January 1970. In the wake of winning both the American and British Open Championships he had just received an OBE from HM the Queen. He was the first Briton to win the British Open in eighteen years. In America, the former Scunthorpe apprentice steelworker had beaten greats such as Jack Nicklaus and Arnold Palmer to win the US Open in Jacksonville, Florida.

England's double Grand Slam in 1992 was also supposed to mark the retirement from international rugby, after a record of thirty-five caps, of a young winger who was a flyer in more ways than one.

That's what took us to RAF Wyton in Cambridgeshire for Michael Aspel to surprise Flight Lieutenant Rory Underwood as he stepped from the Canberra he had just brought in to land.

Back at the studio were his triumphant team mates, including skipper Will Carling. A further reunion was with the pilots Rory had trained with

Rory Underwood greets RAF colleague John Peters, fully recovered after being taken prisoner in the Gulf War.

ten years before, completed by a young man flying in from his base in Germany. He was Flight Lieutenant John Peters, looking rather fitter and happier than the pictures of him as a Gulf War captive which were flashed around the world.

Some time after his Life, Rory decided on a new lease of life in international rugby.

That led to his mother, Anne, becoming the proudest mother in Britain at Twickenham on Saturday 6 March 1993.

Rory's younger brother, Tony, was also selected to play for England

This Is Your Life

We dreamed up an unusual way to tackle England rugby captain Bill Beaumont . . .

. . . and it worked.

against Scotland. Millions of viewers saw Anne dancing with joy up in the stands when Tony went over for a try only minutes after Rory had done the same.

Bill Beaumont had captained England's first rugby Grand Slam victory for twenty-three years when we surprised him with a bizarre pick-up.

Burly Bill had once told a team mate his mini was too small for him to fit inside, but he would accept a lift on the roof rack.

On 31 March 1980, Bill was on a business trip to London. Unknown to him, we had arranged for his driver to take him through Battersea Park. And there he was surrounded by a 'scrum' of minis – a motorcade with his Grand Slam-winning team mates on the roof racks.

The Life shared the halcyon days of Welsh rugby in the Seventies, kicking off with the world's best fly half – Barry 'King' John. Eamonn Andrews was waiting in the players' tunnel at Twickenham after the international against England on 15 January 1972.

John Dawe led the Welsh team on to the set, and scrum half Gareth Edwards recalled his first international.

'How do you want the ball?' he asked 'King' John.

'You just chuck it, boyo, I'll catch it.'

Four years later we caught Gareth Edwards himself. On a business trip to London, he stepped out of an office building, and a motor coach pulled to a halt. Led by skipper Mervyn Davies – another Life subject – the whole Welsh squad piled out.

British Lions captain, Ireland's Willie John McBride – whom we surprised in front of the crowd at Dublin's Lansdowne Road when his turn came – described Gareth as 'the linch-pin of the side'.

Twice world water-ski champion Liz Hobbs MBE almost didn't live for us to do her Life. When she crashed at 80 mph in July 1984, it was 'like hitting a concrete wall'. Her neck was cracked and she had six broken ribs, a smashed breastbone and a punctured lung. She made a miraculous recovery and came to the studios on 23 December 1986 for, she thought, an appearance on the children's programme *Splash*. But Eamonn Andrews was waiting.

Michael Aspel was waiting in Yorkshire to surprise her *Emmerdale* star husband, Frazer Hines, on 11 September 1992. Beamed Liz after the show: 'We've now got bookends.'

Chapter Eleven
Life upon the Wicked Stage

Michael Aspel had good reason to feel extra nervous as he waited for the curtain to fall on the production of Pirandello's *Henry IV* at Wyndham's Theatre on 15 September 1990. As the cast took their curtain calls, Michael was scheduled to walk out from the wings and surprise the play's star – an actor of international stature who had always told friends and colleagues, 'Never let them near me with that Big Red Book.'

And former rugby-playing, hell-raising Richard Harris is not an actor to be messed with. When Michael approached him, with the audience going wild, Richard flung up his arms, flopped down on Henry's throne and blurted, 'I always said I'd run. But now I'm too old!'

Back at Teddington Studios we had a surprise that was unique for the *Life* – both Richard's ex-wives walked on, and sat one on either side of him. He looked delighted, as who wouldn't be with Elizabeth Harris on one side and Hollywood actress Ann Turkel on the other, both cultured beauties straight from the pages of *Vogue*? Both had told us they wouldn't miss the evening for anything, and Ann flew in specially from New York.

Elizabeth, mother of their three sons, had met Richard when they were at drama school. Ann was a schoolgirl when she saw *Camelot* and compiled a scrapbook of the show. Never did she think that one day she would marry King Arthur.

Co-stars of the 1967 film, Vanessa Redgrave (who played Guinevere) and Franco Nero (Lancelot) greeted Richard from Hollywood.

The play in which Richard was currently appearing – from which Isla Blair, Edward de Souza and John Savident joined us – had a special significance for him. As one of five brothers who all won rugby caps for the same province, he had gone to Dublin from Limerick to see Ireland play Scotland. After the game he popped into the Gate Theatre to see a play: Pirandello's *Henry IV*. When the curtain came down he decided there and then he would become an actor.

In the early evening of 15 December 1986, in the strictest secrecy, members of an internationally famous theatrical dynasty gathered in the Green Room at Teddington Studios.

Just a couple of miles down the road in Kingston upon Thames, Lady Redgrave, the actress Rachel Kempson, was arriving at a large

Richard Harris had always said he would do a runner . . .

. . . fortunately he didn't — and he was joined by his two former wives.

book store to sign copies of her book *A Family and its Fortunes*. She was blissfully unaware that Eamonn Andrews was lurking nearby with our book.

Her first surprise came when she saw who the first two customers were – her daughter Vanessa, and Vanessa's daughter Natasha. They joined us at the studios, where Vanessa's younger daughter, Joely, later of *Lady Chatterley* fame, had arrived from the RSC at Stratford.

Lady Redgrave and her late husband, Sir Michael, were married for thirty-nine years and the story of the dynasty they founded continued to unfold, with Lynn Redgrave greeting her mother from Boston, Massachusetts, where she was on tour.

We had a live link to the stage of the Young Vic for the interval in a production of *Julius Caesar*, for a word from Brutus and Portia – Lady Redgrave's son Corin and his actress wife Kika Markham. Corin's children by his first marriage, Luke and the latest acting addition, Jemma Redgrave, joined us.

So did a splendid cast of friends and colleagues, among them Robert Stephens, Dorothy Tutin, Geraldine James, Kenneth Haigh and Patricia Hayes, and there were greetings from Sir Anthony Quayle and Sir John Mills, with Edward Woodward chipping in from location filming on *The Equalizer* in New York.

A last-minute surprise came when Lynn Redgrave rang to say, amazingly, she did not have a performance that night. Instantly we booked her on a plane from Boston, with daughters Kelly and Annabel. They came on set, gave Lady Redgrave a wonderfully warm hug and flew straight back to Boston. The very stuff of drama.

It was the opening night of the stage version of the hit television series *Allo, Allo* when actress Kirsten Cooke, in her French Resistance beret and trenchcoat, whispered to Eamonn Andrews, 'Listen vaire carefully. I will say this only once. You must move in five seconds or all will be lost.'

Eamonn sprinted to the stage of the Prince of Wales Theatre – to become the last customer of the evening at the Café René, and surprise René himself, that marvellous comedy actor Gorden Kaye.

He put up no resistance and we recorded the programme onstage, in the café set, with the whole of the cast of the long-running show.

René's 'wife' Edith, actress Carmen Silvera, sat next to him, as the audience heard how the Huddersfield-born actor reached TV stardom after playing Elsie Tanner's accident-prone nephew Bernard in *Coronation Street* for eight months in 1969. From *Born and Bred* came Kate Williams, Gillian Raine and James Grout, and from *All*

Creatures Great and Small, in which Gordon had made a guest appearance, Christopher Timothy.

Dennis Waterman was well and truly 'nicked' when Eamonn burst in on *The Sweeney* . . .

. . . and so was his colleague Jack Regan − John Thaw − when Eamonn called at the National Theatre.

When Michael Aspel surprised Alec McCowen on stage at the Strand Theatre on 4 October 1989, where he was appearing in the Jeffrey Archer play *Exclusive*, set in a Fleet Street newspaper office, the programme made real-life headlines, and for a reason no one could have predicted.

On stage with him were Paul Scofield and Eileen Atkins, and we had assembled surprise contributions from some famous names who had worked with this three-times Stage Actor of the Year winner. Phyllis Calvert, Anna Massey, Alan MacNaughtan, Margaret Courtenay, Julie Walters, George Bernard Shaw's great leading lady Ellen Pollock, and ninety-eight-year-old Gwen Ffrangcon-Davies, all sang his praises.

But the following day, Alec rang to say he was not happy – and it was his reason that made the headlines.

He was concerned nothing had been mentioned of actor Geoff Burridge, his close companion of many years, who had fallen victim to AIDS two years before.

But he was satisfied when Michael Aspel recorded a voice-over after the closing titles to the effect that no life story of Alec McCowen would be complete without mention of Geoff Burridge.

The beer-loving Inspector Morse was still the scotch-drinking Inspector Regan (who had a first name, Jack) of *The Sweeney* when Eamonn Andrews collared John Thaw on 12 March 1980.

He had gone to the National Theatre on the South Bank for a meeting about his appearance in a production there. When he walked into the foyer, gathered round the piano were his wife Sheila Hancock, and a whole gang of friends, including Jack Smethurst, Kenny Lynch, Tony Selby, Ian Hendry, George Sewell, Diane Keen, Carol Drinkwater, James Ellis, writer Ian Kennedy Martin and *Sweeney* producer Ted Childs (later executive producer on *Morse*).

At the television studios that day, his *Sweeney* sergeant, Dennis Waterman, was waiting, fresh from location. And we learned how Jimmy 'Schnozzle' Durante's number 'The Song has got to come from the Heart' got into an episode of *The Sweeney*.

Manchester-born John Thaw told jokes and did impressions in the interval at Saturday morning cinema clubs, so he and his brother could get in free. Down south, Dennis Waterman did the same sort of thing. So they decided to feature as a comedy duo in *The Sweeney*.

It was John's former headmaster who encouraged his acting, and to attend an audition at RADA at the age of just sixteen, he was driven overnight in his Uncle Charley's van. He got a place and left home with a neat, brown paper parcel under his arm – they didn't have a suitcase.

Fellow former student Nicol Williamson greeted from Broadway, and the student he shared digs with, Tom Courtenay, was there, as was Diana Rigg, his co-star in the West End hit *Night and Day*.

'Ma Larkin', Pam Ferris, greets her screen daughter Catherine Zeta Jones.

'Pa Larkin' – David Jason – looks on, still slightly bemused after Michael had made a slip at the pick-up and called him 'David Jacobs'. It featured in *It'll Be All Right On The Night*.

John and wife Sheila met in another West End play, appropriately titled *So What About Love?*

Sheila we had already surprised on 25 November 1976, onstage at the Lyric, Shaftesbury Avenue, where she was appearing in the Ben Travers farce *The Bed Before Yesterday*. We recorded the show onstage, and the first surprise was husband John and daughters Ellie Jane and Abigail appearing in a stage 'box'. She thought they were all at home, babysitting for two-year-old Joanna.

Sheila, too, was at RADA, winning a scholarship, after doing some entertaining, with her sister Billie, at their parents' pub in Kings Cross.

Her big break came in BBC TV's *The Rag Trade* in 1962. Co-stars

155

Peter Jones and Reg Varney were with us, and Miriam Karlin greeted from Leicester where she was on stage.

Sheila had won the *Evening Standard* Best Actress award for her role in *Rattle of a Simple Man,* and her co-star, Edward Woodward, was there, as was another leading man, Richard Briers. Derek Nimmo greeted from Hong Kong.

And to surprise Sheila, the man she called her boyfriend turned up – the author himself, Ben Travers, who was ninety.

Another master of the art of farce, Brian Rix had just made the last of many thousands of West End appearances when Eamonn Andrews surprised him on 23 March 1977, making a charity presentation.

The special team he had worked with over the years were at the studios, including Ray Cooney, John Chapman, Derek Royle, Clive Exton, Andrew Sachs, Michael Pertwee and Joanna Lumley. And, of course, his actress wife Elspet Grey and actress daughter Louisa were there.

Brian, who has a handicapped daughter, is almost as well known for his charity work as for his acting. At the time of his Life he was vice-president of the Stars' Organisation for Spastics, and since 1988 he has been chairman of Mencap, the Royal Society for Mentally Handicapped Children and Adults. His efforts for these organisations have been rewarded with a knighthood in 1986, followed by a peerage in 1992.

Fans of television's long-running series *Emmerdale Farm* perhaps got a surprise when the character of Annie Sugden turned up – in real life Brian's sister, actress Sheila Mercier.

But the surprise that really hit him for six had nothing to do with the theatre. Cricket is Brian's offstage passion, and his all-time hero West Indies fast bowler Wes Hall. We flew him in for the 'curtain'.

Paul Nicholas, one of Britain's most popular television comedy actors because of his performance as Vince in *Just Good Friends,* was wearing another identity when Michael Aspel travelled to the Bristol Hippodrome to surprise him when the curtain came down on the musical *Barnum* on 1 October 1991.

He had started his musical career with the band of Screaming Lord Sutch and the Savages – and we could prove it by running a piece of film showing Paul in the band's leopard-skin outfit. Even better, 'Lord' David Sutch himself appeared to present Paul with his old costume. This time it was the audience who screamed.

Paul bade farewell to the Savages to star in *Hair* in 1968. The controversial musical also launched Oliver Tobias, who joined us in Bristol, as did singer Patti Boulaye. *Hair* coincided with the end of theatre censorship, and there was some nudity in the show, but Patti said she and Paul managed to keep their clothes on.

We heard from Andrew Lloyd Webber, Elaine Paige, and King Herod from *Jesus Christ Superstar*, Victor Spinetti. Wayne Sleep appeared from *Cats* and Michael Ball from *Pirates of Penzance*.

From a clip of *Just Good Friends* – a screen kiss in which they 'crashed' their scooter crash-helmets – came Penny, Jan Francis.

Dora Bryan was starring as Dolly Levi in *Hello, Dolly* when Michael Aspel walked onstage at the Opera House, Manchester. He presented the Life there and then, on 17 January 1989.

The audience was delighted, because 'Our Dora', born just a few miles up the road in Oldham, has been a firm favourite since she started her career at Oldham Rep. When she was assistant stage manager there, she didn't care for the heavy 'mood music' in the interval of a production of Ibsen's *Ghosts* – so she changed it for a swing recording of 'In The Mood'.

With her and Paul Nicholas in *Charlie Girl* was, of course, Hollywood's Cyd 'the Legs' Charisse, who spoke to Dora from Beverly Hills.

From her dressing room in *Follies* at London's Shaftesbury Theatre we heard from Eartha Kitt. Larry Grayson arrived in Manchester, and so did Robert Stephens, who played Dora's shady boyfriend in the 1961 film *A Taste of Honey*.

Thirty-two years on we flew in from Canada the actress who had been Dora's daughter in that film, Rita Tushingham, to say 'Hello, Dora.'

If ever an actor sounded to the theatre born, he has to be Donald Sinden, but this one-time carpenter's apprentice started his career by accident, as we discovered on 10 April 1985, on the stage of the Royalty Theatre in the West End.

This time the pick-up was not onstage, but on location for the long-running television comedy *Never the Twain*, with co-star Windsor Davies as Eamonn's co-conspirator.

Then they were joined by the other regular members of the cast, Maria Charles, Teddy Turner and Derek Deadman.

Donald's two sons, Jeremy and Marc, both actors, were there too. One day Marc, understudying in a play at the Cambridge Theatre, got the chance to go on. His father was appearing in *London Assurance* at the Albery nearby, and stopped the traffic when he strolled down to the

Paul Nicholas was on stage at Bristol in *Barnum*.

Susannah York was starring in TV's *We'll Meet Again* when Eamonn turned up as the 'captain' of the American B17 bomber which featured in the series.

Cambridge to observe his son's performance – still wearing full Regency costume.

It was a far cry from Plymouth, where he was born in 1923, and where his father had a chemist's shop. Donald became an apprentice carpenter with no thought of the stage until he got a call from his

158

cousin Frank. Frank had been called up for wartime service – in fact he was later killed in action – and asked the young Sinden to take his part in an amateur production.

Said the future star: 'Don't be so damned silly.' But he did it, was spotted and invited to join a services entertainment unit. There he got the acting bug and went to drama school.

Then leading man at the Shakespeare Memorial Theatre, eighty-five-year-old Robert Harris, remembered how Donald started to lose concentration, then realised it was because his eyes were on Helen of Troy, who was to become his wife, Diana.

Classical roles were interrupted when he was invited to sign a seven-year film contract after impressing, with Jack Hawkins, in *The Cruel Sea*. Jack's widow Doreen recalled how her husband had hauled non-swimmer Donald from a particularly deep studio 'tank'.

Donald also co-starred in *Mogambo* with Hollywood legend Clark Gable, and with Anne Baxter in *Mix Me a Person*. Anne spoke from New York, and many more reminiscences came from Muriel Pavlow and her husband Derek Farr, Patrick Cargill, Joyce Carey, John McCallum, his wife Googie Withers and their daughter Joanna. Tim Piggott-Smith, direct from his success in *The Jewel in the Crown*, recalled from Paris how Donald had singled him out as a promising talent when judging a school drama competition.

Judi Dench and her husband Michael Williams, Guy Rolfe, Mai Zetterling, Nigel Davenport, Elaine Stritch, Dame Anna Neagle and Sir Peter Hall were also among the guests.

Dame Sybil Thorndike called in to surprise Robert Morley – she had starred in the first play he wrote, in 1935.

The programme closed with a name no one knew, except Donald. It was ninety-one-year-old Mai, mother of cousin Frank, who had asked Donald to take his place in that amateur production all those years ago, only to be told, 'Don't be so damned silly. . . .'

Among the wonderful cast who turned up to pay tribute to Robert Morley on the stage of the Savoy Theatre on 24 April 1974 was a no less legendary figure of the theatre than the then ninety-one-year-old Dame Sybil Thorndike, the star of the first play Robert wrote in 1935.

Robert's wife, Joan, was the daughter of another theatrical Dame, the late Dame Gladys Cooper.

And Robert was co-author with Rosemary Anne Sisson of the play at the Savoy, *A Ghost on Tiptoe*, in which he was co-starring with Ambrosine Philpotts and William Franklyn.

There were greetings from old chums such as Peter Bull, Robert Hardy, Peter Ustinov and his great pal Wilfrid Hyde-White, who summed up Robert's perfect day: 'Stay at the racecourse till dark, and the casino till daybreak.'

That great film director John Huston – he directed Robert in the classic *The African Queen* – reminded Robert of one particular day at the races, a selling plate. Robert was trying to persuade Huston into joining him in a bid for a horse which Robert really rated. Huston was just about to agree and join a bid when the auctioneer took them by surprise and announced, 'Going, going, gone!' and banged down his hammer, whereupon the horse Robert so fancied joint-owning let out a last 'neigh . . .' and dropped down dead.

But it was Dame Sybil Thorndike who summed up Robert Morley, the gentleman actor. Rushing to open a door for her at the BBC, he tripped. 'Get up, you silly old thing,' commanded the Dame. But he couldn't. He'd actually broken his ankle and was taken to hospital by ambulance.

The broken ankle put him out of work – but only temporarily. What did he do? Got himself a part in the television series *Emergency – Ward 10* – as a man with a broken ankle.

The hottest theatre ticket in town on 18 March 1992 was at the Theatre Royal, Haymarket, where two actors were winning rave notices in *Becket*. Derek Jacobi was in on the secret when Michael Aspel walked out onstage at the curtain to surprise King Henry, played by Robert Lindsay, who won a Best Actor Award for his role in Alan Bleasdale's television drama series *GBH*.

Waiting for him at our studios was his partner and mother of their daughter, actress Diana Weston, star of *The Upper Hand*. Also there were long-time friends such as Phyllis Logan, Belinda Lang, Lynda Bellingham, Mel Martin, Julie Peasgood, Stephen Bill and Tommy Vance.

Like so many others who make it in the acting profession, Robert came from unlikely beginnings, his father having been a joiner, his mother a canteen lady.

When he appeared in a school production of *The Pied Piper of Hamelin* his father, Norman, was sitting next to a woman who kept saying, every time Robert spoke, 'He's obviously had elocution lessons and comes from a posh family.'

Norman nudged her.

'He's never had elocution lessons and he's certainly not posh,' he said.

'How do *you* know?' enquired the woman.

' 'Cos I'm his dad!'

Robert got a place at RADA and won huge television success as 'Wolfie' in *Citizen Smith* with Mike Grady, who was there, and Peter Vaughan, who flew in specially from a holiday in Spain.

In the theatre, he was very successful at Manchester's Exchange Theatre (Trevor Peacock and artistic director Braham Murray came from there) and in the West End in the musical *Me and My Girl*, with Emma Thompson.

He transferred to Broadway, and Marianne Plunkett, his Broadway 'Girl', and the rest of the cast greeted him from Sardi's.

Among the many fans he won in New York was that legendary lady of the screen, Katharine Hepburn, who telephoned our studio from her New York apartment to wish Robert well.

From the award-winning *GBH* came Lindsay Duncan, writer Alan Bleasdale and co-star Michael Palin, who revealed that Robert's role of politician Michael Murray had originally been written with him in mind, and the schoolteacher role of Jim Nelson with Robert in mind.

But the role-reversal proved one of television's major successes of the season.

Dulcie Gray and Michael Denison have been in the business just a little longer than Robert Lindsay – even when we surprised Dulcie at the Richmond Theatre on stage in March 1973, she and Michael had been married for thirty-four years, and at the time of writing they are still going strong.

Dulcie co-starred with James Mason in *They Were Sisters*, and the great film actor spoke from his home in Switzerland.

Richard Attenborough spoke of the play *Brighton Rock*, which made

This Is Your Life

Award-winning actor Robert Lindsay gets a pat on the head from his co-star in Alan Bleasdale's *GBH*, Michael Palin.

Leonard Rossiter greets another star of the 1975 TV hit comedy *Rising Damp*, Richard Beckinsale.

162

stars of them both; her big film success with husband Michael was in 1948 in *The Glass Mountain*, featuring opera star Tito Gobbi.

When the tables were turned four years later, Michael was at London's Inn on the Park, believing Dulcie was at home. His name was paged and he was called to a foyer telephone booth to take a call from Dulcie.

Over the phone, Dulcie told him, 'I've got someone with me. Eamonn Andrews.' She put Eamonn on the line, and he said, 'Michael, take a look in the next phone booth.'

When he did, there were Dulcie – and Eamonn with the Big Red Book.

Cathleen Nesbitt, at ninety-two the Life's oldest subject.

Cathleen Nesbitt, ninety-two years young, is the oldest – so far – subject to be surprised by the Life, and it happened on 1 May 1980 outside the New London Theatre, not far from where she had made her first West End appearance seventy years before.

Among her favourite roles was the one she created in the original Broadway production of *My Fair Lady* in 1955, and was about to play again in America, that of Professor Higgins's mother.

The surprise greeting that day was from the stars and cast of the London revival of the show, with Tony Britton and Liz Robertson.

Alan Jay Lerner, the lyricist who turned Shaw's *Pygmalion* into one of the world's biggest musical successes, told us how the late producer Moss Hart had to talk Cathleen into playing the part of Mrs Higgins.

Another former Mrs Higgins was also there – Dame Anna Neagle.

Professor Higgins himself, Rex Harrison, filmed a tribute, and there was an amazing West End turn-out: Clifford Mollison, Dame Wendy Hiller, Roland Culver, Irene Worth, Robert Flemyng, Douglas Fairbanks Junior, Nicol Williamson, Vincent Price and Coral Browne, Jean Simmons and Sir John Gielgud.

It wasn't quite the curtain call. We were holding the 'curtain up' all over the West End for a unique salute from virtually every show then playing theatreland: we had George Layton and Helen Shapiro; Elizabeth Seal; Michael Jayston, Maria Aitken, Jenny Quayle, Ian Collier, Lesley Gregson, William Franklyn and two actors who had just captured television awards for *The Good Life*, Richard Briers and Paul Eddington.

From the RSC's production of *Once in a Lifetime* came Carmen du Sautoy; from *Evita*, John Turner; from *Not Now Darling*, Leslie Phillips, Andrew Sachs, Sylvia Syms and Derek Bond; from *Stage Struck*, Ian Ogilvy and Sheila Gish; and from *Annie*, Charles Weste and Catherine Marte. Cheryl Kennedy, soon to play Eliza in the US revival of *My Fair Lady*, sent greetings, and finally, to the oldest from the youngest, came a tribute from the 'Siamese children' from *The King and I*.

Quite a curtain call for the actress who had been seventy years a leading lady.

Sir John Mills wasn't far off that remarkable record when, bravely, despite failing eyesight and having to use a stick, he appeared with the rest of that remarkable theatrical dynasty when we surprised daughter Juliet at the Richmond Theatre on 1 October 1992.

Both he and Juliet's big sister Hayley had been 'booked' some years before, so they knew what it would mean to Juliet. She was starting a tour – with Hayley – of *Fallen Angels*, a play written by her godfather, Sir Noël Coward. Her godmother, by the way, was Vivien Leigh, then married to Laurence Olivier. Their telegram on her birth read, 'From Uncle Sub-Lieutenant Olivier and Aunt Puss'.

Noël Coward wrote and directed *In Which We Serve*, in which the eleven-week-old Juliet made her screen début, as the daughter of a member of the crew of the famous HMS *Kelly* (played by Sir John). He recalled that in the middle of a deeply moving scene the baby Juliet 'let rip a report from her cot which would have done justice to any one of HMS *Kelly*'s guns'. The whole film studio dissolved into hysterics. When the storm subsided, Sir John and Lady Mills (authoress Mary Hayley Bell) looked at the director, totally mortified.

'The Master' muttered, 'Hereditary, I fear.'

Chapter Twelve
Life and Politics

'It's amazing what God can do with a lad from the Rhondda with a patch on his trousers,' was how the holder of the historic office of Speaker of the House of Commons once described himself.

Few politicians have closed their Parliamentary careers engulfed by such a tidal wave of all-party affection as Lord Tonypandy, formerly George Thomas MP, whose lilting Welsh calls for 'Order! Order!' also made him a firm favourite on the radio.

The newly retired Speaker was due to take up a new post as honorary chairman of the National Children's Home on 25 October 1983. A special concert – in aid of the charity – was being staged at the Royal Albert Hall to honour the incoming chairman. A celebrity gathering at the rehearsal was in on our secret, and included Nerys Hughes, Iris Williams, Siân Phillips, Angela Rippon and Richard Briers.

When Lord Tonypandy arrived, an extra celebrity was there – Eamonn Andrews with the Big Red Book. Back at the studios viewers heard how George's younger brother had gone down the pit at thirteen to help support the family so that George could stay on at school and become a teacher. He went into the Commons in 1945 as MP for Cardiff Central. Elected for Cardiff South was future Prime Minister the Right Honourable James Callaghan, who joined in the tributes along with Lord Wilson and then Prime Minister Margaret Thatcher.

Prince Charles sent his 'warmest good wishes to one of the most distinguished Speakers the House of Commons has ever known in its long and proud history'.

And in the historic Speaker's Rooms at the Commons Lord Tonypandy's coat of arms featured the Crown and Portcullis sign of the House of Commons, surmounted by a miner's lamp.

Welsh rugby legend and veteran broadcaster Cliff Morgan told a story which summed up Lord Tonypandy's eight years as Speaker.

A member from Liverpool with a somewhat thick 'scouse' accent was speaking. A Scottish member complained he could not understand a word. Uproar broke out.

'Order! Order!' called the Speaker. Nothing. The uproar continued. Then, in the full majesty of office, he stood up – decreeing that everyone be silent. He glanced caustically around the chamber, eyes glaring.

'There are many accents in this House,' he said, reprovingly. 'I only wish I had one myself.'

A split second of silence – then the House of Commons rocked with laughter.

Jeffrey Archer, now Lord Archer, was taking an early evening jog over Westminster Bridge on 13 January 1981, perhaps thinking over the plot of his next book, but not knowing of our plot and the Life book.

Jeffrey Archer was out for a jog – and ran into Eamonn with the Somerset county cricket team.

Life-long cricket fan and Somerset supporter, the former Conservative MP for Louth in Lincolnshire couldn't believe his eyes when he found himself jogging towards another group of 'joggers' – England and Somerset's Ian Botham, and the county team, with captain Brian Rose.

Elected to the Commons in 1969, at the age of twenty-nine, Jeffrey resigned in 1974 when his world crashed in financial ruin at the pinnacle of his success. He had invested heavily in a Canadian company claiming to have the answer to pollution from car exhausts. It turned out to be a swindle.

But Jeffrey made another fortune by writing about his bad fortune in *Not a Penny More, Not a Penny Less*.

How that book, first of his many best-sellers, got published was a remarkable example of inter-party co-operation. He sent the manuscript to literary agent Debbie Owen, wife of former Labour Foreign Secretary Dr David Owen.

Being particularly interested in the work of another MP, David Owen read it over the weekend and heartily recommended it to his wife.

It sold two million copies.

Former Chancellor, Secretary of State for Defence and Shadow Foreign Secretary Denis Healey came to Teddington Studios for a programme

Denis Healey's brother Terry sportingly re-created a moment from Boris Karloff's 1930s film *The Ghoul* — which terrified them as youngsters. His 'ghoul' trousers turned out to be a little oversized round the waist, with hilarious results.

Denis Healey's reaction when he saw his brother on *our* big screen as *The Ghoul*.

about famous people and their hobbies – his being photography. And was his face a picture when Michael Aspel stepped from the studio shadows!

Michael glanced at the book and said, 'I thought that might raise your eyebrows.'

In the Life studio were key members of the South-East Leeds constituency he had held for Labour for thirty-six years, despite being christened Denis Winston Healey, because his parents were Churchill supporters when Winston was a Liberal MP.

As Major Healey, he was Beachmaster for the Allied landings at Anzio, and at the end of the war he became International Secretary at Labour Party Headquarters, working closely with Ernest Bevin and Hugh Gaitskill.

By 1964 he was Secretary of State for Defence, and on a visit to the Far East, the Special Boat Service put on a display which involved parachuting into the sea and diving into a submarine. Among the Marine Commandos was Liberal Democrat leader Paddy Ashdown, introduced, in a moment of aberration by Michael Aspel, as 'Dame Peggy' (as in Ashcroft). It could have been edited out but, in fairness, Michael insisted it was kept in. 'Can't think what made me say it,' said Britain's most urbane TV presenter.

From 1970–72 Denis was Shadow Foreign Secretary, and Foreign Secretary Sir Geoffrey Howe, a great rival who we never thought would appear because of the 'like being savaged by a dead sheep' jibe Denis made in the Commons, paid a tribute. Neil Kinnock rushed straight over from the House of Commons with wife Glenys. We had film of Denis, his wife Edna and Neil and Glenys on a visit to Moscow. They were waiting for the train from Moscow to Leningrad when it started to snow. They linked arms and hummed 'Lara's Theme' from *Dr Zhivago*.

At the pick-up Denis said to Michael, 'Could you ring Edna and tell her this is on?' She had been our 'KGB' for weeks and was, of course, there.

From around the world Denis's counterparts as Foreign Secretary paid tribute: Henry Kissinger in Washington, former Secretary of State; Prime Minister Lee Kuan Yew in Singapore; and from Bonn, former Chancellor Helmut Schmidt. Said Michael: 'Thanks, lads.'

Pity Denis could not have been at our afternoon rehearsal with his camera. On the programme he saw his brother Terry re-enacting a childhood prank Denis had played on him after they had been to see Boris Karloff in *The Ghoul*: he hid inside a bedroom cupboard and a gloved hand snaked its way around the door.

For the part, Terry was wearing a pair of extra large trousers from the wardrobe department. He was getting into the part by take two, and flung open the door of the gothic-style cupboard – and the trousers collapsed around his ankles.

Said Terry to the convulsed crew: 'Hope you got that one.'

A minor postscript to the Life on Denis Healey is the story of how I came to be wearing Edna's fur hat in Moscow. Very kindly, she had lent it to researcher Caroline Blackadder who had mentioned that her next research journey would take her to Russia.

Caroline, researcher Sue Green and I set out to confirm the lowly beginnings of tycoon and former Labour MP Robert Maxwell. What a Life *that* was! He *had* been born in poverty, his family *had* been wiped out in Hitler's concentration camps, he *was* decorated for gallantry on the field of battle, and he built, lost, regained and lost again a business empire once worth billions.

All that from one of nine children born in a salt-mine village straight out of *Fiddler on the Roof*.

Our journey had taken us more than thirty hours by train and car to the village of Solotvino. But, on the return journey, how did I come to be wearing Edna Healey's hat?

Fast asleep on the way back to Moscow I was 'mugged'. Not only of 'hard' currency, but of the ski-wear-style clothing I had purchased specially to brave late November in Russia.

When we arrived at Moscow Station it was fifteen below freezing and all I had left was a cotton jacket and jeans. My two charitable researchers pitched in with whatever they'd got to help keep me warm – beyond which I will not go, except to say that someone mentioned I could lose a lot of heat through my head. So, as snow started to fall, Caroline plonked her borrowed fur hat on my head.

Cue 'Lara's Theme' from *Dr Zhivago*.

In the neo-Gothic vastness of Rochdale Town Hall the vastness of Sir Cyril Smith MBE, MP, about to retire from the political arena, made a 'farewell' appearance while a brass band played 'My Way' – only to find Michael Aspel there to do it his way with the Big Red Book.

The audience cheered as though they were at a pop concert when Michael announced we would be telling the story there and then.

Where else could that story be told but Rochdale Town Hall? Cyril's mother had been the Town Hall char – still was when he made her his Lady Mayoress in 1966. Cyril never knew his father.

What a moment of pride it was when his eighty-five-year-old mother

Robert Maxwell greets the man whose bullets missed him by inches. Ex-Private Verdon Bosley was trapped in a German-occupied farmhouse when Maxwell went to the rescue. Maxwell called out orders to the Germans to surrender — and spoke in German. Private Bosley opened fire with his sten-gun, believing Maxwell was a German officer. The burst of fire missed Maxwell by the thickness of the Big Red Book.

The band played his 'signature tune' as Sir Cyril Smith, MP, walked into Rochdale Town Hall for Michael Aspel's surprise. He's sitting on a special 'double-seater' to accommodate his frame. Next to him is his mother, who was once the Town Hall char.

Eva, brother Norman and sister Eunice joined him on the platform at the truly amazing Victorian venue. We had borrowed his old Mayoral chair – a double-seater – to ensure his girth didn't bring the seat with him when he stood to welcome surprise guests.

Our man in midwinter Moscow –
the author in Edna Healey's hat.

These included son-of-Rochdale, then Minister for the Environment
and Countryside, David Trippier (MP for Rossendale) and Lord
Tonypandy (from Cardiff). There was also a moving greeting from
former Liberal leader Jeremy Thorpe.

Suffering from Parkinson's Disease, he had made a supreme effort
to record a few tremulous words to bury the hatchet with his former
colleague, with whom he had fallen out when in his prime.

Sir Cyril knew the effort that had gone into Jeremy Thorpe recording
those few words – his first in public for years – and the effect was there
for viewers to see.

He managed a damp-eyed 'Thank you, Jeremy', and wrote to him,
and to us, to say it was the greatest surprise of his life.

171

A postscript: a small hotel in the shadows of the stern Victorian edifice of Rochdale Town Hall. Michael Aspel, producer Malcolm Morris and our make-up girl go to find a room for Michael's camera make-up. To use any room in the Town Hall itself was too dangerous for security so close to the pick-up.

Michael, Malcolm and make-up girl stand at the postage-stamp 'reception' desk, no luggage between them, apart from the make-up case. Our programme organiser has booked a room.

The Lancashire voice from behind the desk, a totally unimpressed lady, asks, 'Will you be having breakfast?'

Michael: 'We're only here for about an hour.'

'Oh,' she says and hands over the keys, eyes returning to the bookings book.

Michael and Malcolm had to wait for our signal before they left the room, but the make-up girl was needed back at our HQ.

Mischievously, Michael told her, 'Go out weeping and clutching a handful of money.'

Half an hour later he himself left in full make-up.

The Rochdale lass behind the desk didn't even look up.

'Our committee room is above Barclay's the butchers where they sell the best sausages in town' was the 'commercial' made in his speeches by Liberal Party leader Jo Grimond, thirty-three years MP for Britain's most remote and widely scattered constituency, the Orkney Islands and Islands of Shetland.

On 11 February 1983, Jo was being interviewed by Michael Parkinson at TV-AM about his coming retirement, when Eamonn Andrews met him in the foyer, crammed with Young Liberals singing 'For He's A Jolly Good Fellow'. Which few would deny.

Appointed leader of his party in 1956, Jo was one of the most amicable characters in politics, a fact vouchsafed by so many of his constituents who had a day trip to London for the show – crofters, farmers, fishermen and that village butcher himself, Peter Barclay, of sausage fame.

Jo's wife, Laura, came from a famous Liberal family, her brother being former MP Mark Bonham-Carter.

Son of a jute-works owning family in Dundee, Jo went to Eton and Oxford, and was called to the Bar in 1937.

When he was appointed Liberal leader, a young ITN newscaster, Ludovic Kennedy, wrote to him, and became Liberal candidate for

On 11 February 1983, Eamonn 'gatecrashed' the studios of the newly launched TV-AM to surprise Jo Grimond – there for an interview with Michael Parkinson. Jo was about to retire from politics after more than thirty years. As he left the building for our studios the former leader of the Liberal Party had another surprise: the foyer was packed with young Liberals giving a rousing chorus of 'For he's a jolly good fellow'. On the programme there were many who agreed, including the then ninety-five-year-old former Labour MP, Lord Brockway.

Rochdale. His wife Moira Shearer (of *The Red Shoes* fame) campaigned with him, and both were there for the Life. David Steel greeted from Edinburgh University, and one of Jo Grimond's political favourites was there in person – the Labour peer Lord Brockway, formerly Fenner Brockway, at the age of ninety-five.

Amazing enough that Jack Ashley started out in life as a fourteen-year-old labourer, went on to become President of the Cambridge University Union Society, was elected to Parliament and became champion of the underprivileged. Even more amazing was the fact that he carried on as a campaigning MP after becoming totally deaf at the age of forty-six when he was poised for ministerial office.

He was playing badminton with his three daughters in the garden of his Surrey home when Eamonn Andrews popped in to say 'This Is Your Life'. Knowing Jack Ashley could not hear a word, Eamonn was pointing to the printed words on the book, though there was little need, for Jack was by that time an expert lip-reader.

Jack Ashley was only five when his nightwatchman father died. The only man in the tiny cottage in Widnes, he went to work as a labourer in an asbestos factory at the age of just fourteen. At twenty-two he was the youngest borough councillor in the country.

He won a scholarship to Ruskin College, Oxford, and moved on to Cambridge where he had the proud distinction of becoming its first-ever working-class President of the Union. By 1966 he was MP for Stoke-on-Trent South.

He met his wife Pauline at Cambridge when she went to interview him for the University newspaper *Varsity*. Eamonn had interviewed Jack Ashley on television after he had been stricken with total deafness. Pauline sat out of the range of the cameras. Because, obviously, he could not hear his own voice, a vital contribution of hers was to signal when to modulate his tones.

The then Shadow Minister for Education, Conservative MP Norman St John Stevas, had known Jack at Cambridge, and the Minister for Economic Affairs, the Rt Hon Michael Stewart, the Minister for the Disabled, Alf Morris, and the Secretary of State for Social Services, the Rt Hon Barbara Castle, all paid tribute to the MP who had fought for compensation for the children who were the victims of the drug Thalidomide.

Jack Ashley, with a little help from Pauline, lip-read every word on the programme. The fighting spirit of the former teenage labourer who became President of the Cambridge Union was still there.

Cabinet office may have eluded him; sheer guts didn't.

Chapter Thirteen

Life in Broadcasting

Gloria Hunniford was broadcasting live as usual at 2 p.m. on 12 January 1983, and her studio guest was actor/comedian Stan Stennett. A regular in *Crossroads* at the time, he had been the subject of the Life the week before, and Gloria was interviewing him about the experience.

Gloria ran a phone-in show. 'Right, the last caller is on the line,' she said. 'Who's calling?'

The voice on the line was one of the most famous in Britain.

'Hello, Gloria, this is Eamonn Andrews calling. I've been listening to you and Stan talking about *This Is Your Life* last week when Stan was the subject, and there's something I'd like to ask him myself.'

Eamonn then put down the phone in the studio next door, and to Gloria's astonishment walked 'live' into her studio with the Big Red Book, and her name on it.

At our television theatre Gloria's future star presenter daughter, Caron Keating, was waiting to greet Mum, as was Terry Wogan, who called her 'Grievous Bodily Hunniford'. Val Doonican was there – he had advised the Belfast broadcaster on her career in London when she started at the BBC as Jimmy Young's holiday replacement.

One of the highlights of that year's Royal Variety Show had been a song-and-dance trio featuring Gloria, Jan Leeming, who joined us, and Esther Rantzen, who had taken a real showbiz booking – she greeted Gloria from panto in Bognor Regis.

Esther Rantzen was at BBC Television Centre presenting her new programme *Hearts of Gold* on 10 November 1988, when Michael Aspel returned to his old BBC stamping ground, walking into Esther's studio to surprise her in front of the audience.

'Let's go before they ask me to stay and read the news,' said Michael.

Waiting for Esther on the Life set back at Teddington Studios were members of her *That's Life* team going back fifteen years: Maev Alexander, Gavin Campbell, Bill Buckley, Doc Cox, John Mould, Michael Groth, Paul Heiney, George Layton, Adrian Mills, Joanna Monro, Kieran Prendiville, Chris Serle, Molly Sugden and Glyn Worsnip. Plus, of course, Esther's documentary-maker husband Desmond Wilcox. Cyril Fletcher greeted his old *That's Life* team mates from his home in Guernsey.

Gloria Hunniford thought Eamonn was on the phone — he was, but from the next studio . . .

. . . and she was greeted by someone soon to be a broadcaster herself — her daughter, Caron Keating.

From her first job in radio – rattling Mrs Dale's tea-cups in the sound effects department on *Mrs Dale's Diary* – to that year's Richard Dimbleby Award at BAFTA, Esther had come a long way.

Sue Lawley, who had presented the award, came along in person to pay tribute to her then BBC colleague.

Judith Chalmers started broadcasting for the BBC in Manchester on *Children's Hour* when she was just thirteen.

On 17 March 1981, she had been attending a charity event at Number 11 Downing Street with husband Neil Durden Smith. As they came out of the famous street, waiting for them was a special bus draped with a giant 'Wish You Were Here?' sign.

On board the bus, to Judith's amazement, was a star-studded passenger list of friends and colleagues who had all been a part of her broadcasting life: Pete Murray, Patrick Mower, Nicholas Parsons, Anita Harris, Willie Rushton, Mavis Nicholson, Elaine Grand, Chris Kelly, Mick McManus, Marjorie Anderson, Dickie Henderson and her *Come Dancing* colleague Peter West.

When she had got over her surprise, clearly Judith was very happy to be there.

Filming for Angela Rippon's Life cost researcher Maurice Leonard his raincoat: her horse liked the taste and 'ate' it. Maurice was to become Angela's producer on *What's My Line?* and dined out on the story. We surprised Angela at a book signing at Brent Cross on 20 November 1981, and sprang her colleagues from 'the forthcoming breakfast television' – Peter Jay, David Frost and Anna Ford.

For more than twenty years ITN's award-winning war correspondent Michael Nicholson had been in the thick of the action all over the world, bringing the front-line stories to the nation's front rooms.

But on 10 December 1991 Michael himself was the story – our story.

ITN Editor-in-Chief Stewart Purvis was giving a cocktail party, attended by colleagues, including Carol Barnes, Trevor McDonald, Alistair Stewart and Julia Somerville, to welcome him back from his latest dangerous assignment in Yugoslavia. We had hastily postponed our surprise when he had to stay on to cover suddenly intensified fighting.

But Michael Nicholson had an unexpected guest at that ITN home-coming party – Michael Aspel.

Of all his death-defying adventures, from Africa to the Middle East, Vietnam to the Falklands, the most tense came in Angola in 1978 when

This Is Your Life

Our bus-load of celebrities pulls up at Downing Street . . .

. . . and Judith Chalmers had no idea we were there.

he flew in to cover the civil war. For four months he and his crew were in the jungle surrounded by trigger-happy guerrilla troops.

The urbane Anthony Carthew, former Royal correspondent, organised a rescue plane, posing as an eccentric millionaire in order to take off from Zaire. Sandy Gall was there to greet Michael when the rescue plane landed in Johannesburg.

For his Falklands coverage he shared the BAFTA award with the BBC's Brian Hanrahan. Michael got an interview with a certain helicopter pilot – Prince Andrew, who wrote to the Life with a special message congratulating Michael Nicholson on his newly announced OBE.

We had dramatic film of his escape, with cameraman Peter Wilkinson and sound man Hugh Thompson, from the besieged American embassy in Saigon in 1975. Ten years later he returned to reunite a refugee family with the son they had not seen for nine years, and bring him back to their new home in Wales. The family came to say their thanks; a moment of genuine happiness from all the tragedy witnessed by the award-winning war reporter. A few months after our programme, Michael also brought happiness into the life of a nine-year-old orphan girl. He added Natasha Mihalcic to his passport to bring her home to leafy Surrey from war-ravaged Sarajevo.

Sandy Gall was celebrating thirty action-packed years and his safe return from covering the fighting in Afghanistan with Michael Nicholson and other colleagues, including Martyn Lewis, Selina Scott, Ivor Mills, Rory McPherson and Gordon Honeycombe, when Eamonn Andrews joined the party with the Big Red Book.

Sandy's war reporting covered Vietnam, Suez, the Congo, Biafra and Uganda. Best-selling author Frederick Forsyth was a BBC correspondent when he met Sandy in Biafra in 1967, where the 'vigilantes' mistook Sandy, with his craggy features and broken nose, for a 'dog of war' – a mercenary, and the title of one of Freddie's later books.

Sandy's most hair-raising moment came in Uganda in 1973 when he was arrested with Reuter's reporter Nick Moore and flung into a prison hut with bullet holes in the walls and newly spilt blood on the ceiling. Another prisoner was taken outside and bludgeoned to death with sledge-hammers. Sandy spoke the Lord's Prayer.

They were marched to another hut, there to join award-winning war photographer Donald McCullin; then, thankfully, they were deported. Sandy had that deportation order framed and he hung it in his loo at home. One night when he was reading the news we had it photographed so we could show it on the Life.

Martyn Lewis was filming outside Buckingham Palace – an introduction to a collection of his reports on Prince Charles in America – when Eamonn Andrews pounced on 25 February 1986.

Sandy Gall, Leonard Parkin, Pamela Armstrong, Carol Barnes, Glyn Mathias and Sir Alastair Burnet were at the studios. So, too, was Martyn's wife Liz, a former HTV announcer.

Martyn had seen his share of the action covering the Turkish-Greek conflict in Cyprus in 1974, and events in Iran in 1979, following the overthrow of the Shah. His turn to be arrested – an occupational hazard of the war correspondent – came in Malaysia where he was covering the plight of the 'boat people'.

We heard that Martyn got his job at HTV as a result of a remarkable letter to the Director of Programmes, legendary BBC war correspondent Wynford Vaughan-Thomas. This reminded Wynford that in 1908 his (Wynford's) father had led a choir in Swansea in which Martyn's grandfather sang.

'It was on these grounds he felt I should audition him,' said Wynford.

Martyn got his audition – and the job.

Trevor McDonald, Britain's first black newscaster, was lunching with colleagues at the White Tower in the West End on 16 January 1990.

He asked for the wine list and Michael Aspel appeared with the book.

Trevor started his broadcasting career as a radio reporter in Trinidad and at ITN was not just desk-bound. He, too, saw plenty of action, including filming by his car headlights during the uprising in the Philippines which ousted President Marcos from office.

Contributions to Trevor's Life came from former US Secretary of State for Defence, Caspar Weinberger in Washington, and the Prime Minister of Pakistan, Benazir Bhutto in Islamabad. Former West Indies captain Clive Lloyd, about whom Trevor wrote a book, was there.

So was comedian Lenny Henry, recalling the days of the cult children's programme *TISWAS* in which Lenny did an impression of Trevor – in his invented character of Trevor McDoughnut.

Michael Aspel – though not as presenter of the Life – and Noel Edmonds were there to greet the doyen of DJs Alan 'Fluff' Freeman when he walked into Teddington Studios on 10 October 1987.

Twenty years before, said Noel Edmonds, at Radio Luxembourg, 'Fluff' had been god, his catchphrases 'Greetings, pop-pickers' and 'Right, all right, stay bright' familiar to millions of listeners.

Every one of his 'disciples' turned out for him: Ed Stewart, David Hamilton, Simon Bates, Nicky Campbell, John Peel, Tommy Vance, Tony Prince, Don Moss, Dave Cash, Johnnie Walker, Roger Scott, Tony Blackburn, Mike Read, Dave Lee Travis, Keith Fordyce, and fellow 'veterans' Pete Murray and Jimmy Saville were there. So was Rolling Stone Bill Wyman.

Michael Aspel told Eamonn Andrews he had first met 'Fluff' at the Radio Show at Olympia thirty years before. Alan Freeman was totally unknown here and had just arrived from Australia.

He told Michael, 'I think I'll be lucky to last until Christmas.'

But he didn't say what year.

Terry Wogan was still a DJ when Eamonn Andrews gatecrashed his BBC radio studio while he was broadcasting live on 19 April 1978. We had a radio car at the front door so he could continue broadcasting on the way to our studio. Said the blarney to the blarney: 'If I'd known about this I'd have shaved.'

Sir James Saville was at the Kensington Hilton with a group of *Jim'll Fix It* youngsters to launch the show's fifteenth season on 12 May 1990, with a bit of magic from Paul Daniels. The extra bit of magic came when Paul 'sprang' Michael Aspel.

The contributions reflected Jimmy's wide-ranging Life, from Tom Jones to Big Daddy, a former wrestling opponent. David Jacobs was there as joint pioneer presenter of *Top of the Pops* – in 1964.

Margaret Thatcher sent a personal letter of congratulation, and Jimmy received a warm tribute for all his work at Stoke Mandeville Hospital from the chief consultant, Dr Hans Frankel.

One simple statistic summed up Jimmy's work for charity: if every marathon he had run for charitable causes were laid out in a straight line, he would have run all the way from Britain to the USA. How's about that then, guys and gals?

On 11 February 1986, Derek Jameson, the former Fleet Street editor, was about to embark on presenting Radio Two's morning show. His regular spot on TV-AM, with Anne Diamond and Nick Owen, had established a firm following, though Gloria Hunniford offered the view that it was only because the gravel-voiced Cockney had been having elocution lessons from Henry Cooper.

Born in London's East End, son of an unmarried mother who scraped a living working in a laundry, Derek had started work as a fourteen-year-old messenger boy at Reuter's. He had gone on to hold the editorship of no fewer than four national newspapers, so where better to surprise him than in Fleet Street.

As he walked down the famous street in the gloom of that winter evening he spotted a newspaper billboard for the *Evening Standard*. 'Big Surprise For Fleet Street's Derek Jameson!' it declaimed. The surprise was that Eamonn was the newsvendor.

Also surprised was a genuine passer-by who offered a pound coin and found a newspaper thrust at her with the words, 'Forget the money!' Derek had that very moment strolled into view.

At our television theatre, just around the corner in Kingsway, waited some of Fleet Street's finest: Sir Larry Lamb, Philippa Kennedy, Charles Wintour, Marjorie Proops and the former Page Three Girl Samantha Fox.

From his new career in radio were Mike Read, Ray Moore, Ken Bruce, David Hamilton, Jimmy Young and Gloria Hunniford.

From New York there was a rare sighting, and greeting, from the boss of the multi-million *Penthouse* empire Bob Guccione, Derek's cartoonist in 1960 when Derek edited the *London American*, and whose offer of a partnership he had turned down. A bare cheek.

Twenty-five years of television journalism, two million miles of travel under his blazer, an opinion poll saying the majority of people would love his job, and the press launch of his book *Within Whicker's World* – 8 March 1982 was perfect timing to surprise the vintage broadcaster still travelling well.

Everybody here was a part of Whicker's World.

Starting on his local newspaper at five shillings a week, working with Montgomery for the Army Film and Television Unit in North Africa during the war, then joining the Exchange Telegraph agency, Alan Whicker had put in some tough groundwork on his glittering career, including covering the Korean War.

Veteran *Sunday Times* Far East correspondent Richard Hughes flew in to tell us how surprised his colleagues were when he walked into the press HQ in Tokyo during the Korean War. The *Daily Mail* had reported Whicker 'lost in action'.

He started his television career as a freelance for the *Tonight* programme, and BBC colleagues Cliff Michelmore, director Jack Gold, Sir Huw Wheldon and Trevor Philpott were all there to pay tribute. Reflecting Whicker's fascination with the rich and famous, the wife of one of the world's wealthiest men, former *Vogue* model Baroness Fiona Thyssen flew in specially.

Whicker had won BAFTA's 1977 Richard Dimbleby Award. But he remained convinced that when he freelanced for *Tonight* there was a behind-the-scenes conspiracy to send him anywhere in the world where it was raining.

Presenter of *Tonight* Cliff Michelmore featured as a joint Life with his wife, Jean Metcalfe, and we opened with Eamonn Andrews on the roof of Broadcasting House as the signature tune of *Two-Way Family Favourites*, 'With a Song in my Heart', faded up.

In 1945 the programme linked loved ones long parted by the war. Sunday at noon was a special time for millions. It also proved to be a special time for Cliff and Jean, two people who had never met, but who found a song in their hearts.

Jean presented the programme in London, and Sergeant Derek Jones was in Hamburg. But one day Derek was taken ill and had to go to hospital. A certain Squadron Leader Cliff Michelmore was his stand-in and fell for the girl 'with a lilt and smile in her voice'.

On leave in London, Cliff finally got to meet Jean, in the basement studio from where she worked. We had arranged for the BBC to return them there for a sentimental journey and a radio interview.

With Eamonn were old *Family Favourites* colleagues, including Bill Crozier, Paul Hollingdale, Brian Matthew and Tim Gudgeon; waiting in the studio were Judith Chalmers, David Jacobs, Keith Fordyce, Ed Stewart and Robert Dougall.

We had also invited some of the stars whose records had been requested so frequently: the Beverley Sisters, Lita Roza, Humphrey Lyttelton and Acker Bilk.

From the *Tonight* show there was quite a reunion, with Sir Geoffrey Johnson Smith MP, Chris Brasher, John Morgan, Polly Elwes, Julian Pettifer, Fyfe Robertson, Ned Sherrin, Jack Gold and Donald Baverstock.

And, of course, Alan Whicker – but he said hello to his old pal from Perth, Western Australia.

The only son of a Methodist minister was having dinner with his mother at a London restaurant on 12 January 1972 when the waiter turned out to be Eamonn Andrews.

For one of the rare moments in his globetrotting life, David Frost was speechless; his mother, Mona, just relieved she had managed to keep the secret.

His colleagues from *That Was The Week That Was* were waiting back at the studio: Al Mancini, Patrick Campbell, David Kernan, Kenneth Cope, Lance Percival, Roy Kinnear and another old pal from *Frost Over Britain*, Ronnie Corbett.

David Frost was enjoying a quiet dinner, unaware the waiter was Eamonn.

David had been the first English chat-show host to have a five-nights-a-week spot on network television in America. Pinning him down was a major problem, but we knew he would do anything for Mum. Once, when she was ill, he had flown by helicopter to the Suffolk village where she lived and parked it in the road opposite her bungalow. She was with him when he received the OBE.

But what even the supreme TV professional didn't know was that that night at Quaglino's the 'diners' at the next table were our production assistant and cameraman; the camera was under the table.

184

The man who inherited David's chat-show crown was Michael Parkinson, who brought a first-rate journalistic brain to the job. He certainly had plenty to write home to Barnsley about when Eamonn Andrews arrived by boat at the bottom of his garden on the riverside at Bray, near Maidenhead, on 18 October 1978.

Waiting back at our studios were George Best (Michael wrote a book about him), Geoff Boycott, umpire Dickie Bird, Jimmy Tarbuck, Marian Montgomery, her husband Laurie Holloway, Russell Harty, Ronnie Scott, Stephane Grappelli, Pet Clark and the Harry Stoneham Five. Not surprisingly, for the jazz-loving 'Parky' we ended with a 'jam session'.

Fifteen years before 28 November 1990, we had thought of presenting the Life of Bernard Braden, but the plot was 'blown' by one of his grandchildren.

But Bernie had no idea what was happening when Michael Aspel sprang the surprise outside the Aldwych Theatre in the West End where, forty years before, Bernard Braden had co-starred with Vivien Leigh in *A Streetcar Named Desire*, directed by Laurence Olivier.

They meet at last on the Life:
Barbara Kelly and Eva Bartok.

Back in those days Bernard and his wife Barbara Kelly, newly arrived from Canada, were hailed as entertainment's 'golden couple'.

In Vancouver he had left school at sixteen to work at the local radio station as engineer, announcer and singer.

Bedtime With Braden established Bernard and Barbara, and from those halcyon radio days came writers Frank Muir and Denis Norden, Pearl Carr, Benny Lee, Nat Temple and announcer Ronald Fletcher.

And an international Canadian film director, penniless when he arrived in London with only a letter of introduction to Bernard and Barbara, greeted them from the location, in Connecticut, of his latest film – Norman Jewison.

Bernard had helped us surprise Barbara in October 1978. She had once appeared in a film starring Eva Bartok. Eva flew in from Hollywood at great expense, including a suite at the Savoy, and a chauffeur-driven Rolls-Royce at her disposal.

Researcher Maurice Leonard told Bernard, enthusiastically, 'We've just landed a great surprise for Barbara's Life – Eva Bartok has flown in.'

Drawled Bernard: 'It'll sure be a surprise all right. They've never met.'

They had shot their scenes for the film on totally separate locations.

Happily for us, both proved consummate actresses when they met on the Life -- for the very first time.

Chapter Fourteen
Life's Best-Sellers

Barbara Cartland had just completed her five-hundredth book when Michael Aspel arrived in a horse-drawn carriage at the studios of Gainsborough Pictures on 8 November 1989.

He was in the glamorous company of actress Lysette Anthony, one of the stars of the film being shot there based on one of Barbara Cartland's novels, *A Ghost in Monte Carlo*. Producer Laurie Johnson had arranged a visit to the set for the world's most prolific writer.

After Michael had sprung the Life book, Lysette and the other members of the cast, Fiona Fullerton, Liz Fraser, Francesca Gonshaw, Lewis Collins, Gareth Hunt, Jolyon Baker, Neil Dickson, Marcus Gilbert and Ron Moody, joined us back at the studios.

Waiting on the Life set were many friends, including Clare Duchess of Sutherland, Margaret Duchess of Argyll, Princess Helena Moutafian, Bishop Mervyn Stockwood and legendary bookseller Christina Foyle.

From the Spencer family seat at Althorp, Barbara's daughter, Raine, Countess Spencer, and Earl Spencer sent their greetings from a setting straight out of one of her novels.

Sir John Mills and Michael York, both of whom had appeared in films of her books, spoke to her from location in Zagreb.

Barbara wrote her first novel when she was a Twenties 'flapper' and called it *Jigsaw – Mayfair with the Lid Off*.

War had brought tragedy to her family, her father being killed in action in the First World War, and her two brothers within forty-eight hours of each other at Dunkirk.

As a captain in the ATS her romantic spirit came to the rescue of services brides. She advertised in *The Lady* for second-hand wedding dresses, which could be hired at one pound a day, because the girls hated getting married in their uniforms.

One such bride, Vera Kelly, and her husband George, came to say thanks forty-four years on.

Lady Pamela Hicks told a story which emphasised the worldwide popularity of Barbara Cartland's books. Her late father, Lord Louis Mountbatten, had been asked to take with him a collection of her latest books for the wife of Egyptian President Sadat.

'Thank you very much,' said the President. 'But I'm going to read them first.'

'This time next week, where shall I be? Sitting by the fireside, scoffing my tea. Plenty of comics, lots of books. No more Matron's dirty looks.'

So sang a group of Dr Barnardo's 'old boys' as Eamonn Andrews walked in on Leslie Thomas, himself a former Barnardo's boy, as he opened a new wing at their hostel in Kingston, Surrey, on 1 November 1978.

This Time Next Week – based on his life at Barnardo's – was the first book Leslie had written.

The former newspaper reporter rocketed to fame with the hilarious *The Virgin Soldiers*, and many more best-sellers were to follow. International film producer Carl Foreman – who made the hit movie of the book – and star Hywel Bennett were at the studios to greet Leslie, and hear his remarkable story.

'Virgin Soldier' Leslie Thomas found himself surrounded by his old Barnardo's pals.

He was just twelve when his father, a merchant navy stoker, died at sea in the war, and his mother died shortly afterwards. Leslie and his younger brother, Roy, were put into the care of Barnardo's, but in separate homes. Roy was then found a foster home. After eighteen months apart, Leslie 'did a bunk' and set out to find Roy, which he did, part of his transport being a bicycle which he 'borrowed' from outside a police station.

But it worked, and the brothers were reunited, as indeed they were the night of the Life – we flew in Roy from his home in Australia.

Jilly Cooper couldn't believe it when Eamonn walked in the pub.

Another best-seller who started literary life as a humble local newspaper reporter was Jilly Cooper – she worked for the old Middlesex *Independent* at their Brentford office.

On 18 March 1980, she was in an East End pub doing interviews for a television programme based on her book *The British in Love*.

Long before her runaway best-sellers *Riders, Rivals* and *Polo* Jilly found journalistic fame after sending an article to the *Sunday Times* describing her frantic, and funny, experiences as a working wife. The then editor, Harold Evans, immediately offered Jilly a regular column because she was someone so many young working women could identify with.

Jilly's flat-sharing experiences became the situation comedy *It's Awfully Bad For Your Eyes, Darling* starring Joanna Lumley, who was also there, along with Jilly's friends and neighbours from Putney's 'Media Gulch' – as she called it – David and Josceline Dimbleby.

Jilly had written a dedication in her book to her former English teacher, 'who seemed to fill the dusty classroom with light'. We brought her along for a twenty years reunion. Miss Aphra Lloyd said she was the only member of the staff who could take Jilly's work seriously. It was covered in ink blots and 'dreadful crossings out'.

Very Jilly Cooper.

The film based on his book *The Eagle Has Landed* had just opened in Leicester Square on 10 May 1978, when author Harry Patterson – he took the pen name Jack Higgins from a deceased relative – was 'ambushed' by Eamonn Andrews and one of the stars of the film, Judy Geeson.

The former office boy in the Leeds Corporation Cleansing Department had written no fewer than forty books under five different pen names – and did not become a full-time writer until he was forty.

His daughter, Sarah, had written a best-seller *The Distant Summer* when only fourteen.

Harry had taken a BSc by correspondence course to become a college lecturer. The story of how he risked all to become a writer might have come from a novel.

He was on holiday in Cornwall, visiting the ancient church of St Kew. The vicar spotted him and thought he looked like a man with something on his mind. They got talking and the vicar advised Harry to follow the example of Winston Churchill: list the pros and cons of being a college lecturer and compare them with a similar list of being a full-time writer. Follow whichever came out on top.

Harry Patterson did exactly that, following the advice of the vicar at that one and only meeting nine years before. Their second meeting was on the Life, and the Reverend Reginald MacKenzie had no idea – until we told him – that the man he advised that day was now an internationally best-selling author.

The Concorde pilot on the concourse at Heathrow on 13 September 1989, when Barbara Taylor Bradford flew in from New York for dinner with publishing tycoon Rupert Murdoch, turned out – to her astonishment – to be Michael Aspel.

The creator of so many high-flying heroines had travelled a long way since her birth in a terraced house in Armley, near Leeds.

A 'coach party' of her relatives from there were waiting at our studios, and there were no firmer fans than they of books such as *A Woman of Substance, Hold The Dream, To Be The Best* and *Act of Will*.

James Brolin and Lindsay Wagner, who had starred in television blockbusters based on Barbara's books, spoke from Hollywood.

Barbara's literary inspiration came when, as a little girl, she had a story published in a children's magazine for which she received a postal order for seven shillings and sixpence. She spent it on a green vase from Woolworth's for her mother.

Once again newspapers featured strongly in the early career of the future best-selling author. She worked on the *Yorkshire Evening Post*, then went to London as fashion editor of *Woman's Own*.

Among her close friends in those early London days was the

actress who found fame as Miss Moneypenny in the James Bond films, Lois Maxwell, who flew in from Toronto.

Barbara moved to Los Angeles when she met her American husband, Bob. There she had a column for the *LA Times*, 'Designing Woman', writing about the homes of the stars, including Edward G. Robinson and Vic Damone.

She first started writing thrillers before drawing on her Yorkshire background to write *A Woman of Substance*.

The programme featured one of the most unusual long-distance greetings ever seen on the Life. Barbara now lives in Manhattan, and her faithful dog Gemmy sits beside her all the time she is writing at her desk in her Park Avenue penthouse.

We filmed there, and when Barbara looked at the screen it gave the impression Gemmy had 'typed' a message on her machine: 'Come home soon, miss you. . . .'

Barbara loved it.

My Family and Other Animals was just one of the entertaining books by Gerald Durrell, who received his Life surprise on 15 February 1983, after his OBE investiture at Buckingham Palace.

Gerald, through his Jersey Wildlife Preservation Trust, had saved scores of species of wildlife and led expeditions to the jungles and forests of the world in order to do so.

Of course, the programme included another best-selling writer – brother Lawrence Durrell, author of, among many others, the *Alexandria Quartet*.

Gerald's day had started on a high note with the investiture by the Prince of Wales, and the Life finished with a glowing compliment on his work from the vice-chairman of the World Wildlife Fund, Sir Peter Scott, who came in person to say, 'We have a richer planet thanks to the work of Gerald Durrell.'

From workhouse laundry to millionaire status after fifty-eight books translated into fourteen languages: that was the story which took the Life to Tyneside on 14 December 1982.

Catherine Cookson's *The Mallens* trilogy was enjoying huge success in a television adaptation, and she had accepted an invitation to be interviewed by Tom Coyne on her favourite programme, Tyne Tees Television's *Northern Life*.

Catherine was born just eight miles from those City Road, Newcastle, studios, illegitimate and in dire poverty. As a child she picked driftwood from the Tyne and scraped cinders from the refuse tip to make a fire.

Until she was seven, she thought her grandmother was her mother, and her mother her sister. And, like Harry Patterson, she came to writing late – she did not start her first novel until after her fortieth birthday.

From *The Mallens* came the Squire, John Hallam, and the governess, Caroline Blakiston; two great fans, Windsor Davies and Melvyn Hayes greeted her from panto in Sunderland, and two more favourite Tynesiders, Lawrie and Anne McMenemy were there.

From the Harton Institution – the 'workhouse' – to selling fifty million books worldwide; a few Geordie tears were shed in the City Road studio that night.

Monica Dickens, great-granddaughter of Charles Dickens, had a far more privileged upbringing, her father being a barrister and her grandfather, son of Charles, Sir Henry Dickens. Eamonn Andrews surprised her when she came to London on 31 March 1971 for the publication of her twenty-first book.

Family friend Sir Compton MacKenzie, then aged eighty-eight, greeted her from his home in Edinburgh.

Though from a comfortable middle-class background, Monica showed the true Dickens spirit to come to grips with the subjects of her books. Her experiences as cook and servant girl, wartime nurse and working at a factory bench, all fuelled her writing. *One Pair Of Hands* – about her life below stairs – was her first novel, and it sold a million.

Her book about nursing, *One Pair of Feet*, inspired another hospital-based author to write his 'doctor' books – and Richard Gordon was there to tell us so.

Noel Barber was lucky to survive his career as a Fleet Street foreign correspondent to write novels – during the Hungarian uprising against the Russians in 1956 Noel received forty-two stitches in a head wound after a Russian soldier opened fire on his car.

The incident happened when Noel was making his delivery of 'copy' to colleague Jeffrey Blyth, who waited nightly at the frontier-post for the despatches.

His great rival, Sefton Delmer of the *Daily Express*, got the wounded Noel to the Britain Legation. Still in pyjamas, Noel got a car and drove through snow and minefields into Austria to file his story.

Noel Barber wrote nineteen books before he got one published; at the time of our Life, his latest book was *The Fall of Shanghai*. He was the youngest brother of the former Chancellor of the Exchequer Anthony, later Lord, Barber, who was there to offer congratulations.

Few lived life more dangerously than legendary foreign correspondent and author Noel Barber. He survived a vicious stabbing in Algeria to cover the Hungarian uprising where his car was blasted by a hail of bullets from a Russian soldier's sub-machine gun. Noel had forty-two stitches in a head wound — without anaesthetic.

Alan Whicker and a galaxy of Fleet Street by-lines (including Fyfe Roberton, George Gale, Leslie Thomas, Cecil Wilson, Olga Franklin and Patrick Sargeant) were on hand to help him get a tender head by far more pleasant means.

Eamonn Andrews surprised Noel as he stepped out of a car outside the White House in London, and famous Fleet Street colleagues, including Olga Franklin, Cecil Wilson, Colin Reid, Alan Whicker, Leslie Thomas, Patrick Sargeant and, of course, Jeffrey Blyth, all turned out to take part in the Life's story of a great reporter – and best-selling novelist.

Lena Kennedy's Life was an East Ender's story to rival the BBC soap opera. A remarkable grandmother, she started her working life in the rag-trade 'sweat shops' of Hoxton, at thirteen, and didn't have her first book published until she was sixty-five.

Her best-sellers include *Lily My Lovely, Autumn Alley, Nelly Kelly* and the one she was there to autograph at Bentall's in Kingston on 14 April 1986, *Down Our Street*.

It was based on the real street where Lena was born and brought up. For the first time in half a century the programme reunited the neighbours of Witham Street, Hoxton, long since demolished.

Lena's novels evoked the hardship of life there, but romance, too.

She was fifty-eight when she heard the local council had started creative writing classes at night school. Students had to read out what they had written.

Lena took hers in a huge hold-all. It was her first-ever crack at writing a novel and she called it *Maggie*. So entranced were the rest of the night-school class they asked her to read an instalment each week.

What followed no *EastEnders* writer would have dared to invent. Her daughter Angela and son Keith looked up 'publishers' in the Yellow Pages, found one nearby, and left the manuscript of *Maggie* there in a carrier bag. The book came back with the message, 'Sorry, we only publish cartoons.'

Then Angela got a job as secretary at the Theatre Royal, Stratford East. One night in the bar she was introduced to 'a publisher'. He was the next recipient of *Maggie*, but Terry Oates turned out to be a *music* publisher.

So Lena's first novel gathered dust on his office shelf for two years until one night he met a pal who was a publisher's editor. John Man read it to his wife Angie – a brief passage from *Maggie* every evening, just like the night-school class. Angie liked it. And that's how *Maggie* was finally published.

After nine novels, all best-sellers, had Lena changed? According to Bob Arnott, captain of the *QE2*, definitely not. Sailing to New York on the luxury liner for a promotional tour, Lena was offered the wine list at dinner – a list containing some of the world's great vintages.

Lena ordered a Guinness.

Lena's world was light years away from that of the best-selling writer Michael Aspel surprised in the roof garden at the BelAge Hotel in Los Angeles on 21 February 1993.

Jackie Collins was celebrating the launch of the video of her novel *Lady Boss*. Michael was the surprise guest at the party, which continued at the nearby studios of CBS.

One hundred and seventy million copies of her books have been sold in more than thirty countries; not bad for someone who first arrived in Hollywood at sixteen hoping to emulate her sister's acting career. Except Jackie had always described herself as 'an out-of-work writer'.

Her Hollywood experiences were to get her writing career underway.

Joan told us she met her 'baby' sister – eight years younger – at the airport in LA, tossed her the keys to her apartment, before flying off to some exotic location, and advised her, 'Learn to drive.'

That she did, bought a car, and drove to interminable auditions. The result of that period in her life was her novel *The World is Full of Married Men*.

When *she* married night-club owner Oscar Lerman, she plucked up the courage to show him the manuscript. It was he – who died only a short while ago – who told her she had a best-seller on her hands.

She followed it with *The Stud*, the film of which revived Joan's then slightly flagging career.

Last word went to Joan: 'By the way, darling, could I have the keys to my apartment back sometime?'

Chapter Fifteen
Living Life Dangerously

Explorer Lieutenant-Colonel John Blashford-Snell had just been the guest on, appropriately enough, *Desert Island Discs* and was crossing the road outside Broadcasting House with presenter Roy Plomley when we surprised the man who thrives on danger.

What we didn't know was that the incident might have been dangerous for Eamonn Andrews. The colonel had served in Northern Ireland and on 6 October 1976 still had an armed bodyguard. He was instantly on alert when he heard the Irish accent, but fortunately also instantly recognised the Life host.

One of the colonel's proudest achievements came in 1968 – the Great Abbai Expedition, seeking the start of the Blue Nile, flowing from the Ethiopian Highlands to the plains of the Sudan. 'Blashers' and his party navigated five hundred miles of crocodile-infested waters and were twice attacked by marauding bandits. He put on his pith helmet and walked towards one heavily armed group, calling through a loud-hailer, 'Tanasterling, tanasterling, salaam!' Translated, that

Explorer John Blashford-Snell had just recorded an edition of *Desert Island Discs* with Roy Plomley when Eamonn Andrews arrived on another island – a traffic island outside Broadcasting House.

means, 'We come in peace' – whereupon he was shot at. One member of the party was already wounded.

Armed bandits staged a night raid on his camp. The colonel emerged from his tent wearing only his pith helmet and fired his flare-gun into the ground, producing great bouncing balls of fire into the path of the bandits and frightening them off for a few precious moments to allow the party to escape – with the colonel grabbing his clothes.

Few have lived more dangerously than the RAF's most outstanding fighter pilot of the war – Air-Vice-Marshal J. E. 'Johnnie' Johnson CB, CBE, DSO and Two Bars, DFC and Bar, whom we surprised with a special VE Day tribute on 3 May 1985.

Those decorations for gallantry were won by risking his life when 'the Few' flew into battle with the Luftwaffe's Messerschmitts. Johnnie Johnson beat the Battle of Britain record of thirty-two enemy aircraft shot down, held by fighter ace 'Sailor' Malan. He got his thirty-third on the last day of June 1944, when he led the first Spitfire wing into Normandy.

The author of *The Story of Air Fighting* had flown into battle with Douglas Bader and other Battle of Britain heroes, such as Air Chief Marshal Sir Denis Crowley Milling and Group Captain Hugh Dundas. All had fought in what Johnnie Johnson called 'that hot, sweaty, tiny greenhouse of a cockpit'.

What he wanted most was 'a joust' with a particular German air ace, built up by the press into a personal challenge. Alas, the German pilot had been shot down and wounded. After the war he wrote to Johnnie regretting he had been unable to accept the challenge.

Forty years on we flew in that German fighter ace, Major Walter Matoni, for a more peaceful meeting with Air-Vice-Marshal Johnson.

Major-General Robert Foote VC, CB, DSO we surprised when he was visiting the Royal Armaments Research and Development Establishment at Chertsey, on 30 September 1986.

General Foote won his Victoria Cross in the Western Desert in 1942 in an action south of Tobruk along the Sidra Ridge, christened 'the Cauldron'.

There he certainly lived life dangerously. His tank hit, he got out and walked in front of the tanks under his command, leading them on foot in the height of battle.

His adjutant and gunner Major John Maclean told viewers, 'It was a sight I will never forget – Robert striding out in front of the tanks, signalling orders and directions, with the Germans throwing everything they had at us. He even had a smile on his face.'

HM King George VI presented the general with the VC on 12 December 1944 for what must have been one of the most amazing acts of bravery of the war.

Sir Richard Attenborough, who had just directed *A Bridge Too Far* – the story of the airborne assault on Arnhem – had invited to Twickenham Film Studios a legendary hero of that battle, even among a host of heroes, Major-General John Frost CB, DSO, MC. And that's where we picked him up. Anthony Hopkins, who played the general in the film, greeted him from Hollywood.

For thirty-three years Major-General Frost had been trying to locate his former batman. With the general wounded, the batman had dragged him to a wall, propped him up, cocked his revolver for him and said, 'If anyone comes through that door, sir, shoot.' Then he rushed off to find a stretcher-bearer.

General Frost had even gone to the lengths of taking a newspaper advertisement to find ex-private Dennis Wicks. It was a challenge the Life research team could not resist. Private Wicks was alive and well – and on the general's programme.

Canny are the ways of the Scots, and it remains a mystery how the Queen Mother discovered we were having difficulty prising the man Ian Fleming is generally believed to have based James Bond on from his Scottish lair.

What is not a mystery is that she invited him to lunch at Clarence House on 30 November 1984 – the day we had planned to surprise him.

While in London he received an invitation from Thames TV to be interviewed about the books he had written of his countless daring exploits during the war – exploits which had earned him the nickname 'the Tartan Pimpernel'. In real life, he was diplomat, former MP, writer, soldier and war hero, Sir Fitzroy MacLean.

He was one of the original founders of the SAS, and served with the founder himself, David Stirling, in the Middle East, where – very James Bond-like – Sir Fitzroy managed to abduct a pro-enemy Persian general, at gunpoint.

Little wonder Winston Churchill personally chose him to lead one of the most vital and dangerous missions of the war. He was parachuted into enemy-occupied Yugoslavia to set up a British Military Mission, and organise the partisans. He accomplished his mission with 007 élan. But, that day of the Life, he was hoodwinked by the Queen Mother's luncheon invitation.

Wednesday 7 November 1990 was the Golden Jubilee of a very special and exclusive organisation – 'the Guinea Pig Club'. Members had to have survived a wartime burning aircraft and received 'body repairs' at the famous burns centre at the Queen Victoria Hospital, East Grinstead, where pioneering plastic surgeons, under the inspired leadership of Sir Archibald McIndoe, saved hundreds of lives.

The Chief Guinea Pig was Group-Captain Tom Gleave CBE, Légion d'Honneur, Croix de Guerre. He was invited to the RAF museum at Duxford, Cambridgeshire, to take part in a documentary about the Golden Jubilee.

Instead, he bumped into Michael Aspel with the Big Red Book, and back at the studios the whole audience comprised the heroic membership of the Guinea Pig Club.

Actor Nigel Havers was there, too. He had got to know them when about to film for the television series *Perfect Heroes*, based on that East Grinstead hospital.

'They are a breed apart,' said Nigel.

Group-Captain Gleave was shot down on 31 August 1940 and his cockpit was engulfed in flames. When his wife went to see her badly burned husband in hospital, all he could say was, 'I had a row with a German.'

A modern-day victim of the flames of war was former Welsh Guards Falklands veteran Simon Weston – stories of the Guinea Pig Club had kept him going through the darkest days of his own living hell when his face was virtually burned off.

The battle of the Falklands hero told the Battle of Britain hero, 'I have never been prouder to call anybody a real Pig of a man.'

Chay Blyth CBE, the former paratroop sergeant who found fame battling with the sea, was moored at Westminster Pier on 23 October 1974 when Eamonn Andrews popped aboard.

The Scot, from Hawick, was by then one of the world's most daring adventurers, having sailed the oceans of the world through gale and hurricane. With Captain John Ridgway he had rowed three thousand miles across the Atlantic, then made maritime history by sailing single-handed around the world *against* the oncoming winds in a boat less than sixty feet long.

Sir Alec Rose sailed single-handed around the world from the opposite direction. He told viewers that what Chay did was 'like riding a bike up Snowdon'. What he had achieved in sailing terms was simply incredible.

Chay Blyth's voyage was 'like riding a bike up Snowdon', according to another famous mariner, Sir Alec Rose.

Tracy Edwards MBE, who captained the first all-female crew in the Whitbread Round the World Race, all 33,000 miles of it, was due for a photo-call on board *Maiden* at St Katharine's Dock in London on 12 September 1990. What she didn't know was that her all-female crew was hiding below deck, with Michael Aspel.

Yet the woman who had created her own bit of history by captaining that all-girl crew in the world's most demanding yachting event used to suffer from seasickness. That was when she worked on a yacht in the Greek Islands.

When we surprised her she had just been voted the first woman 'Yachtsman of the Year'.

There was a warm greeting from another brave woman of the sea, Clare Francis, and from a royal sponsor, King Hussein of Jordan.

We had surprised Clare Francis on 5 March 1980, at the Savoy Hotel, where she was having a business meeting in the River Room. Unknown to her, her round-the-world crew (of men) – in 1977 she was the only female captain of a crew in the race – had moored outside, stolen through the Savoy's river-facing rear garden, and 'gatecrashed'.

Clare, who went on to become a successful novelist, had previously sailed the Atlantic single-handed in the fastest ever time for a woman.

Remarkable for a slip of a girl who spent five years at the Royal

Ballet School, dreaming of being a ballerina. Struck by the debilitating illness ME, she brought the same courage to fighting it in order to become a successful novelist.

Eamonn Andrews joined the all-male crew to surprise Clare Francis – the only female skipper in the round-the-world race.

Round-the-world mariner Dame Naomi James, whom we surprised on 22 December 1980, had devoted a chapter in her memoirs to Tom McClean: he had recaptured his own world record against the might of the Atlantic in nothing but a rowing boat in fifty-four days, twenty-three hours.

He thought he was helping Dame Naomi's book launch when he turned up for pictures rowing his Atlantic boat on the Thames. Instead, his two young sons, who he thought were back home in Scotland, James, aged seven, and Ryan, five, called to him through loud-hailers, 'Hello, Dad! Bet you didn't expect to see us!'

A moving moment for Tom, who had never known his own parents and had been brought up in an orphanage.

As he stepped ashore on 22 September 1987, Eamonn Andrews was there with the Big Red Book to tell the story of the ex-Para and SAS soldier who had become the first man in the world to row the Atlantic single-handed.

He had seen active service in Arabia and Borneo, and the mark of respect in which he was held was the fact that the man who played the role of his father at his wedding was General Sir Cecil Blacker, former Adjutant-General of the Army and former ADC General to HM the Queen. He had helped Tom set up his adventure centre in Scotland.

Korean war hero General Sir Anthony Farrar-Hockley, known as 'Farra the Para', also greeted Tom.

Two men who had rowed the Atlantic as a pair said they had thought it couldn't be done single-handed – Captain John Ridgway, and Tom McClean's former Para platoon sergeant, Chay Blyth.

The Banqueting Hall of the Old Brewery in the City of London was the scene of a gala evening on 9 September 1990 – the occasion of the 501st edition of the Life since Thames Television first started broadcasting the programme.

Every guest had been the Life's guest of honour over a period of twenty-one years. As Michael Aspel said, 'I doubt if there has ever been such a stunning array of people, from all walks of life, gathered together: show business, sport, politics, courage in war, bravery in peace, light-hearted lives and lives of self-sacrifice.'

The man whose name was on the book that night covered them all. Our co-conspirator was Countess Mountbatten of Burma, and the man from whom she was keeping the secret was her husband, the host at that table, international film producer Lord Brabourne.

Said Michael Aspel as he sprang the surprise: 'As our dinner guests might say, "Welcome to the club." '

The curtains onstage parted to reveal friends, colleagues and family, including daughters Joanna and Amanda, sons Michael-John, Philip and Timothy, and Lord Mountbatten's second daughter Lady Pamela Hicks.

Before the war, Lord Brabourne's father had been Governor of Bombay and Bengal and Acting Viceroy of India as, of course, was Lord Mountbatten. So, uniquely, both grandfathers of Lord Brabourne's children were Viceroys of India.

In 1941, Lord Brabourne lied about his age – he was in fact seventeen – to enlist in the Coldstream Guards. By a coincidence he was among the troops drafted in as extras on Noël Coward's wartime classic *In Which We Serve*, based on the exploits of Lord Louis and HMS *Kelly*.

Lord Brabourne's younger brother, Norton, an officer in the Grenadier Guards, was taken prisoner in 1943. He attempted an escape, but was recaptured and shot to deter others.

Himself commissioned, Lord Brabourne was in the thick of the action as the Guards swept through Europe following the Normandy landings in 1944. He was wounded in the shoulder.

Next he became ADC to General Sir William Slim of the 14th

Army in South-East Asia. One day, the general invited the Supreme Allied Commander, Lord Louis, to tea at his Ceylon HQ. He took Lady Patricia with him, and that is when they met. The following year he became army ADC to Mountbatten, and he and Patricia were married in 1946 at Romsey Abbey.

Prince Charles wrote, 'Just tell him he and my godmother Patricia have been a part of my life since my earliest childhood recollections and they both mean a great deal to me.'

After demob, he went to work for film producer Herbert Wilcox and met a newly demobbed third assistant director, Richard Goodwin. They were to set up their own company, and the first film Lord Brabourne produced was *Harry Black and the Tiger,* starring Stewart Granger, who greeted him before going on stage.

International directors Lewis Gilbert, Sidney Lumet and Franco Zeffirelli paid tribute, as did producer David Puttnam.

The lives of Lord Brabourne and Lord Louis Mountbatten were inextricably linked from the moment he first met Patricia. And, with Patricia, he was at Lord Louis's side at the very end. A family fishing trip, a mile from Mullaghmore Harbour in County Sligo, on 27 August 1979, ended in a tragedy that made world headlines.

A bomb had been planted in the boat, resulting in the death of Lord Louis, Lord Brabourne's mother, Doreen Lady Brabourne, and his son Nicholas, aged fourteen, twin of Timothy. Local youngster Paul Maxwell, aged fifteen, also died in the blast. Lord Brabourne himself, Patricia and Timothy were all seriously injured. Patricia ensures her father's memory lives on with the title she now so proudly bears: Countess Mountbatten of Burma.

A moving example of this family's fighting spirit came from Lord Mountbatten's family home at Broadlands, where we filmed Lord Brabourne's son Norton, Lord Romsey, his wife Penny and their children Nicholas, aged nine, Alexandra , seven, and five-year-old Leonora, who was battling against cancer, and had been allowed home from Bart's Hospital for a few days.

Lord Romsey and Penny joined us live, and the family picture was completed with more grandchildren, Joanna's daughter Eleuthera, four, and surprise fly-ins from Portugal, Michael-John's wife Melissa, with their daughter whose name keeps alive the memory of Lord Mountbatten's heroic wartime experiences – two-year-old Kelly.

Alas, only thirty-six hours after a visit from Princess Diana, little Leonora lost her battle against cancer and died on 22 October 1991.

Chapter Sixteen
It's a Funny Old Life

The constant quest of the Life team to spring the show's surprises does not always go smoothly. Sometimes they can backfire. That's when we look at each other and mutter, 'Funny old life. . . .'

In its early BBC days, Life took quite a lot of criticism from the press. 'Intrusion' was a favourite word; even 'unfair' and 'torture'. But viewers watched, and the subjects didn't complain. Well, apart from Danny Blanchflower.

Eamonn knew the footballer also as a radio colleague, and was totally relaxed before the pick-up. ('For the last time,' he recalled later.)

Blanchflower was booked for a soccer discussion with Eamonn at Broadcasting House. The book hidden under a table, Eamonn opened a newspaper to make the scene look casual as Blanchflower walked into the news studio. He even stopped to comb his hair. Said Eamonn, 'Do you see that camera, Danny?'

Danny said he knew it to be an automatic camera, controlled from upstairs. He'd worked with it before. Eamonn told him it was on – and for a special reason. Eamonn reached down for the book . . . 'because tonight, Danny Blanchflower, This Is. . . .'

But there was no Danny; the boy had bolted. Sports Editor Angus Mackay grabbed him by the jacket, but Blanchflower wriggled out of it and exited in shirt sleeves, bellowing, 'Let me out! Let me out!'

Jackie Collins turns the pages of her own Life at the studios of CBS in Hollywood.

Eamonn hared after him, and told him there was a packed theatre and friends waiting to greet him. Said Blanchflower: 'You invited them, not me.'

As Eamonn said later, 'Danny was completely within his rights in refusing to go on and owed no explanation to anyone.'

Attractive, dark-haired, immaculately groomed researcher Elizabeth Ross became our own 'James Bond girl' when we started building up our surprise guest list for the Life of Richard Harris.

007 himself, Sean Connery, had been a great pal of Richard's for years. When Elizabeth telephoned Sean's wife Micheline, at their home in Spain, she was confident Sean would like to contribute to the programme.

Elizabeth established he was playing golf at Gleneagles, was suitably briefed by our own 'M' (producer Malcolm Morris) and given instructions to rendezvous with a camera crew in Scotland. The idea was that as soon as she made contact with Connery, all she had to say was, 'It will only take a few moments and I've got the crew here all ready to go.'

As it turned out, it wasn't possible for Elizabeth to do a SMERSH operation at the all-male Gleneagles. She couldn't get in. But, as the camera crew waited eagerly, she did get through to Connery on the club telephone.

'Don't you people ever give up?' barked the urbane Bond.

'Then he told me where I could go in no uncertain terms,' said the extremely well-brought up Elizabeth. Ah well, he might have changed his mind had he actually seen her. Or maybe his back swing was really off that day.

We were hoping Connery's golf would be on form when we were working on the Life of another pal of his, comedian Jimmy Tarbuck.

This time, a researcher was sent to Marbella with a camera crew to film Sean. Forward intelligence informed us that if they were poised somewhere on the golf course, they should wait for golf fanatic Connery to hit a perfect shot to the green, then step forward and ask permission to film there and then.

Connery hit a dream shot. The crew sprang into action. The request was made. But the gaze of 'James Bond' was transfixed on the right foot of one of the team.

He had trodden on Connery's ball. There was no Sean Connery on Tarbuck's programme. And, considering the fate of some of those Bond villains, the crew was fortunate to arrive back in one piece.

Anjelica Huston filmed for us for Roddy McDowall's Life. We sent a crew to the set of *The Addams Family II* in Pasadena, where she did an amusing piece for us in the character of Morticia.

But it was us who got the surprise that night. As we were leaving our hotel, with Michael Aspel, to spring our surprise on Roddy at the Pacific Design Centre, who should get out of the lift at the BelAge? Anjelica Huston.

Former world champion Mike Tyson was missing from Frank Bruno's Life, but needed no excuses: he was still in prison. Researcher Sarah Cockcroft persuaded the warden to allow Tyson to film a message for us. Alas, Tyson had become depressed and reclusive, and wouldn't face the camera.

Jimmy Greaves has made it clear he would give Michael the red card if he saw the Red Book.

One morning in January 1990 Jimmy was on TV-AM with Michael as studio guest. Lorraine Kelly asked Michael the inevitable Life question, 'Why don't you do more ordinary people?'

Jimmy said he thought that everybody had something a bit extraordinary in them. Michael agreed that was true, but pointed out that would not necessarily make compelling viewing for millions at peak time.

Interviewer Mike Morris asked Jimmy how he would feel if he were approached with the Big Red Book?

Jimmy: 'I'd run a mile, mate.'

Mike Morris: 'You'd do a Danny Blanchflower?'

Jimmy: 'You bet.'

Benny Hill told producer Dennis Kirkland the same. Dennis and the great comedy star were inseparable, and when the two were 'sacked' by Thames Television, the chances of doing a Life on Benny became even more remote.

But when things started looking up – they had filmed in New York for an independently produced programme – and a book by Benny's brother was about to be published, we tried an approach again.

Dennis shook his head. Although the book had been written with Benny's approval, said Dennis, the two brothers had fallen out years ago and had never properly made it up.

Frank Bruno shapes up to our co-conspirator in his surprise, comedian Freddie Starr.

As for the Life, Benny put on his 'little boy' act and told Dennis, 'If you ever let them near me I'll kill you and chop you up and hide your body in the bushes. So there.'

We never did do Benny.

'Rumpole of the Bailey' has issued a permanent brief not to allow the Big Red Book near him. Leo McKern told his producer he thought the programme an intrusion; our view is that it is a surprise party. So strongly did he feel that he would not even contribute to the Life we did on his colleague in chambers, Phyllida Erskine-Browne QC, actress Patricia Hodge – though Rumpole was recording in the studio next door.

In the vaults there are a few film tributes viewers will never see.

Producer Malcolm Morris went to Number 10 Downing Street for Prime Minister Margaret Thatcher to video-record a message to disc jockey Jimmy Young.

So keen was she to get it right, she did it again, promising our secret was safe with her. Unfortunately it wasn't quite so safe with others. Jimmy discovered our plans, and we pulled out.

Jill Ireland, battling against cancer, bravely made one of her last appearances in front of a camera, with husband Charles Bronson, to record a tribute to Michael Winner, who had directed them both.

Alas, because of non-availability of others, we felt we could not get together in time a sufficiently strong programme to do justice to Winner's career.

Hollywood nearly got in the works on the Life of Richard Harris. Frank Sinatra's office sent him a telegram congratulating Richard on his Life. Unfortunately it was sent the day before the programme. Fortunately, the message went to the wrong theatre, and finally caught up with Richard the day *after*.

'If I'd got that I'd have pulled out,' said Harris. And Ol' Blue Eyes would have caused a few tears at the Life, too.

The Duchess of York had agreed to film a tribute to round-the-world yachtswoman Tracy Edwards: then out came that vast colour-picture spread in *Hello* magazine, for which the Yorks were said to have picked up enough to redecorate 'South-York'.

A script had been written and Fergie had approved it. But after the *Hello* exposure clearly someone at the Palace had told her 'no' to any more.

Instead, she signed the script I had written as a letter.

Prince Michael of Kent agreed to video a tribute to the wildlife artist David Shepherd. Director Brian Klein went to Kensington Palace with a crew, and the prince decided he would like to stand up while he was speaking.

Brian persuaded him to sit. 'You'll feel much more relaxed,' he said.

So the prince delivered his message sitting down. He asked for the tape to be replayed for him. He viewed it and said, 'Why is it Royals always come over as pompous?'

Oliver Reed had taken the 'pledge' to behave himself for the 501st *This Is Your Life* bash at the Old Brewery in the City, but decided he'd like to take a bash at actor Patrick Mower instead. Ollie was legless.

'I'm only here for my old mate Eamonn,' he slurred. Ollie was escorted from the banqueting hall by former subjects wrestler Jackie Pallo and stuntman 'Nosher' Powell.

One man who missed it all was disc jockey Alan 'Fluff' Freeman.

All decked out in black tie he arrived for the gala evening the night *after* the event. He telephoned to say he must have got his dates mixed.

Researcher Maurice Leonard (nowadays Michael Barrymore's producer) waited with eager anticipation at Heathrow for the arrival of Hollywood legend Danny Kaye, flying in for the Lord Mountbatten Life.

Maurice, a film buff and great, outgoing enthusiast, couldn't wait to spot his hero coming through the arrivals barrier, followed by a porter with his luggage. Maurice greeted the star effusively, delighted to meet him at last, his limousine was waiting etc. Kaye didn't so much as look at him.

'Tip the ******* porter,' he grunted.

Maurice was rather more fortunate when he went to Heathrow to greet Ursula Andress, flying in from Los Angeles to appear on the Life of Charles Aznavour.

She arrived with a Hollywood-star-sized suitcase which Maurice – a muscular lad – bent down to lift into the boot of the waiting car. To his embarrassment he instantly pulled a muscle and remained bent double. The star helped bundle him into the car and proceeded to massage his bare back.

This is what she was doing, with the gallant researcher lying face down in her lap, as the car pulled into the Teddington Studios.

The agony and the ecstasy.

Where was 'Lara' the night we surprised 'Dr Zhivago'? Alas, reclusive Julie Christie was not even able to film a message the night of the Life of Omar Sharif, though Rod Steiger and director Sir David Lean managed to do so. But for the many viewers who enquired of Miss Christie, we did ask.

Did we get a surprise when actor Warren Mitchell went into his Alf Garnett character on seeing his old friend Richard Burton on our live link to Germany!

Our line on the link went down on us – for more than an hour. We got urgent calls from Germany to tell us that Richard was whiling away the time by making inroads into a case of vodka.

When the technical problems were sorted out that famous face appeared on our big screen to greet the *'Til Death Us Do Part* star.

But by now that smooth, rich voice had been well lubricated.

'Hello, my old friend,' slurred he.

Warren Mitchell scrutinised him carefully and summed up in finest Alf Garnett tones: 'You're pissed.'

Motorcycle world champion Barry Sheene soon learned that we had safer (and more luxurious) transport to take him to our studios.

Rhyming slang had eluded the Dublin-based Eamonn Andrews, and the night we did the Life of motorcycle world champion Barry Sheene, it showed.

Former Beatle George Harrison came along to say he was a keen fan, but until he met the amazing speed merchant he had thought he was a bit of a 'Midland banker'.

The audience stifled chuckles, as did the crew. Eamonn carried on regardless, and afterwards wanted to know why it had never appeared in any of the research that George had once worked for the Midland.

One night we were entertaining friends and relatives – and husband – of a star performer in a luxury London hotel. I left our private room for a moment to buy an evening newspaper in the foyer. In the cocktail bar who did I spot but our subject – and with a handsome young man who had not been unearthed in our research.

As mentioned earlier, the oldest recipient of the Big Red Book was actress Cathleen Nesbitt, aged ninety-two. The youngest was Twiggy, who was only twenty. She was our chosen subject on 10 December 1969 – the plan being to fade out on the 'Swinging Sixties' with its fashion icon, named in 1966 'the Face of the Sixties'.

But as the drinks flowed at the party where we'd planned to surprise her, one face was missing – Twiggy's.

The girl born Leslie Hornby, in Neasden, was at the Twickenham home of her parents, Norman and Nell, doing her knitting.

We sent her then manager and mentor, former hairdresser Justin de Villeneuve – in his Lamborghini – to bring her to the party 'for Japanese film cameras' at Justin's mews house in town.

There was a final moment of panic when it looked as though she was refusing to get out of the car and enter the party. Eamonn pounced before she could change her mind, so we could tell the story of the most famous fashion model in the world.

Frankie Vaughan holds a Life record – he is the only star ever to have appeared as guest of honour on both American and British versions of the Life. Ralph Edwards pounced in Hollywood when the young singer from Liverpool arrived to make the film *Let's Make Love* – with Marilyn Monroe. Eamonn Andrews caught him in cabaret at Caesar's Palace, Luton, where we made the programme.

The Life surprise on comedy duo Cannon and Ball came close to backfiring.

Eamonn loved elaborate pick-ups, and very good he was in them, so the names of Tommy Cannon and Bobby Ball were too good not to suggest an idea.

They were about to appear in the West End and a photo-call was being staged. Outside the Theatre Royal, Drury Lane, we had a giant 'props' cannon built, and the 'ball' was supposed to be Eamonn. So he was bundled inside the 'barrel', all set to pop out and surprise the couple. But they walked straight past our 'cannon' – not knowing Eamonn was stuck inside.

The camera crew hauled him out in time to chase after Cannon and Ball with the book.

One of the most bizarre contributions to the Life was Rex Harrison's for Cathleen Nesbitt.

Rex and Eamonn had met before and not got on. To get Rex to contribute anything to the Life – and what a subject he would have made – was nigh impossible.

What was also nigh impossible was for him not to acknowledge the Life Eamonn was presenting on Miss Nesbitt. Harrison's agents said he was flying back to America the morning of our programme.

We persisted, and eventually he agreed to record – sound only – from the Rolls-Royce taking him to the airport.

Then we had a suggestion: would he object to our camera filming him recording the message from another car alongside?

That was the explanation for that strange contribution, looking at a man in the back seat of a car travelling at speed down a motorway, talking into a tape-recorder. Rex might have thought it a wheeze to cock a snook at Eamonn, and that we would never use it.

But we did. Who could resist?

Princess Diana was in on our secret when she attended the London charity opening of the film *Hear My Song*, based on the life of Josef Locke.

But viewers almost didn't get to see the wonderful shot of the princess bursting into delighted laughter and applause when Michael walked onstage to surprise Josef, who responded with, 'You b . . . b . . . blaggard!' Then looked towards where the princess was sitting – he had met her in the line-up before the film – and gasped, 'Did the princess know?'

Pick-up director Steve Minchin, a veteran outside broadcast man with vast experience of royal coverage, afterwards, and quite rightly, played it by the book and dropped a line to the palace. It had been agreed that all coverage of the line-up before the show was totally in order. But the shot *after* the show of the delighted – and delightful – reaction of the princess? Steve thought he ought to clear it with the palace.

There was no reply, so in it went and out on air it went.

The day after came a letter from the palace expressing doubt about its use. We'll put that one down to the luck of the Life.

Just as we did years ago when the brother of our celebrity flown in from New York got into a bit of a fracas the night before and was due to appear in court a few hours before we recorded. All was explained to the magistrate, who let him off and released him in the 'good behaviour' custody of the Life. The magistrate was a fan of the show.

And, I suspect, of TV's *Special Branch*. Our subject was its star, George Sewell, and the young man who had been 'collared' was his brother Danny.

But our planned pick-up of a wonderful 'unknown' – foster mother Kitty Wilson – is perhaps the classic of the 'biter bit' surprise that can sometimes happen. Eamonn lay in wait at Liverpool Street Station. The train came in, Eamonn moved swiftly through the crowds, the hidden cameras following him. Gently he put his hand on the woman's shoulder.

'Hello, Kitty,' he said.

The woman turned and looked at him in total confusion.

Wrong woman.

Chapter Seventeen
Life's a Party

The scene: the crowded Moonlight Tango Café, Ventura Boulevard, Los Angeles, with its singing waiters and non-stop swing band.

By special request, the band is belting out the conga. The swaying conga of customers snakes around the tables, led by the Life team, including Michael Aspel, letting down his well-groomed hair.

The band switches to a hot jazz number and we're all jiving like crazy: Michael, secretaries, researchers, producer and, needless to say, writer. We pause only to toast our hosts at the studios of CBS, where we have just recorded our last programme of the season – movie legend Ann Miller.

As the wine waiter recharges my glass he grins, 'Hey, you guys sure know how to party.'

We sure do. We are celebrating springing thirty surprise parties on Life guests of honour in the last six months.

What's more, once again our show has rarely been out of the top ten in the ratings, averaging audiences of more than fifteen million (sixteen and a half million watched Frank Bruno's Life).

We 'warmed-up' for the Moonlight Tango (they know us, we've celebrated there before) with drinks and buffet for the playback of Ann Miller's Life, climaxed by the appearance of Ginger Rogers. Ginger is in great form at the party, too.

Also there is another part of Hollywood history, the creator of *This Is Your Life*, Ralph Edwards. Can it really be over forty-seven years since his brainchild first made its mark – on radio?

Countless millions have watched the show on television since, in nine different countries.

Ralph tells me the American Movie Classics channel will continue replaying 'vintage' Lives for the next two and a half years, and adds, 'We are constantly considering the possibility of bringing back the format as a first-run series, or specials.' Said Ralph: 'This Is Your Life is a long and rich story which is not over yet.'

He is delighted the programme is now as much a television institution in Britain as it is in America.

It is fascinating to hear from the man who created the format how it evolved; especially since, as far as we are concerned, it is still evolving. We have transmitted from theatres, aircraft hangars, the circus Big Top, hotel ballrooms, regional studios for regional subjects.

The format's adaptability is endless. The total transmission period in the UK, including its time with the BBC, covers a span of almost thirty-five years.

'Won't you ever run out of subjects?' is a question we are asked. The best reply I can recall came from producer Malcolm Morris when the gynaecologist about to deliver his son asked the same question: 'You keep bringing them into the world, and I'll keep doing their Lives.' His son, Greg, is now twenty.

I remind him of this as, even at the Moonlight Tango, it's getting time for chairs on tables.

Michael Aspel and associate producer John Graham are busy signing a napkin, witnessed by our friends at CBS. It turns out to be a 'contract' pledging our return.

It will join the bizarre collection of Life memorabillia on the walls of the office at Teddington Studios.

Exhausted, but happy, we climb into the cars taking us back to the hotel.

At Teddington, the 'Dream Board' is full. What's more, at the request of the network, we have made four extra programmes, taking our transmission period to well beyond Easter.

At CBS, they have put our 'Hollywood' set and scenery in storage.

I glance back at the Moonlight Tango and think of a special party to come. At the turn of the year, *This Is Your Life* celebrates twenty-five years on ITV as a Thames production.

For what started as a 'pilot' and six shows, not a bad run.

And for as long as the viewers keep watching, Life will go on.

Finally, a book about *This Is Your Life* would not be complete without a big surprise ending, and this has now been provided by the BBC. After its twenty-fifth season (1993–1994) on ITV, the programme will return to BBC Television for a further three years at least, made by Thames Television as an independent production company and still presented by Michael Aspel. In the words of BBC1 Controller Alan Yentob, 'It is a bit like having one of the family jewels returned.'

Although she had to make her appearance confined to a wheelchair, nothing would keep the legendary Ginger Rogers away from the Life of her friend Ann Miller, another legend of the great days of Hollywood musicals.

Appendix

An A–Z of Life Subjects

Featured by Thames Television

The following is a complete list of Life subjects since the first Thames Television transmission in December 1969. Sometimes our 'subject' has been more than one person; in a very few cases and for various reasons we have 'done' the same subject twice.

From the mid-1970s the security-conscious *This Is Your Life* team invented a system of codenames to disguise the identity of its intended subjects. If you had stumbled across the codenames below, would you have been able to identify the Life concerned?

Name	Codename	Transmission Date	Name	Codename	Transmission Date
Ackland, Joss	Stick	15.12.76	Barlow, Thelma	Till	13.11.91
Adams, Janet		14.3.73	Barraclough, Roy	Wedding	21.10.87
Adamson, Peter	Dad	23.12.81	Barrett, Norman	Tower	31.10.90
Alderton, John		6.2.74	Barron, Keith	Knight	9.1.85
Ali, Muhammad	Three	25.12.78	Bart, Lionel	Abbey	3.4.91
Alliss, Peter	Town	3.4.85	Bass, Alfie		11.3.70
Anderson, Jean	Alice	30.1.85	Bassey, Shirley	Feather	29.11.72
Anderson, Moira	Heather	26.3.75	Bates, Michael	Sahib	16.4.76
Andrews, Eamonn		15.5.74	Beacham, Stephanie	Powder	31.1.90
Andrews, Harry	Kent	6.3.85			
Aquinas, Sister	Zero	24.2.93	Beaumont, Bill	Bees	9.4.80
Archer, Jeffrey	Dan	14.1.81	Beckinsale, Richard	Gruel	23.11.77
Arnott, Bob	Duke	14.12.77			
Ashley, Jack	Extra	10.10.74	Bee Gees, The	Hits	20.2.91
Askey, Arthur	Eyes	25.12.74	Bellamy, David	Five	20.12.78
Aspel, Michael	Detective	14.5.80	Bellingham, Lynda	Cube	27.1.93
Ayres, Pam	Verse	24.11.76	Benson, Ivy	League	1.12.76
Aznavour, Charles	Sparrow	19.12.79	Berg, Jack 'Kid'	Ice	14.1.87
			Berglas, David	Deck	25.12.91
Bachelors, The	Peas	4.1.78	Berryman, Gwen	Target	25.2.76
Baden-Semper, Nina	Neighbour	12.3.75	Berwick, Lin	Will	21.12.77
			Best, George		17.11.71
Bader, Douglas	Reach	31.3.82	Bevan, Brian	Ernie	2.4.80
Bailey, Robin	Barnum	27.1.82	Beverley Sisters, The		31.12.69
Baker, Hylda		1.3.82			
Baldock, Michael	Bottle	18.4.90	Bewes, Rodney	Trio	10.12.80
Ball, Kenny		3.3.71	Biddlecombe, Terry		17.4.74
Banks, Gordon		8.3.72			
Barber, Noel	Snip	12.12.79	Bird, Dickie	Bail	7.10.92
Barkworth, Peter	Game	14.3.79	Blackburn, Tony	Legend	22.1.92

This Is Your Life

Name	Codename	Transmission Date	Name	Codename	Transmission Date
Blackman, Honor		17.12.69	Carson, Frank	Cracker	6.2.85
Blackman, Honor	Obey	17.2.93	Carson, Willie		17.1.73
Blair, Lionel		6.3.74	Cartland, Barbara	Pink	13.12.89
Blashford-Snell, John	Star	10.11.76	Cazenove, Christopher	Guard	25.2.87
Bleasdale, Alan	See	5.2.92	Chalmers, Judith	Visa	8.4.81
Blessed, Brian	Victor	4.4.84	Champion, Bob	Wonder	13.10.81
Bluebell, Miss (Margaret Kelly)	Flower	3.5.79	Charlton, Bobby		26.11.69
			Charlton, Jackie		2.5.73
Blyth, Chay	Loner	27.11.74	Chas 'n' Dave	Couple	31.12.85
Boht, Jean	Yeast	22.11.89	Chipperfield, Mary	Sawdust	2.3.77
Botham, Ian	Bit	4.11.81	Clark, Petula	Paris	30.4.75
Bowen, Jim	Bull	10.4.85	Coles, William		23.1.74
Bowles, Peter	Manor	5.11.80	Collins, Jackie	Lucky	24.3.93
Bowness, Felix	Jockey	11.12.85	Collins, Joan	Esther	3.11.82
Boyce, Max	Touch	22.2.78	Collins, Lewis	Sussex	8.12.82
Boyle, Katie	Europe	10.11.82	Collins, Pauline		5.4.72
Brabourne, Lord	India	17.10.90	Collins, Phil	Jacket	26.10.88
Brace, Mike	Belt	13.1.82	Compton, Denis	Captain	18.2.87
Braden, Bernard	Beat	16.1.91	Connolly, Billy	Rig	31.12.80
Branson, Richard	Island	20.11.85	Conteh, John	Greyhound	13.11.74
Briers, Richard		3.5.72	Cookson, Catherine	Katie	22.12.82
Briggs, Barry		27.3.74			
Briggs, Johnny	Agent	26.1.83	Coombs, Pat	Bread	8.2.78
Brightman, Sarah	Shine	1.10.89	Cooney, Ray	Minstrel	15.1.75
Britton, Tony	England	26.1.77	Cooper, Henry		14.1.70
Brooke-Taylor, Tim	Stitches	18.2.81	Cooper, Jilly	Butterworth	19.3.80
			Corbett, Harry	Hand	21.12.88
Broome, David	Sweep	11.1.78	Corbett, Ronnie		1.4.70
Brown, Faith	Hope	20.1.82	Cormeau/Farrow, Yvonne	Luck	8.11.89
Brown, Janet	Margaret	3.12.80			
Brown, Joe		23.12.70	Corrigan, James		14.2.73
Bruno, Frank	Glove	3.2.93	Cotton, Henry	Reel	5.2.86
Bryan, Dora	Honey	25.1.89	Coupland, Diana		28.2.73
Buckman, Rob	Panther	18.11.81	Courtney, Tom		23.2.72
Busby, Matt		12.5.71	Cousins, Robin	Lake	26.3.80
Butterworth, Peter	Yellow	5.3.75	Crabtree, Shirley ('Big Daddy')	Apple	7.3.79
			Craig, Wendy		11.2.70
Caine, Marti	Tomato	22.3.78	Craven, Gemma	Slipper	4.3.81
Cairoli, Charlie		25.2.70	Cribbins, Bernard	Cot	25.2.81
Calvert, Phyllis		20.12.72	Cricket, Jimmy	Stump	4.11.87
Cameron, Gloria	Bench	27.12.83	Croft, Michael	Youth	15.2.78
Campbell, Patrick		30.12.70	Croucher, Norman	Horn	5.5.76
Cannon & Ball	Armoury	11.11.81	Crowther, Leslie		28.3.73
Capes, Geoff	Cloak	6.2.80	Cushing, Peter	Baron	21.2.90
Carey, Joyce	Lady	26.12.85			
Cargill, Patrick	Parent	28.12.85			
Carpenter, Harry	Wood	27.3.91	Dale, Jim		21.11.73
Carr, Pearl & Johnson, Teddy	Diamond	12.11.86	Dalglish, Kenny	Park	16.2.73
			Daniels, Paul	Father	2.11.88
Carrier, Robert	Pigeon	19.1.83	Dankworth, John		27.2.74

Name	Codename	Transmission Date	Name	Codename	Transmission Date
Davidson, Jim	Face	1.2.84	Fincher, Terry	Snap	21.4.76
Davies, Dickie	Wallop	19.3.75	Finney, Tom	Cap	9.11.88
Davies, Windsor	Whisper	7.1.76	Flanders, Michael		26.1.72
Davis, Carl	Theme	29.10.86	Fletcher, Cyril	Odd	16.3.77
Davison, Peter	Shandy	24.3.82	Floyd, Keith	Soup	23.10.91
Davro, Bobby	Double	11.4.90	Foote, Robert	Valour	22.10.86
Dawn, Liz	Dusk	10.1.90	Foster, Barry	Canal	23.1.91
Dawson, Les		22.12.71	Fowlds, Derek	Beat	31.3.93
Dawson, Les	Ada	23.12.92	Francis, Clare	Drake	12.3.80
De Burgh, Chris	Red	15.4.92	Francis, Dick	Thriller	18.12.74
Denham, Maurice	Pipe	27.11.85	Franklyn, William	Tonic	26.4.78
Denison, Michael	Writ	23.2.77	Fraser, Bill	Shoes	21.10.81
Dickens, Monica		7.4.71	Freeman, Alan	Chart	14.10.87
Distel, Sacha		15.12.71	French, Harold		27.5.70
Dodd, Ken	Stick	7.5.90	Fresco, Monty	Al	19.11.86
Doheny, Fathers, Michael & Kevin	Father	17.10.84	Friend, Harry	Mate	4.2.87
			Frost, David		12.1.72
Dolin, Anton	Plus	12.4.78	Frost, John	Snow	6.4.77
D'Oliveira, Basil		17.3.71			
Donegan, Lonnie	Dust	17.4.91			
Dooley, Arthur		4.2.70	Gabor, Zsa Zsa	Star	29.11.89
Doonican, Val		6.5.70	Gall, Sandy	Beach	30.3.83
Dors, Diana	Diamond	27.10.82	Galway, James	Bay	24.1.79
Dotrice, Roy		20.3.74	Geldof, Bob	Mice	16.1.85
Dougall, Robert		2.1.74	George, Susan	Straw	3.12.86
Dougan, Derek		16.1.74	Gittins, Chris	Angel	8.2.84
Douglas, Jack	Sneeze	17.4.85	Gleave, Tom	Prop	9.1.91
Drake, Gabrielle	Swan	9.4.87	Glennie, Evelyn	Chime	6.3.91
Driver, Betty		11.2.76	Glitter, Gary	Sparkle	1.1.92
Driver, Harry		3.12.69	Goddard, Liza	Polish	15.1.84
Dukes, Ronnie	Duchess	12.11.75	Godfree, Kitty	Centre	6.2.88
Dunn, Clive		24.3.71	Goldberger, Alice	Lifeline	25.10.78
Dunn, Richard	Ring	28.4.76	Gooch, Graham	County	24.10.90
Durrell, Gerald	Jersey	23.2.83	Good, Jack		18.3.70
			Goodyear, Julie	Bar	22.10.80
			Goolden, Richard	Willow	8.3.78
			Gordon, Noele		7.2.73
Edwards, Gareth	Ball	7.4.76	Gordon, Richard		28.2.74
Edwards, Tracy	Skip	24.10.90	Gormley, Joe	Pit	3.3.82
Ellaway, David	Mission	4.12.85	Granger, Stewart	Clan	5.3.80
English, Arthur	Tie	18.1.78	Grant, Russell	Sign	13.2.85
Evans, Geraint	Tone	4.1.84	Grappelli, Stéphane	Grape	21.2.79
Evans, Richard		4.3.70	Gray, Dulcie		7.3.73
			Grayson, Larry		27.12.72
Fairbanks Junior, Douglas	Salad	20.12.89	Green, Hughie		16.2.72
			Gregson, John		25.4.73
Fairfax, John		7.1.70	Greig, Tony	Reg	30.3.77
Faith, Adam		28.4.71	Grey, Beryl		10.4.74
Faye, Alice	Band	19.12.84	Griffiths, Bill		22.11.72
Feather, Vic		28.11.73	Griffiths, Terry	Pocket	16.1.80
Ferris, Pam	Wheel	18.12.91	Grimond, Jo	Sprint	2.3.83
Fiennes, Ranulph	Vault	20.10.82	Guyler, Deryck		9.1.74

This Is Your Life

Name	Codename	Transmission Date	Name	Codename	Transmission Date
Hailey, Arthur	Comet	6.2.91	Illingworth, Ray		12.4.72
Hailwood, Mike	Wheels	26.11.75	Inman, John	Store	22.12.76
Hamp, Johnnie	Tag	10.2.93			
Hampshire, Susan	Dance	8.4.92			
Hancock, Sheila	Honeymoon	5.1.77	Jackley, Nat	Walk	10.4.80
Hanson, John	Shadow	12.2.75	Jacklin, Tony		18.2.70
Hare, Doris		29.12.71	Jacks, Brian	Lad	21.1.81
Harewood, Lord	Opera	27.2.85	Jacobs, David	Hit	25.3.87
Harper, Gerald	Bazaar	9.1.80	James, Naomi	Lionheart	10.1.79
Harris, Anita	Skate	6.1.82	Jameson, Derek	Street	19.2.86
Harris, John	Tweed	22.1.86	Jeffries, Lionel		21.4.71
Harris, Richard	Tweed	14.11.90	Jennings, Pat	Hands	16.11.83
Harris, Rolf		1.12.71	Jewel, Jimmy		30.1.74
Harty, Russell	Hale	17.12.80	John, Barry		19.1.72
Hatch, Tony & Trent, Jackie	Song	13.2.91	Johnson, Harry	Guard	29.1.75
			Johnson, Joe	Powder	26.11.86
Hauxwell, Hannah	Dale	25.3.92	Johnson, Teddy & Carr, Pearl	Diamond	12.11.86
Havers, Nigel	Hero	8.1.92	Johnston, Brian	Cake	24.11.82
Hayes, Melvin	Redhill	28.1.81	Johnston, 'Johnnie'		8.5.85
Hayes, Patricia		19.4.72	Jones, Anthony	Rope	20.1.93
Hayles, Margaret	Stone	1.2.89	Jones, Gwyneth	Voice	30.10.91
Healey, Denis	Camera	8.2.89			
Hemery, David		8.5.74	Kaye, Gorden	Romeo	5.11.86
Henderson, Dickie		17.2.71	Keegan, Kevin	Mighty	14.2.79
Hendry, Ian	Lotus	15.2.78	Keen, Diane	Fox	17.11.82
Hendry, Stephen	Chalk	28.11.90	Kelly, Barbara	Dry	15.11.78
Henry, Paul	Hat	27.3.85	Kelly, Matthew	Plug	21.12.83
Henry, Stuart	Lux	30.11.83	Kempson, Rachel	Dynasty	17.12.86
Herbert, Wally	Fur	24.2.82	Kennedy, Lena	Memory	16.4.86
Higgins, Alex	Gale	11.2.81	Kennedy, Nigel	Bow	14.3.90
Hill, Graham		20.1.71	Kent, Jean	Country	1.1.75
Hill, Vince	Vale	3.3.76	Kerr, Graham		29.3.72
Hines, Frazer	Beans	14.10.92	Kerr, Pat	Air	21.10.92
Hobbs, Liz	Wave	7.1.87	Kinnear, Roy	Ash	13.2.80
Hodge, Patricia	Light	28.1.87	Kydd, Sam		20.2.74
Holness, Bob	Block	4.4.90			
Hope, Bob		18 & 25.11.70			
Housego, Fred	Chair	4.2.81			
Howard, Jim	Pipe	19.2.92	La Rue, Danny	Street	18.4.84
Howarth, Jack	Hall	20.11.74	Langford, Bonnie	Good	29.1.86
Howerd, Frankie	Roman	27.2.76	Law, Denis	Barrister	19.2.75
Hudd, Roy	Lines	4.1.89	Law, Robert	Line	21.3.79
Hughes, Emlyn	Horse	27.2.80	Lawless, Terry	Order	25.1.84
Hughes, Nerys	Bird	22.2.84	Laye, Evelyn	Adam	19.12.90
Hull, Rod	Attack	3.2.82	Lee, Christopher		3.4.74
Humperdinck, Engelbert	Name	30.11.88	Lethbridge, Matthew	Gospel	11.1.84
Hunniford, Gloria	Bee	12.1.83	Lewis, Martyn	Wales	12.3.86
Hunter, Rita		21.3.73	Lindsay, Robert	Kane	18.3.92
Hyde-White, Wilfrid	Races	3.11.76	Lister, Moira		10.2.71
			Lloyd, Clive	West	21.5.80

Name	Codename	Transmission Date	Name	Codename	Transmission Date
Lloyd, Kevin	Ben	26.2.92	Metcalfe, Jean & Michelmore, Cliff	Favourites	31.12.86
Lloyd Webber, Andrew	Joseph	26.11.80			
Locke, Josef	Key	11.3.92	Michell, Keith		5.1.72
Lofthouse, Nat	Lion	7.4.93	Milburn, Colin		8.4.70
Logan, Jimmy		4.4.73	Milburn, Jackie	Coal	9.12.81
Loss, Joe	Found	15.10.80	Miles, Lord	Robin	1.3.85
Lovat, Lord	Green	7.2.79	Milland, Ray	Sunshine	19.11.75
Love, Geoff	Band	8.1.75	Miller, Ann	Kate	14.4.93
Lucas, 'Laddie'	Wings	11.4.84	Milligan, Spike		8.4.70
Lulu		10.5.72	Mills, Cyril	Ring	11.12.89
Lynn, Vera	Harry	1.1.79	Mills, Gladys	Joyful	24.12.75
Lynne, Gillian	Cat	15.2.89	Mills, Hayley		5.12.73
			Mills, John	Glory	26.10.83
			Mills, Juliet	Romeo	28.10.92
McBride, Willie John	Pride	23.4.75	Minter, Alan	Dawn	23.4.80
McClean, Tom	Solo	13.2.88	Mitchell, Leslie	Air	6.12.72
McColgan, Liz	Line	4.12.91	Monkhouse, Bob	Abbot	10.2.82
McCowan, Alec	Smart	6.12.89	Monro, Matt	Carpet	23.3.77
McDonald, Trevor	Burger	24.1.90	Moore, Bobby		6.1.71
McDowall, Roddy	Planet	3.3.93	Moore, Dudley		13.12.72
McElnea, June ('Sister Mac')	Child	12.2.86	Moore, Dudley	Arthur	4 & 11.3.87
McGuigan, Barry	Motor	7.12.88	Moore, Patrick		13.2.74
McKellar, Kenneth	Glen	6.3.91	Moreland, Mo	Jam	15.1.92
Macken, Eddie	Jump	7.3.84	Morgan, Cliff	Face	28.12.88
McKenzie, Julia	Neighbour	2.12.81	Morley, Robert		1.5.74
McKenzie, Precious	Metal	2.4.75	Most, Mickey	Disc	31.12.81
MacLean, Fitzroy	Chief	12.12.84	Mountbatten, Earl	Uncle	27.4.77
McMenemy, Laurie	Matt	29.10.80	Mower, Patrick	Lawn	21.1.76
Macnee, Patrick	Bowler	24.10.84	Mullery, Alan	Broadway	24.3.76
Madoc, Ruth	Camp	28.11.84	Murdoch, Richard	Ministry	3.5.78
Magri, Charlie	Fly	23.3.83	Murphy, Glen	Ladder	16.12.92
Manning, Bernard	Gag	27.11.91	Murray, Pete		12.12.73
Mansell, Nigel	Wheels	22.2.89			
Marks, Alfred		24.11.71	Neagle, Anna	Spring	9.3.83
Marsden, Gerry	Ferry	18.12.85	Neal, Patricia	Hud	13.12.78
Marsh, Billy	Field	28.3.90	Nesbitt, Cathleen	Festival	7.5.80
Marsh, Terry	Pete	18.3.87	Newby, Eric	Windjammer	6.12.78
Marshall, Arthur	Dawn	6.4.83	Newley, Anthony	Dodger	2.12.92
Martin, George	Air	30.1.80	Nicholas, Paul	Saint	16.10.91
Martin, Millicent	Modern	26.12.84	Nicholson, Michael	Wire	11.12.91
Masham, Lady	Triumph	4.2.76	Nixon, David		26.11.73
Maskell, Dan	Voice	24.4.85	Noble, Richard	Land	14.12.83
Maxwell, Robert	House	14.12.88	Noone, Peter		31.3.71
Maynard, Bill	Reprise	4.12.74			
Melly, George	Foot	21.4.93			
Mercer, Joe		25.3.70	O'Connor, Des		19.11.69
Mercier, Sheila	Country	13.11.85	O'Connor, Tom	Clock	12.1.77
			Ogilvy, Ian	Bernard	18.4.79
			O'Hara, Mary	Vow	8.11.78

This Is Your Life

Name	Codename	Transmission Date	Name	Codename	Transmission Date
O'Leary, Francis		9.5.73	Rhodes, Zandra	Greece	20.2.85
O'Neil, Paddy	Afternoon	23.1.80	Richards, Stan	Land	10.4.91
O'Neill, Jonjo	Gold	25.3.81	Richards, Viv	Willow	21.11.84
O'Neill, Terry	Jazz	11.12.85	Ridley, Arnold	Albert	10.3.76
O'Shea, Tessie	Orlando	5.12.84	Rippon, Angela	Reader	25.11.81
O'Sullivan, Richard	House	11.12.74	Rix, Brian	Torquay	13.4.77
Owen, Bill	Wine	7.1.81	Roache, William	Scholar	16.10.85
			Robson, Bryan	Train	23.1.85
			Rogers, Ted	Go	26.3.86
Paige, Elaine	Book	31.1.79	Rooney, Mickey	Andy	19.10.88
Painting, Norman	Art	6.11.91	Rossington, Jane	Oak	20.1.88
Paisley, Bob	Pattern	28.12.77	Rossiter, Leonard	Rising	5.2.75
Pallo, Jackie		18.4.73	Rothwell, Talbot		3.12.70
Parkinson, Michael	Windsor	1.11.78	Roux, Albert &	Menu	13.1.93
Parkinson, Norman	Snap	2.11.83	Michel		
Parsons, Nicholas	Clergy	1.3.78	Rudkin, Alan		15.3.72
Patterson, Harry (Jack Higgins)	Henry	17.5.78	Rushton, William	Beard	1.4.87
Pavey, Alfred	Switch	16.2.77			
Pearce, Joyce	Justice	11.4.79	Sachs, Andrew	Avenue	2.1.80
Pertwee, Jon		14.4.71	Sachs, Leonard	Variety	9.3.77
Peters, Mary		31.1.73	Sanderson, Tessa	Point	18.11.92
Phoenix, Pat		15.11.72	Sassoon, Vidal		2.12.70
Pickles, Wilfred		24.2.71	Saunders, Peter	Ruby	25.11.92
Pitman, Jenny	Mine	28.3.84	Saville, Jimmy		28.1.70
Pollock, Ellen	Shaw	11.11.92	Saville, Sir James	Row	12.12.90
Porter, Nyree Dawn	Morning	20.2.80	Schlesinger, John	Midnight	19.11.80
			Scott, Derek	Great	21.1.87
Pountney, Robert	King	5.12.90	Scott, Sheila		13.3.74
Powell, Fred 'Nosher'		26.4.72	Scott, Terry	Watford	13.3.78
			Scudamore, Peter	Letter	14.2.90
Powell, Robert	Watch	28.2.79	Secombe, Harry	Road	17.3.90
Powell, Sandy		27.1.71	Seed, Pat	North	28.11.79
Price, Margaret	Vote	15.4.81	Semprini, Alberto	Caravan	20.4.79
Priest, Florence	Lamp	19.1.77	Sewell, George		19.12.73
Proops, Marjorie		10.3.71	Shand, Jimmy	Box	29.11.78
Pyke, Magnus	Fish	10.12.75	Shane, Paul	Extra	16.12.81
			Shankly, Bill		10.1.73
			Sharif, Omar	Sand	25.10.89
Quayle, Anthony	Partridge	9.2.77	Shatner, William	Beam	27.12.89
Quilley, Denis	Pen	30.4.86	Shearing, George	Velvet	12.2.92
			Sheene, Barry	Gloss	25.1.78
			Shepherd, David	Tiger	28.2.90
Rantzen, Esther	Queen	16.11.88	Sheridan, Dinah	Song	28.3.79
Ray, Ted	Beam	17.12.86	Shilton, Peter	Medal	19.3.86
Rayner, Claire	Sun	11.1.89	Silvera, Carmen	Café	30.1.91
Reardon, Ray	Break	14.1.76	Sinden, Donald	Butler	1.5.85
Reed, Oliver	Book	8.1.86	Slater, Larry	Water	9.4.86
Reid, Beryl	Sister	17.3.76	Sleep, Wayne	Rest	27.10.81
Reid, Pat		21.2.73	Smethurst, Jack		24.1.73
Remedios, Alberto	Quaver	28.1.76	Smith, Cyril	Access	15.11.89
Revie, Don		24.4.74	Sobers, Gary	Bat	7.5.75

Name	Codename	Transmission Date	Name	Codename	Transmission Date
Solti, Georg	Ring	28.10.87	Varney, Reg		20.5.70
Soutter, Robert		13.1.71	Vaughan, Frankie		15.4.70
Spanier, Ginette		9.2.72	Vernon, Richard	Pools	26.2.86
Speight, Johnny		13.1.71			
Spencer, John P.	Marks	2.2.83			
Spencer, Peggy	Mark	17.3.93	Waddington, Bill	Game	15.10.86
Spring, Mike	Season	29.2.84	Wade, Virginia	Sixteen	7.12.77
Staff, Kathy	Legs	21.3.84	Wallace, Ian	Recovery	29.3.78
Stardust, Alvin	Twinkle	13.3.85	Ward, Bill	Ten	10.12.86
Starr, Freddie	Planet	14.3.84	Waterman, Dennis	Bill	5.4.78
Stennett, Stan	Minstrel	5.1.83	Watt, Jim	Steam	11.3.81
Stewart, Andy	Scottie	31.12.70	Watts, Queenie	Sparrow	22.1.75
Stiles, Nobby	Gate	20.11.91	Weedon, Bert	Fret	9.12.92
Styne, Jule	Secretary	24.5.78	Weir, Molly	Flood	2.2.77
Sugden, Mollie	Mother	9.4.75	Welch, Elisabeth	Shanty	6.11.85
Sullivan, Clive		3.1.73	Wells, Alan	Water	29.12.82
Surtees, John	Flag	30.12.92	Wells, Joan	Dee	25.12.80
Sweeney, H.J. 'Todd'	Barber	20.3.85	Weston, Simon	Tall	7.2.90
			Whicker, Alan	Bamboo	17.3.82
Sykes, Eric	Boundary	25.12.79	Whillans, Don		8.12.71
			White, Jimmy	Snow	10.3.93
			Whitfield, June	May	14.4.76
Tarbuck, Jimmy	Pool	13.4.83	Whittaker, Roger	Kenya	10.3.82
Tarmey, William	Cellar	4.11.92	Wicks, Jim	Corner	8.12.76
Taylor, Dennis	Black	23.10.85	Wilde, Marty	Tame	15.12.82
Taylor Bradford, Barbara	Will	3.1.90	Willetts, Dave	Jet	20.3.91
			Williams, Charlie		2.2.72
Te Kanawa, Kiri	Katie	25.12.81	Williams, Eluned	Home	21.3.90
Tetley, Mike	Tea	16.4.80	Williams, J.P.R.	Arms	4.4.79
Thaw, John	Warm	18.3.81	Williams, Simon	Saint	2.4.86
Thomas, George (Lord Tonypandy)	Chair	7.12.83	Wilmot, Gary	Cat	24.12.86
			Wilson, Kitty	Mum	16.3.83
			Windsor, Barbara	Castle	30.9.92
Thomas, Leslie	Soldier	17.1.79	Windsor, Frank	Trotsky	3.12.75
Thrower, Percy	Root	31.3.76	Winters, Mike & Bernie		16.12.70
Tidy, Bill	Tripe	17.12.75			
Todd, Bob	Farmer	15.2.84	Wisdom, Norman	Laugh	11.2.87
Todd, Richard	Heart	23.11.83	Wise, Ernie	Join	26.12.90
Tomlinson, David	Broom	13.3.91	Withers, Googie		5.5.72
Topol, Chaim	Slate	9.11.83	Wogan, Terry	Two	19.4.78
Toshak, Jon	Tall	17.2.82	Wood, Michael		22.3.72
Toye, Wendy	Dream	29.1.92	Woodhouse, 'Skipper' John	Safe	27.2.91
Trent, Jackie & Hatch, Tony	Song	13.2.91	Woodward, Edward		3.2.71
Trueman, Freddie	Fast	5.12.79			
Turner, Eva	Diva	9.2.83	Wright, Billy	Left	17.1.90
Twiggy (Leslie Hornby)		10.12.69			
			Yarwood, Mike	Terry	31.5.78
			Yarwood, Mike, RN	Hand	12.12.80
Underwood, Rory	Wing	1.4.92			
Ustinov, Peter	Russian	30.11.77	York, Susannah	Surrey	23.11.83

Index

Figures in italics indicate pages on which photographs appear. A full list of subjects of *TIYL* appears in the Appendix.

ABC Television, 34–5
Ali, Muhammad, 55–9, *55*
Andress, Ursula, 208
Andrews, Eamonn, 9, 15, 29–30, *12, 30, 31, 79, 189*; own *TIYL*, 32–4, *30, 31*; leaves BBC, 34, 40; and ITV, 34, 35, 39–40; death, 41–42; comparison with Michael Aspel, 49–50
Andrews, Grainne, 32, 34, 40–1, 42
Andrews, Harry, 108
Aquinas, Sister, 130
Archer, Jeffrey, 166–7, *166*
Ashley, Jack, 173–4
Aspel, Michael, 15, 26, *22, 46, 47, 90*; background, 49–51; succession to Eamonn Andrews, 44–5; comparison with Eamonn Andrews, 49–50; script reading, 24, 25; the pick-up, 27; own *TIYL*, 17, *51*

Bader, Sir Douglas, 59–62, *60*
Barber, Noel, 192–3, *193*
Barker, Ronnie, 11
Barraclough, Roy, 110–11
Barrett, Norman, *47*
Bartok, Eva, *185*
Bassey, Shirley, 77–8, *78*
Baverstock, Donald, 34
BBC and *TIYL*, 29–30, 34, 213
Beacham, Stephanie, 101
Beaumont, Bill, 149, *148*
Bee Gees, 122–4, *123*
Best, George, 132–3, *132*
Bevan, Brian, 90–1
Big Red Book, 11, *74*
Blackadder, Caroline (researcher), 169
Blanchflower, Danny, 11, 203–4
Blashford-Snell, John, 195, *195*
Bleasdale, Alan, 21
Blyth, Chay, 198, *199*
Botham, Ian, 143, *144*

Bottomley, Patti, 35, 36, 43
Bottomley, Roy, 12, 17, 125, *171*; takes *TIYL* to ITV, 34–5
Boycott, Geoff, *144*
Brabourne, Lord, 52, 53, 201–2, *52, 54*
Braden, Bernard, 15, 185
Bradford, Barbara Taylor, 190–1
Bradley, General Omar, 28
Briggs, Johnny, 117
Brightman, Sarah, 124–5
Brockway, Fenner, Lord Brockway, *173*
Bruno, Frank, 140–1, 212, *206*
Bryan, Dora, 157
Burton, Richard, 208
Busby, Sir Matt, 64–6

Caine, Marti, 77
Cannon (Tommy) and Ball (Bobby), 210
Cartland, Dame Barbara, 187
Cazenove, Christopher, 101–3
Chalmers, Judith, 177, *178*
Champion, Bob, 137–8, *138*
Channing, Carol, *121*
Charlton, Bobby, 131, *10*
Christie, Julie, 208
Clark, Irene (PA), 18
Clark, Petula, *126*
Clifton, Bernie, *47*
Cockcroft, Sarah (researcher), 21
Collins, Jackie, 194, *203*
Collins, Joan, 103–4, *104*
Collins, Phil, 45–6
Compton, Denis, 144–5
Connery, Sean, 69, 204, *73*
Connolly, Billy, 76
Conteh, John, 139–40, *139*
Cookson, Catherine, 191–2
Cooper, Henry, 140
Cooper, Jilly, 189, *189*
Cooper, Tommy, 72–3, *72*
Corbett, Ronnie, 74–5
Cormeau, Yvonne, 87–8

Coronation Street, 110–20
Cotton, Henry, 146
Cricket, Jimmy, 41
Cushing, Peter, *107*

Davidson, Jim, 79–80, *80*
Davies, John Howard, 44–5
Davies, Windsor, *33*
Davis, Bette, *106*
Dawn, Elizabeth, 116–17, *119*
Dawson, Les, 83, *82*
Day, Sir Robin, *71*
Denison, Michael, 161–2
Diana, Princess of Wales, 69, 211, *70*
Dickens, Monica, 192
Dodd, Ken, 29
Doherty, Frs Michael and Kevin, 84–5
D'Oliveira, Basil, 145
Driver, Betty, 115
Driver, Harry, 37–8
Dunn, Clive, *31*
Durrell, Gerald, 191

Edwards, Gareth, 149
Edwards, Ralph, 28–9, 31, 43, 212, *30*
Edwards, Tracy, 199, 207
Ellaway, David, 86–7
Evans, Sir Geraint, 127–8
Evans, Richard, 91

Fairbanks, Douglas, 66–7
Faye, Alice, 96–7
Ferris, Pam, 20, *155*
Floyd, Keith, 20, *22*
Foote, Major-General Robert, 196–7
Fowlds, Derek, *46*
Francis, Clare, 199–200, *200*
Francis, Dick, 138
Freeman, Alan, 180–1, 207
Frost, David, 184–5, *184*
Frost, Major-General John, 197

Gabor, Zsa Zsa, 100–1, *73, 99*
'Gala Performance' tune, 11

Gall, Sandy, 179
Geldof, Bob, 129
Gleave, Group Captain Tom, 198
Glennie, Evelyn, 128–9, *130*
Glitter, Gary, 21, *23*
Godfree, Kitty, 136
Gooch, Graham, 144
Goodyear, Julie, 112
Gordon, Richard, 11
Graham, John (associate producer), 12, 14–15, 17, 25, 27, 59
Granger, Stewart, 104–5
Gray, Dulcie, 161–2
Greaves, Jimmy, 205
Green, Sue (researcher), 19, 21, 123
Grimond, Jo, 172–3, *173*
Gruenberg, Axel, 31
Gutteridge, Reg, 56, 57

Hancock, Sheila, 155–6
Harris, Richard, 150, 207, *151*
Harris, Rolf, 80–1
Harrison, George, 209
Harrison, Rex, 210–11
Havers, Nigel, 19, 21, 24, 25, *23*
Healey, Denis, 167–8, *167*
Hendry, Stephen, 136–7, *135*
Higgins, Alex, 137
Higgins, Jack (Harry Patterson), 189–90
Hill, Benny, 205
Hobbs, Liz, 149
Hope, Bob, 62–4, *63*
Hornby, Leslie ('Twiggy'), 209–10
Huston, Anjelica, 205
Howard, Jim, 21, 85–6
Howarth, Jack, 114–15
Howerd, Frankie, 74, *39, 123*
Humperdinck, Engelbert, 24
Hunniford, Gloria, 44, 175, *176*
Hyde-White, Wilfrid, 105

Ireland, Jill, 206

Jacklin, Tony, 146–7
Jameson, Derek, 181–2
Jason, David, *155*
John, Barry, 149
Johnson, Air-Vice-Marshal Johnnie, 196
Jones, Dr Anthony, 92–3

Kaye, Danny, 208
Kaye, Gorden, 152
Keegan, Kevin, 133
Kelly, Barbara, 186, *185*
Kempson, Rachel, 150, 152
Kennedy, Lena, 193–4
Kennedy, Nigel, 125–6
Kerr, Pat, 93, 95, *95*
Kirkland, Dennis (producer), 205
Klein, Brian (director), 18, 19, 25, 26, 27

La Rue, Danny, *75*
Law, Denis, *132*
Lee, Christopher, 107–8, *107*
Lee, Mandy (programme co-ordinator), 13, 96
Leonard, Michael (researcher), 56, 208
Lethbridge, Matthew, 91
Lewis, Martyn, 179–80
Lindsay, Robert, 11–12, 160–1, *162*
Lloyd, Kevin, *111*
Locke, Josef, 69, 211, *70*
Lockyer, Daphne (*Today*), 48

McCartney, Paul and Linda, *139*
McClean, Tom, 200–1
McColgan, Elizabeth, 21, 145–6
McCowen, Alec, 153–4
McDonald, Trevor, 180
McDowall, Roddy, 205
McElnea, Sister June, 88
McKern, Leo, 206
McLaglen, Victor, 30
MacLean, Sir Fitzroy, 197
Manning, Bernard, 21, 24–5, 78–9, *26*
Mansell, Nigel, 9, 142
Martin, George, 126
Matthews, Stanley, 31
Maxwell, Robert, 169, *170*
Melly, George, *3*
Mercer, Joe, 65
Metcalfe, Jean, 183
Michael of Kent, Prince, 207
Michelmore, Cliff, 183
Miller, Ann, 108–9, 212, *214*
Milligan, Spike, 81–2, *72*
Mills, Freddie, 32
Mills, Juliet, 164, *14*
Minchin, Steve (director), 211
Mitchell, Warren, 208

Monkhouse, Bob, *74*
Moore, Dudley, 97–9
Morgan, Cliff, 41
Morley, Robert, 160, *159*
Morris, Malcolm (producer), 12, 16, 17, 20, 43, 45
Mountbatten, Earl (Lord Louis), 52–5, 63, *52, 63*

NBC Radio Station, New York, 28–9
NBC TV, 29
Nesbitt, Cathleen, 163–4, 210–11, *163*
Nicholas, Paul, 20, 156–7, *158*
Nicholson, Michael, 177–9
Nimmo, Derek, 15
Nixon, David, 33–4
Nixon, Mandy (researcher), 83
Norton, Avril (producer), 14

O'Connor, Des, 38–9

Paige, Elaine, *12*
Parkinson, Michael, 76, 185
Peters, Mary, 145
Philip, Prince, Duke of Edinburgh, 83
Phoenix, Pat, 112, 114, *113*
Pitman, Vic, 91–2
Pountney, Robert, 92, *94*
Powell, Vince, 37
Power, Elizabeth, 51, *51*
Price, Margaret, 88–9

Rantzen, Esther, 17, 175, 177
Reed, Oliver, 207
Rippon, Angela, 177, *71*
Rix, Brian, 156
Roache, William, 20, 114
Robson, Brian, 133–4
Rogers, Ginger, *214*
Rooney, Mickey, 46–8
Ross, Elizabeth (researcher), 204
Rossiter, Leonard, *162*

Sachs, Andrew, *13*
Sanderson, Tessa, 146
Saville, Sir Jimmy, 181
Secombe, Sir Harry, 82–3
Sewell, George, 211
Sharif, Omar, 108
Shatner, William ('Captain Kirk'), 101, *102*
Shearing, George, 128, *127*
Sheene, Barry, 141, 209, *2, 209*

Shepherd, David, 207
Sinatra, Frank, 207
Sinden, Donald, 157–60
Slater, Larry, 92
Sloan, Tom, 31
Smith, Sir Cyril, 169–71, *170*
Sobers, Sir Garfield, 143
Solti, Sir George, 40
Speight, Johnny, *72*
Staff, Kathy, *81*
Starr, Freddie, *76, 106*
Status Quo, 18
Stiles, Nobby, 10, *10*
Strich, Elaine, 19
Styne, Jule, 121–2, *121*
Sugden, Mollie, *79*
Surtees, John, 142
Sykes, Eric, *72*

Tarbuck, Jimmy, 75–6, 204
Tarmey, William, 120, *119*
Te Kanawa, Dame Kiri, 126–7
Teddington Studios, 11–27
Tesler, Brian, 34, 35, 36
Thames Television, 35, 36
Thatcher, Margaret, 206
Thaw, John, 154, *153*

This Is Your Life, hiccups and hitches, 11, 20–1; researchers, 13–14, 18; the pick-up, 15; security and losses of programmes, 15–16; codenames, 16–17; 'Dream Board', 18; origin, 28–9; transfer from BBC TV, 34; change of presenter, 43–5; comparison of presenters, 49–50; first repetition of personality, 65
Thomas, George, Lord Tonypandy, 165
Thomas, Leslie, 188, *188*
Thorndike, Dame Sybil, *159*
Tiplady, Sue (film researcher), 14, 24
Tranter, Laurence, 28–9
Trueman, Fred, 142–3
Truth or Consequences, 28
Twiggy (Leslie Hornby), 209–10
Tyson, Mike, 205

Underwood, Rory, 147–8, *147*

Ustinov, Sir Peter, 105, 107, *106*

Vaughan, Frankie, 210

Waddington, Bill, 115–16
Wade, Virginia, 134, *135*
Waldman, Ronnie, 29–30
Waterman, Dennis, *153*
Webber, Andrew Lloyd, 125
Wells, Alan, 145
Wells, Joan, 89
Whicker, Alan, 182–3, *182*
Whitehall, Michael, 19–20
Wilson, Kitty, 89, 211
Wilton, Mavis, 20, 118–20, *118*
Windsor, Barbara, *14*
Winner, Michael, 206–7
Wise, Ernie, 68–9, *71*
Wogan, Terry, 42, 44, 181
Wood, Dr Michael, 86
Woodhouse, Jack, 90–1, *90*

York, Sarah, Duchess of, 207
York, Susannah, *158*
Young, Jimmy, 206